The Universi

The University and Social Justice

Struggles Across the Globe

Edited by Aziz Choudry and Salim Vally

PLUTO PRESS

First published 2020 by Pluto Press
345 Archway Road, London N6 5AA

www.plutobooks.com

British Library Cataloguing in Publication Data
A catalogue record for this book is available from the British Library

ISBN 978 0 7453 4067 8 Hardback
ISBN 978 0 7453 4068 5 Paperback
ISBN 978 1 7868 0574 4 PDF eBook
ISBN 978 1 7868 0576 8 Kindle eBook
ISBN 978 1 7868 0575 1 EPUB eBook

This book is printed on paper suitable for recycling and made from fully managed and sustained forest sources. Logging, pulping and manufacturing processes are expected to conform to the environmental standards of the country of origin.

Typeset by Swales & Willis

Simultaneously printed in the United Kingdom and United States of America

Contents

List of figures and tables

Acknowledgements

As researchers and educators working in universities in Montreal and Johannesburg, we are greatly inspired by and have supported and participated in struggles of student activists and movements, academic and non-academic workers, campus action groups and campaigns. These organisations have not only fought for accessible, critical and quality public education, acted against the interests of political and economic elites, and also advocated for broader progressive change and radical visions for a fairer world. After Québec's 2012 *printemps érable* ('Maple Spring'), and as Rhodes Must Fall/Fees Must Fall spread across South Africa, it seemed inevitable that we would work on a collection like this one.

This book examines university-based activism and its relationship with wider social and political change. Besides the accounts of the politics of resistance from within higher education, in the context of multiple crises of capitalism, ecology, xenophobia and fascism, many more are urgently needed. We dedicate this book to these collective struggles past, present and future.

Our deepest gratitude goes to all of the contributors to this collection for their time, energy and generosity of spirit in completing their chapters, sometimes under adverse conditions. We greatly appreciate David Shulman, Neda Tehrani and the team at Pluto Press for their enthusiastic support, as well as the reviewers of the original book proposal for their helpful suggestions. Many thanks are due to Désirée Rochat who assisted us in preparing and formatting the book manuscript with professionalism, a critical eye, patience and good humour. We thank Melanie Marshall, Adam Bell and Swales and Willis for their invaluable help with the final pre-production stages. We also acknowledge support from Aziz's Canada Research Chair in social movement learning and knowledge production.

While completing this book, we lost Mudney Halim (Johannesburg) and Vicky Pearson (Montreal), both long-time educators and social justice activists. All royalties from this book will be donated to the Centre for Education Rights and Transformation at the University of Johannesburg.

1

Lessons in struggle, studies in resistance

Aziz Choudry and Salim Vally

While the commodification of education and the spectre of the corporate university (private and public) haunts, and has indeed materialised in many locations, many campuses remain sites of struggle, whether erupting, dormant or under the radar. Over 50 years have passed since the 1968 wave of rebellion reverberated around the world against authoritarian rule, war and colonialism when students, often alongside workers, organised mass protests, sending shockwaves of alarm among political, economic and military elites (Dubinsky, Krull, Lord, Mills & Rutherford, 2009; de García, 2005; Pensado, 2015; Vrana, 2017). Throughout the 1950s, 1960s and 1970s – and since – in Thailand, Pakistan, South Korea, Iran and other parts of Asia, Latin America, Africa, Europe and the Pacific, campuses have frequently erupted in protest.

At the start of the twenty-first century, struggles within higher education continue in the context of deep social and economic inequalities, global ecological and capitalist crises, multiple forms of state violence and repression, demands for rethinking the framework and purpose of formal education and universal access to free quality education (on recent student movements, see, for example, Brooks, 2017; Ferguson, 2017; Hensby, 2018; Myers, 2017; Solomon & Palmieri, 2011; Weiss & Aspinall, 2012; Zamponi, 2018). Demands for institutional change, and calls to decolonise (however this term is defined) institutions, programmes of study and curricula have spread across campuses and countries (Bhambra, Gebrial & Nişancıoğlu,

2018; Rhodes Must Fall Oxford, 2018; Sian, 2019). As labour precarity bites deeply across sectors and societies, in many countries, university workers – academic and non-academic – and students have organised to resist further cuts to education and social spending, the imposition of neoliberal governance models, reorientation of education along market lines and the suppression of dissent. In some instances, students have also supported staff in universities struggling for a living wage and opposed the practice of outsourcing workers. In many countries, students, academic and non-academic staff have organised against military research on campus, formed an anti-sweatshop movement against apparel manufacturers, opposed university investments in fossil fuels, mining and other environmentally destructive businesses and demanded institutional/structural changes to address sexism, racism and economic marginalisation (see Chatterjee & Maira, 2014).

Some of these struggles draw on or implicitly continue longer histories and traditions of popular resistance and have been connected to broader movements for progressive social, political and economic change and radical visions of a fairer world. But while intergenerational knowledge may be sometimes passed on within organisations, movements and activist networks, this does not always happen. Among other reasons, the transitory nature of student life at universities poses challenges to recovering useable histories of earlier struggles. As well as a critical geohistorical lens which attends to specific histories, contexts and politics, we believe that these movements need to be theorised within the context of wider understandings of contemporary capitalism and authoritarianism and their potentials explored.

In recent years, from RhodesMustFall/FeesMustFall in South Africa to the 'Maple Spring' in Québec, from Chile to Palestine, student demands, and those of teaching faculty and non-academic workers have sometimes connected to broader struggles for social, economic and political justice – and indeed wider politics of people's movements for liberation, and against authoritarianism, austerity and fascism. In many cases, student movements have met with violent police and state security responses. But they have also sometimes made significant gains. As we write, across the globe, students and professors are again being targeted by the state and right-wing political activists, criminalised, vilified, jailed and assaulted for speaking out against violence, injustice, fascism and repression.

From Palestine to Puerto Rico (Martinez & Garcia, 2018), some student/education justice movements still play important roles in resisting occupation and colonial rule, as in earlier periods. For example, Walker (1990) notes the role of Nga Tamatoa, which emerged from Maori students at the University of Auckland in the 1970s in the Maori movement for self-determination in Aotearoa/New Zealand, in successfully pressuring the New Zealand government for Maori language to be taught in schools. As with other movements, student movements also have their own internal contradictions. Important examples of this are feminist challenges about ways in which dominant forms of gender relations and sexual violence can be reproduced within these movements, as well as anti-racist challenges to student politics and higher education (see for example, hampton, Campos-Martínez and Olavarría, and Abdulhadi and Shehadeh chapters in this volume), including challenging the ways in which decisions are made during student struggles and relations with political parties.

Throughout the twentieth century, in many countries, students were involved in anti-colonial and anti-imperialist politics as well as mobilising to transform higher education either after independence or in the context of challenges to racism, colonialism and imperialism in countries such as the US (Chatterjee & Maira, 2014; Biondi, 2018; Kelley, 2018). Today, neoliberal policies and forms of authoritarianism are deeply intertwined as we can see most clearly perhaps in the chapters on India and Turkey. While student activism is often characterised as inherently left-wing, not all student activism is progressive. Indeed, as history (and some chapters in this book) tells us, campus politics often includes conservative, oppressive and anti-democratic tendencies. Prem Kumar Vijayan (in this volume) contends:

Perhaps the first task for any student political enterprise is to re-examine the identity 'student' – to see it, not as constituted by age or biology, class or gender, but as a particular element in a larger political-economic dynamic; and to see therefore, that not all student politics are necessarily either progressive or democratic, however much they may claim those qualities. It is to see that the terms 'progressive' and 'democratic' themselves need to be reviewed, given that they are increasingly defined by corporate and finance capitalist interests.

(p. 55)

3

While the ephemeral nature of students' time in universities is seen as an impediment to organising, Alberto Toscano (2011) argues that:

> the fragile, transitory nature of student politics can also be read as a strength: they allow for a fleeting if repeated formation of a peculiar form of collectivity ... the university can also unify students in ways that corporativist or fragmented interests cannot ... students do not constitute a class, rather they find themselves situated in a temporal condition: they are apprentice intellectual workers who the moment they gain self-consciousness as a community are dispersed and find themselves neutralized. But in the brief interlude of their preparation they constitute a compact group which has demonstrated an enormous political impulse in country after country.
>
> (p. 83)

This collection explores movements and activism in higher education across diverse contexts. Taken as a whole, its chapters explore the scope for, and moments when, student activism and other struggles that emerge from within institutions of higher education influence, effect or participate in wider social change. We begin this chapter by addressing some dynamics of education, learning and the politics of struggle, linking the book's overarching theme to the areas of critical adult education and critical literature on higher education, while noting some concerns about the fetishisation and securitisation of youth/students. Second, we note the corporatisation, marketisation, managerialism and neoliberalism of higher education and the dialectics of resistance. Third, we present a selective review of campus struggles and legacies and fourth, we turn to considering solidarities between students and workers/labour struggles and the university as a site of struggle. Finally, we reflect on alternative modes of organising and challenges to the politics of knowledge that have emerged from some of these movements. While we are writing, from Brazil and Argentina to Bangladesh and Sudan, new student mobilisations are challenging authoritarian rule and neoliberal cuts to education. In October 2019, student protests forced Chile's government to suspend proposed metro fare increases. As you read this, across the world there will be more.

EDUCATION, LEARNING AND STRUGGLE KNOWLEDGE

Regarding learning, our primary interest is not in the formal degree and diploma programmes, courses and curricula but rather in the spaces in which students, faculty and non-academic workers find themselves planning, mobilising and resisting together, including official student organisations, trade unions, campaigns and informal networks and modes of activism.

As university academics and educators with backgrounds in popular/movement radical adult education, research and organise outside of universities, we are keenly interested in the politics of knowledge production and the relationships between informal/non-formal learning in the course of struggles for change, and processes of more formal education. We take a sympathetic, but unromantic view of social movements and social movement knowledge production, well aware of internal tensions, contradictions and limitations that can be produced and reproduced as well as powerful visions and ideas that emerge from struggles for change.

Globally, within activist networks and social movements, there is a rich history of processes and practices combining informal, perhaps incidental learning with more programmatic political education – and indeed theory (Choudry, 2015; Choudry & Vally, 2018). Scandrett and Ballantyne (2019) note that:

> [i]n the university, formal education (for credit) is given privilege and priority above non-formal education. Non-formal education however can be more self-directed, collective and democratic. A dialectical relationship between formal and non-formal education is a dynamic struggle in which both forms of education are valued and critically interrogate one another.
>
> (p. 176)

Some chapters in this book explicitly build on and discuss activist knowledge and learning that arises in the course of campus mobilisations, occupations and protests and some of the possibilities, limitations and ambivalences as struggles and communities connect in the course of these activities (see Woodcock, Naidoo and Gamedze; hampton, in this volume).

Discussing the relationship between formal university education and non-formal/informal learning, Austin (2009) recalls the work of the

Montreal-based group Caribbean Conference Committee (CCC) and New World Group in the 1960s:

> Reflecting on his experience within the CCC and the C.L.R. James Study Circle while living in Canada, [Jamaican historian, Robert] Hill (2009) recently remarked: 'Education was preparation to take part and play a role in the new stage of Caribbean history ... more specifically, the next stage in the centuries-long struggle of the Caribbean people for freedom, dignity, and nationhood' (p. 100). Hill continues: 'To undertake this role outside the Caribbean ... these students launched a series of community-based initiatives that were both a defence of their community as well as a testing of their intellectual cultural resources. They had one great advantage,' he goes on, 'namely, they saw no distinction between the campus and the community and they based their actions on this mutual convergence of interest.'
>
> (p. 113)

After receiving the first drafts of their chapters we posed the following questions to all the book's contributors: What can be learned from the strategies, tactics, demands and visions generated by student movements? What are their possibilities and limitations? How have these struggles resonated (or not) with other parts of society? How do current/recent movements/forms of activism relate to earlier moments in history/ periods of struggle over education and society? In order to tackle, and indeed attempt to answer these questions, we seek to locate recent movements in a framework that attends to critically understanding them in relation to history, politics, power and context, but also one that avoids fetishising youth activism (Sukarieh & Tannock, 2015). Carpenter and Mojab (2017) write that the field of adult education should embrace 'the category of youth not as distinct from adults but as a social category that is being equally regulated and invoked by the same social, cultural, economic, and political forces' (p. 2).

The construction of university students as 'unruly subjects' (see Chapter 3) and as security threats is nothing new, as colonial and Cold War histories from around the world reveal, as well as more contemporary examples, such as the surveillance and policing of Palestine solidarity activism (Maira, 2019), and the 'counter-terrorism' and 'deradicalisation' ideology that has been enacted as law throughout Britain's education system.

Giroux (2008) argues that youth have become:

one of the most visible symbols onto which class and racial anxieties are projected. The very troubled state of young people confronts us with the broken promises of capitalism in the age of outsourcing, contract work, deindustrialization, and deregulation. It also represents a collective fear of the consequences wrought by systemic class inequalities, racism, and a culture of downsizing and deficits that have created a generation of unskilled and displaced youth who have been expelled from shrinking markets, blue-collar jobs, and any viable hope in the future.

(p. 203)

Sukarieh and Tannock (2018, p. 855) contend that '[t]hough there have been precedents – in the 1960s, for example, the US Central Intelligence Agency raised the alarm over the global spread of a rebellious university student movement', 'the transition of youth from being primarily a local and national "problem" to a global security concern' – is largely a new development. They argue that since the 1990s,

> on the one hand, the social category of youth has become an increasing concern for international development policy and discourse, in part due to its utility for the neoliberal project of renegotiating and eroding welfare and development state entitlements; and on the other, development policy and discourse has become ever more closely tied to global security concerns, following the end of the Cold War and rise of the 'war on terror'.

This security logic also targets dissident faculty (along with student activists and others) who have over the years been jailed, assassinated, assaulted, disappeared or intimidated – in countries such as apartheid South Africa, military dictatorships in Latin America, Asia, Africa and the Middle East. Student activists, some university programmes and critical scholars are targets of smear campaigns and concerted attacks by anti-intellectual and ahistorical strains of the 'populist' right and indeed mainstream political parties and commentators (see also Abdulhadi & Shehadeh, Chapter 7 in this volume). In India, 'anti-national' labels are used by Narendra Modi's BJP government to vilify, intimidate and criminalise student activists, along with others opposing the Indian state's occupation of Kashmir, caste discrimination and injustices against Dalit and Adivasis and Hindu nationalism. Progressive scholars such as GN Saibaba (Delhi University) and Shoma Sen (Nagpur University) remain in jail on trumped-up charges.[1] Özcan's chapter (in this volume) documents two periods of the securitisation and repression – and assesses the resistance strategies – of Turkish academics (see also Baser, Akgönül & Öztürk, 2017; and Erdem & Akın, 2019). In different contexts, such as US and Canadian campuses, as Maira (2019), Ziadah and Hanieh (2010) and Dawson and Mullen (2017) note (see also Chapter 7 in this volume), with the growth of student and faculty activism in support of justice for Palestine and the spread of the Boycott, Divestment and Sanctions (BDS) movement, student organisers and professors have worked together in informal and formal networks (as noted by Woodcock in this book[2]). They have also faced and resisted campaigns of demonisation and intimidation (see Abdulhadi & Shehadeh in this volume) by university administrations and powerful organisations and donors off-campus. As many contributors note, repression is often met with resistance, solidarity and organising against these attempts to silence and demonise.

TO MARKET, TO MARKET: THE CORPORATE UNIVERSITY, EDU-PRENEURS AND MANAGERIALISM

Across the world, universities are confronted by renewed privatisation, intensive marketisation and a challenge to the very notion of the university as a mechanism for addressing social inequality and facilitating the circulation of knowledge. Universities are recast from a public to a commodified sphere, with students as consumers and staff as sales consultants replete with corporate values and corporate planning frameworks. In the face of mass unemployment, aligning skills to the competitive global 'new knowledge economy' has become the obsession of most nation states. Solidarity and learning that addresses the self to public life and social responsibility to robust public participation and democratic citizenship is marginalised and often ridiculed in favour of a culture of crass commercialisation and consumerism (Vally, 2006). Educators and students are cajoled 'to ultimately see all meaning in terms of what can be bought, sold or made profitable' (Shumar, 1997, p. 5). They seek to do so through reifying socially constituted and produced educational processes as measurable things (Canaan, 2002, p. 4).

The emphasis on subjects and disciplines that have a purchase in the marketplace are valued more highly, even as critical education scholars have challenged dominant market capitalist orthodoxies that have become ascendant in framing understandings about the relationship between higher education, society and the economy (see, for example, Torres & Schugurensky, 2002 on Latin America; Vally & Motala, 2014 on South Africa; Breeze, Taylor & Costa, 2019 on Britain). The Edu-Factory Collective (2010) refers to a '"double crisis" (i.e. the global economic crisis and the crisis of the university in ruins)' (n.p.). Worldwide, the adoption of corporate culture as the appropriate form of management and leadership in higher education has become commonplace. Through this model, which divides the university community into a small group of highly paid managers and 'the rest of the staff' (academics and administrative), power and control firmly reside at the top, and leaders are handsomely rewarded. Corporate culture in higher education results in rationalisation and austerity measures which place an increased work burden on faculty and staff while the new corporate and managerial executives receive exorbitant salaries. Faculty autonomy is declining and power is increasingly concentrated in the hands of a few. Corporate managerialism dismantles models of good governance and accountability, tenure and conditions of service, reasonable workloads for staff and access to university for marginalised communities. Further, it weakens, instrumentalises and commodifies community links and resources for research to advance the ideals of critical citizenship and democracy in favour of corporate interests – including that of the increasingly corporate university itself (Baatjes, Spreen & Vally, 2012).

Slaughter and Rhoades (2004) address academic capitalism whereby academic staff are channelled into entrepreneurial ventures as part of the university's income-generating ethic and the embedding of universities within the logic of academic capitalism. The relevance of academic work is linked to productivity as measured by rating and ranking scales. The theory of academic capitalism aims to explain the integration of the university into the global economy, more specifically how faculty, students, administrators and academics use 'a variety of state resources to create new circuits of knowledge that link higher education institutions (HEIs) to the new economy' (Slaughter & Leslie, 1997, p. 210). It reflects the encroachment of the profit motive into the academy, and represents 'a shift from a public good knowledge/learning regime to an academic capitalist knowledge/learning regime', where students become consumers and institutions the marketers

(Slaughter & Leslie, 1997, p. 210). Kelsey (2008) notes how international trade, investment and economic architecture such as the World Trade Organisation's General Agreement on Trade in Services and similar provisions in other regional and bilateral agreements have been largely scripted and driven by, and further facilitate, the needs and priorities of a rapidly growing global educational services sector, which includes universities, further commodifying education and alienating it from its emancipatory possibilities in the service of profit.

Universities worldwide are accommodating a practice that demonises social justice and genuine social responsibility, and where critique can be a risky endeavour. Some universities portray themselves as community-engaged and committed to social justice, equity and diversity but this is often critiqued as a neoliberal exercise in managing social difference and a corporate branding strategy consistent with market competition, rather than reflecting actual practice and institutional change (see for example Ahmed, 2012; Breeze, Taylor & Costa, 2019; and Sian, 2019 on the UK). And as Raymundo and Mongala contend in Chapter 13 of this volume (while remembering the roles students played in many countries' struggles for independence), higher education still serves a 'colonial function as a tool for imperialist control in the "post-colonial era"'.

More concretely, academics, particularly those who dissent, are constantly evaluated. It is a form of accountability premised on distrust, individual advancement and promotion and the devaluing of collegiality and a commitment to the public good. Rampant individualism, entrepreneurship and competitiveness are encouraged. Monitoring mechanisms for producing 'appropriate' research are vigorously adhered to. Critical scholars note the rise of a narrow, utilitarian vocationalism, the notion that the only conceivable point of going to university is to get the right sort of corporate job (Bailey & Freedman, 2011). In their chapter on Mexico, Maldonado-Maldonado and Bañuelos Astorga note that this trend is sometimes met with student protest. Entrepreneurial forms of techno-utopianism, robotics and blind faith in educational technology are often uncritically embraced by university administrations as Mirrlees and Alvi (2014) and Selwyn (2013) contend. An increasing number of university administrations ardently promote the so-called Fourth Industrial Revolution (Maharajh, 2018). While technology and the development of technological skills can be useful, we need to equip students to ask critical questions (including about the political economy of technology itself, and the pedagogical and social implications of educational technology) which they can only do through critical consciousness (not simply higher order critical technical skills – the two are often confused), to engage in democratic debate and to make informed choices about social priorities (Selwyn, 2013; Vally & Motala, 2014).

Faulkner (2011) laments the state of Britain's universities as a result of the 'neo-liberal counter-revolution', writing that:

> To enter the main campus complex of the University of Hertfordshire – to take my local example – is like entering the atrium of a City bank. There is the same numbing brainlessness, the same suffocating absence of thought and imagination, the same absoluteness about the unquestioning conformity. So drained of intellect, culture, and politics are they that many of these places are the very negation of 'universities'. There is nothing 'higher' about them. They are skills factories turning out labour units in an environment that combines the clinical functionalism of Huxley's Brave New World, the political conformity of Orwell's 1984, and the bureaucratic absurdity of Kafka's The Trial. Is the contrast overdrawn? If it is, the procedure remains valid.
>
> (p. 28)

Many universities have become major real estate players, major urban developers in many US cities (and elsewhere), providing new revenue streams and profit (Wiewel & Perry, 2008). Yet in many countries – and not only the US and the UK, where this has perhaps been more documented, with the increase of tuition fees (in countries where higher education is not free), levels of student debt are not only crippling, but also a major feature of national economies (see Figart, 2017, on the US). Doherty (2018), notes that compared to 1979 'the cost of tuition in the US is up nearly 200 per cent at state colleges and nearly 300 per cent at private ones' (n.p.). She notes that US higher education fails to fulfil the promise of social mobility: '38 per cent of students from low-income families will stay poor, even if they graduate. The majority of graduates begin their post-college lives saddled with debt, in jobs or internships that don't provide enough money to live on' (n.p.).

What role has student debt played in the US in disciplining students and containing dissent on campus in recent years? To what extent is this a factor in other contexts, north and south, where higher education, if accessible at all to working-class students, places intolerable debt burdens on them? Meanwhile students in many countries across the world who have protested against fee increases frequently meet with violent state responses (see for example, hampton, Chapter 5 in this volume, on Québec, Woodcock, and Chapter 2, on the UK).

Undoubtedly, despite these negative developments globally, progressive spaces, while constrained, do exist in the academy and individuals in many universities are able to connect with community organisations and social movements and accomplish valuable counter-hegemonic work. Often these spaces have been won through struggles supported by student organisations, staff unions and associations, and by pressure from organisations outside. They must be expanded through a vigorous defence of higher education as a public good, sphere of critical democratic citizenry, and resistance against commercial and corporate values that shape the form, purpose and mission of our institutions. The emphasis on technical rationality, simplistic pragmatism and undemocratic managerial imperatives must be countered. Proactively, initiatives should include linking programmes, projects and resources to community needs and struggles.

CAMPUS RESISTANCE OVER TIME AND SPACE

Although as Toscano (2011) notes earlier, student struggles are often ephemeral, their actions can catalyse or incubate wider struggles.

As some authors in this volume remind us, alongside the use of higher education for domestication and the production of elites, anti-colonial, anti-capitalist and pro-democracy movements have long emerged from campuses across the world. In 1956, students, later joined by workers, sparked the Hungarian Revolution against Stalinism only to be crushed by the Soviet army. As Le Mazier notes in Chapter 10 of this book, left-wing French students were active in opposing France's war in Algeria. In 1968 in Paris student protests sparked a workers' revolt as trade unions joined demonstrations and a general strike was called on 13 May of that year. In the US, student activism – and that of progressive faculty played an important role in the civil rights movement, as well as Puerto Rican independence and the anti-Vietnam War movement.

The brutal crackdown against the occupation of Tiananmen Square, in Beijing, China in 1989 by 100,000 students and hundreds of thousands of residents and workers supporting them was another significant event.

Writing about Africa's student movements,[3] past and present, Hodgkinson and Melchiorre (2019) urge that we should not forget older lesser-known experiences of student protests in other African countries, besides South Africa. They note that there was no single decolonisation project in this era, which saw many students draw on Pan-African and socialist thinking in their struggles. Considering both the challenges of student activists to state authority as well as the ways in which former student activists variously took their political ideas and experiences into careers as opposition politicians or state leaders in many African countries, they suggest: 'By looking back, scholars can understand the potential that such activism has for emancipating people from the legacies of colonialism. It's also a useful way to identify the limits that student decolonisation projects can hold for both broader politics and society, as well as for the activists themselves' (n.p.). In a recent book on Tanzania, Hirji (2019) recounts how after the first flush of independence, students from the University Students African Revolutionary Front together with some progressive staff members such as Walter Rodney, John Saul and others contributed to making the University of Dar es Salaam a beacon of progressive scholarship. They championed decolonisation and while critically supportive of President Nyerere's humanism and policies of *Ujamaa*, also warned of the dangers of neocolonialism. Their critiques celebrated as the 'Dar es Salaam Debates' remain germane to revitalising the African academy today.

SOLIDARITIES AND SITES OF STRUGGLE: STUDENTS, WORKERS, FACULTY AND OTHERS

Forging solidarities across different groups of staff, students and faculty within universities, and beyond is not inevitable. Government ministries and corporate university administrations, faced with challenges to their authority, often use tactics of divide and rule and co-optation. But recent mobilisations in South Africa illustrate some possibilities for student/worker alliances and solidarities despite the use of private security and revelations that the state employed a network of informers within FeesMustFall (Gichanga, 2019; Kalla, 2018; Pauw, 2017).

In the 2015 protests – the biggest university protests in South Africa since the end of formal apartheid in 1994 – students and workers in universities across South Africa powerfully expressed their dissatisfaction with the status quo. Their demands against financial exclusion – encapsulated in the 'FeesMustFall' hashtag – was a call for a higher education system in the interest of the public good. The movement gave meaning to Fanon's (1963, p. 41) dictum, often quoted in this period, 'Each generation must, out of relative obscurity, discover its mission, fulfil it, or betray it'. A significant number of this generation spoke to the intersectionality of class exploitation, racism, different forms of oppression and patriarchy in concrete ways. The national FeesMustFall student movement promoted solidarity between students and workers. For this cause, students were prepared to close their institutions, occupy campus buildings, challenge authority and power and courageously put their bodies on the line. In their mass marches to the ruling ANC headquarters in Johannesburg on 22 October, the Union Buildings in Pretoria and the Parliament in Cape Town on 23 October 2015, students and workers en masse expressed their support for the movement. Two of the participants write (Luckett & Mzobe, 2016, p. 94):

> Protests began with a focus on the student fee increase for 2016, but demands soon expanded to include issues such as free education, the cancellation of student debt, the decolonisation of the curriculum, and the insourcing of all university workers. While the protests have been widely analysed as a student movement, low-paid and outsourced university workers have also been key actors. At the University of the Witwatersrand, outsourced workers joined protesting students from the first day … In a dramatically short space of time major victories were achieved. The ANC government agreed to no fee increase for 2016, and one by one university managements started to agree, in principle, to insource workers, meaning that all outsourced support staff would be directly employed by the university … This is arguably the biggest victory against the privatisation of the public sector in South Africa since 1994.

This was a victory that trade unions were not able to achieve over many years.

Luckett and Pontarelli (2016) urge that '[t]he battle against exploitative labor relations and for a decent life in post-apartheid South Africa does not stop at the university's boundaries' (n.p.) and must be extended to other parts of the South African economy, necessitating linking with struggles beyond the university. They argue that 'the victory of South African outsourced workers shows the global working class that reversing the processes of neoliberalism is still possible' (n.p.). Although these gains are very important, more could have been achieved around the student demands with better coordination between established trade union federations and students – a dynamic that may well resonate in other contexts.

Where they exist, labour and student unions can be important organisations of resistance at universities. Lagnado (2016) documents the organising and campaigns of precarious migrant worker cleaners at British universities which garnered support from students and other university workers (see also Woodcock, Chapter 2, on student/worker connections, and Meari and Abu Duhou in the Palestinian context, Chapter 8 in this volume). Bailey and Freedman (2011, pp. 7–8) emphasise the importance of the University and College Union (UCU) in the UK, citing examples of international and campus solidarities, noting conference resolutions supporting a boycott of Israeli academic institutions in response to the BDS call, while contending that the union's politics have been sharpened because:

> its members find themselves in a fast-changing 'industry' where they are forced to act collectively in relation not only to 'bread and butter' issues (for example, massive casualization, increased workloads and now deteriorating pay and pensions) but the more 'political' questions concerning curricula, research outcomes and, of course, the very 'idea' of the university.

They argue that UCU members must win support amongst other campus staff and students, overcome sectional barriers between professors and visiting tutors, between staff and students, between academics and support staff through organising together, holding joint meetings and running united campaigns. They urge going beyond defensive union action and using 'the site of the university as a space in which to consider and press for radical responses to the privatization of higher education. Partly, this will help build union militancy but it is also an important way of legitimizing our concerns and strategies inside the university itself.' There remain many possibilities for building cross-campus solidarities between students, faculty and other workers, whether through formal organisations such as unions (where these exist, and where their structures and orientations encourage, or are open to a politics of resistance) or through informal networks and forms of struggles where these do not exist (see Vijayan, Chapter 3, this volume, on these tensions in Indian student politics).

ALTERNATIVES

In the context of a panel discussion on social movements, education and learning, Sangeeta Kamat recently articulated a challenge for those working in universities to build and sustain a 'school to movement pipeline'.[4] It is important to engage with radical ideas, learning and knowledge from social movements, community struggles and what Gramsci (1971) termed 'organic intellectuals', and Shivji (2018) calls 'revolutionary intellectuals' outside of universities. As the chapters here suggest, many of them written by scholars who are or have been active in the movements that they write about, there is not such a neat binary between 'scholars' and 'activists' (see also D'Souza, 2009 on this question). We need to consider the limitations and possibilities of ideas and visions for social change largely forged on campuses without involvement or engagement of movements and communities that are outside. What are the horizons of possibility to reimagine education for liberation outside of the limited imagination of the neoliberal university and educational capitalism? And, indeed, outside of the parameters of the liberal imagination?

Alternative models and practices for organising, educating and learning arise in these struggles and commitments to broader society, from the popular education 'groundings' of Guyanese historian Walter Rodney with Jamaica's urban poor (Rodney, 2014), to experiments with popular education through FeesMustFall (see Benson, Gamedze & Koranteng, 2018; and Gamedze and Naidoo in this volume). Often in mass struggles such as FeesMustFall popular education manifests itself through creative visual representation, song, graffiti, posters and plays (Thomas, 2018; Moosa, 2019). Özcan (this volume), and Erdem and Akın, 2019, discuss the creation of the solidarity academies (what the latter call 'communities of communing') after the recent purge of Turkish universities. There are many other examples.[5] Significant learning, including about power and building counter-power can also take place in the 'universities' of the streets and occupations, on demonstrations and in the confrontation with university authorities, state and private security forces. We cannot underestimate the importance of experience for those participating in student movements and who take part in occupations and strikes. Critical reflection on modes of organising, strategies and tactics, decision making, making connections across struggles, campaigns and coalition work, all contribute to incidental learning. Such praxis also builds participants' sense of agency, confidence and consciousness.

Many questions remain about the relationship between campus struggles and broader social and economic transformation. Any critical assessment of this must attend to the historical moment or specific contexts. As noted, universities – not least through important waves of student struggles across many continents and eras – remain contested spaces, as do their relationships to society, and the national and global economies. It is important that the histories of the roles played by those in universities in movements for social change are not forgotten. Perhaps at its most potent, campus activism has gone hand in hand with organising with communities and movements both inside and outside of universities to bring about social change. As with other movements, it is sometimes from the margins, tensions and contradictions of such struggles that powerful challenges to power and the status quo emerge. An important (and far from a new phenomenon), is the generations of feminist organising on campuses confronting patriarchal power relations, sexual violence and harassment.

In 1970, Ernest Mandel wrote that the university as an institution 'remains bound with golden chains to the power of the ruling class', and that any lasting radical transformation of the university could only occur if there was a radical transformation of society. 'But what is impossible for the university as an institution is possible for students as individuals and groups. And what is possible for students as individuals and groups can, on the collective level, temporarily emerge as a possibility for the university as a whole' (n.p.). Following Gramsci, Chatterjee and Maira (2014) support the need for insurgent spaces within the academy as a form of counter-hegemony through engagement with movements and organic intellectuals beyond the academy. Salaita (2014) agrees:

There is remarkable energy in the world beyond the academy for ground-level change, a site of action where theorization is often more germane and sophisticated than in formal institutions, as we saw in the early stages of the Egyptian and Tunisian revolutions. By confining ourselves to the spaces inhabited by the supposedly unimpressionable elite, we ensure a recirculation of intellectual and material resources into limited and specialized institutions ...We need to think more about how the work we do as scholars coheres with the struggles of projustice advocates in all social and economic strata.

(pp. 233–234)

IN THIS BOOK

In Chapter 2, Jamie Woodcock discusses the trajectory, key moments and the limitations of the 2010 UK student movement, arguing that it was underpinned by the earlier anti-war movement, campus Palestine solidarity activism and the 2008 financial crisis. Woodcock highlights the connections between student and worker organising. In reflecting on how university students are frequently perceived as 'unruly subjects', Prem Kumar Vijayan looks at higher education and the landscape, tensions and possibilities of student organising in India. Gülden Özcan's chapter seeks to understand the purges of Turkish academe after the 1980 military coup and in the post-2016 period as well as spaces of resistance of academics in both periods as well as their possibilities and limitations. Critically focusing on the 2012 Québec student strike against a 75 per cent tuition hike, rosalind hampton analyses the Québec student movement to examine how it both challenges and reproduces dominant narratives and relations of settler colonialism. Javier Campos-Martínez and Dayana Olavarría's contribution maps the trajectory of students' practices of resistance during Chilean student struggles between 2006 and 2016, exploring their gains, widespread public support as well as the co-optation of their demands by the state. Documenting the concrete example of advocacy for justice for Palestine at San Francisco State University, Rabab Abdulhadi and Saliem Shehadeh discuss sustained campus repression with the assault on free speech and efforts to fight back, connecting the political economy of the Israel lobby with the corporatisation of this US public university. Lena Meari and Rula

Abu Duhou examine the scope of student activism in Palestine and its potential to exceed the post-Oslo impasse through forging a space for renewing the Palestinian anti-colonial, anti-capitalist and social justice struggle. They discuss how faculty and staff union struggles against neoliberal governance at Birzeit University played a role in this renewal, breaking through the impasse caused by the Oslo Accords. Alma Maldonado-Maldonado and Vania Bañuelos Astorga analyse three Mexican student/youth movements of the last decade, #YoSoy132, Ayotzinapa and #TodosSomosPolitécnico. Julie Le Mazier covers French student mobilisations of the late 2000s, looking at their tactics, modes of action and organisation. Asher Gamedze and Leigh-Ann Naidoo share insights from a collective process emerging from recent campus revolts across South Africa around *Publica[c]tion*, a Black student-driven publication which aimed to archive, extend and continue the work of the student movement, while challenging and critiquing standard academic knowledge production. Rhoda Nanre Nafziger and Krystal Strong critically appraise the history of Nigeria's student radicalism and the past, present and future horizons of the Nigerian student movement. Sarah Raymundo and Karlo Mongaya discuss struggles within and over higher education in the Philippines, what they term the struggle between postcolonial and transformative education at the University of the Philippines, and the ways these dynamics are linked to broader movements for social and economic justice.

NOTES

1 See for example: EPW Engage (2018); Free Saibaba (n.d.); Free Them All (n.d.); Sen, K. (2019).
2 Ismail (2011) notes that there were 27 university occupations in Britain protesting the Israeli assault on Gaza in early 2009.
3 This article refers to a special themed edition of the journal *Africa* which the authors co-edited.
4 Sangeeta Kamat, 'Comment at Panel on Social Movements, Education, and Learning' (62nd Comparative and International Education Society conference, Mexico City, Mexico, 25 March 2018).
5 See for example, Edu-Factory Collective (2009).

REFERENCES

[Date last accessed for all links: 1 August 2019]

Ahmed, S. (2012). *On Being Included: Racism and diversity in institutional life*. Durham, NC: Duke University Press.

Austin, D. (2009). Education and Liberation. *McGill Journal of Education*, 44(1), 107–117.

Baatjes, I., Spreen C. A. & Vally, S. (2012). The Broken Promise of Neoliberal Restructuring of South African Higher Education. In B. Pusser, K. Kempner, S. Marginson & I. Ordorika (eds), *Universities and the Public Sphere: Knowledge creation and state building in the era of globalization* (pp. 139–158). New York: Routledge.

Bailey, M. & Freedman, D. (eds). (2011). *The Assault on Universities: A manifesto for resistance*. London: Pluto Press.

Baser, B., Akgönül, S. & Öztürk, A. E. (2017). 'Academics for Peace' in Turkey: A Case Of Criminalizing Dissent and Critical Thought via Counterterrorism Policy. *Critical Studies on Terrorism*, 10(2), 274–296.

Benson, K., Gamedze, A. & Koranteng, A. (2018). African History in Context: Toward a praxis of radical education. In A. Choudry & S. Vally (eds), *Reflections on Knowledge, Learning and Social Movements: History's schools* (pp. 104–116). New York: Routledge.

Bhambra, G. K., Gebrial, D. & Nişancıoğlu, K. (eds). (2018). *Decolonising the University*. London: Pluto Press.

Biondi, M. (2018). Alternative Imaginaries on US Campuses: Revisiting the origins of Black Studies. In A. Choudry & S. Vally (eds), *Reflections on Knowledge, Learning and Social Movements: History's schools* (pp. 205–222). New York: Routledge.

Breeze, M., Taylor, Y. & Costa, C. (eds). (2019). *Time and Space in the Neoliberal University: Futures and fractures in higher education*. New York: Palgrave Macmillan.

Brooks, E. (ed.). (2017). *Student Politics and Protest: International perspectives*. London and New York: Routledge.

Canaan, J. (2002). Teaching Social Theory in Trying Times. *Sociological Research Online*, 6(4). Retrieved from https://tinyurl.com/y6fhdh8d.

Carpenter, S. & Mojab, S. (eds). (2017). *Youth as/in Crisis: Young people, public policy, and the politics of learning*. Rotterdam: Sense.

Chatterjee, P. & Maira, S. (eds). (2014). *The Imperial University: Academic repression and scholarly dissent*. Minneapolis, MN: University of Minnesota Press.

Choudry, A. (2015). *Learning Activism: The intellectual life of contemporary social movements*. Toronto: University of Toronto Press.

Choudry, A. & Vally, S. (eds). (2018). *Reflections on Knowledge, Learning and Social Movements: History's schools*. New York: Routledge.

Dawson, A. & Mullen, B. (eds). (2017). *Against Apartheid: The case for boycotting Israeli universities*. Chicago: Haymarket.

Doherty, M. (2018, 13 September). Get a Brazilian. *London Review of Books*, *40*(17), 24–26. Retrieved from www.lrb.co.uk/v40/n17/maggie-doherty/get-a-brazilian.

D'Souza, R. (2009). The Prison Houses of Knowledge: Activist Scholarship and Revolution in the Era of 'Globalization'. *McGill Journal of Education, 44*(1), 19–38.

de García, C. I. R. (2005). *Frente a la Torre: Ensayos del Centenario de la Universidad de Puerto Rico, 1903–2003*. San Juan: La Editorial, UPR.

Dubinsky, K., Krull, C., Lord, S., Mills, S. & Rutherford, S. (eds). (2009). *New World Coming: The sixties and the shaping of global consciousness*. Toronto: Between the Lines.

EPW Engage. (2018). Do Universities Threaten National Security? *Economic and Political Weekly*. Retrieved from www.epw.in/engage/article/do-universities-threaten-national-security.

Edu-Factory Collective. (2010, 17 January). To Build up a Transnational Network of Struggles and Resistance: Within and against the global university. *Monthly Review online*. Retrieved from https://mronline.org/author/the-edu-factory-collective/.

—— (2009). *Cognitive Labor, the Production of Knowledge, and Exodus from the Education Factory*. New York: Autonomedia.

Erdem, E. & Akın, K. (2019). Emergent Repertoires of Resistance and Commoning in Higher Education: The Solidarity Academies Movement in Turkey. *South Atlantic Quarterly, 118*(1), 145–163.

Fanon, F. (1963). *The Wretched of the Earth*. New York: Grove Press.

Faulkner, N. (2011). What is a University Education for? In M. Bailey & D. Freedman (eds), *The Assault on Universities: A manifesto for resistance*. London: Pluto Press.

Ferguson, R. A. (2017). *We Demand: The university and student protests*. Oakland, CA: University of California Press.

Figart, D. M. (2017). Swimming in Debt. In *Stories of Progressive Institutional Change: Challenges to the neoliberal economy* (pp. 81–98). New York: Palgrave Macmillan.

Free Saibaba. (n.d.). [Website]. Retrieved from https://freesaibaba.wordpress.com.

Free Them All. (n.d.). [Website]. Retrieved from https://free-them-all.net.

Ganjavi, M. & Mojab, S. (2018). A Lost Tale of the Student Movement in Iran. In A. Choudry & S. Vally (eds), *Reflections on Knowledge, Learning and Social Movements: History's schools* (pp. 55–69). New York: Routledge.

Gichanga W. M. (2019). *Barriers for Control – The Private Security Industry and Student Protests in South Africa, Pretoria: The Private Security Industry Regulatory Authority*. Retrieved from www.psira.co.za/psira/dmdocuments/research/PSIRA%20Barriers%201203.pdf.

Giroux, H. (2008). Youth and the Politics of Education in Dark Times. In P. P. Trifonas (ed.), *Worlds of Difference: Rethinking the Ethics of Global Education for the 21st Century* (pp. 199–216). Boulder: Paradigm Publishers.

Gramsci, A. (1971). *Selections from the Prison Notebooks of Antonio Gramsci.* New York: International Publishers.

Heffernan, A. & Nieftagodien, N. (eds). (2016). *Students Must Rise: Struggle in South Africa before and beyond Soweto '76.* Johannesburg: Wits University Press.

Hensby, A. (2018). *Participation and Non-Participation in Student Activism: Paths and Barriers to Mobilising Young People for Political Action.* London: Rowman and Littlefield.

Hirji, K. (2019). *Under-Education in Africa: From colonialism to neoliberalism.* Montreal: Daraja Press.

Hodgkinson, D. & Melchiorre, L. (2019, 18 February). Africa's Student Movements: History sheds light on modern activism. *The Conversation.* Retrieved from http://theconversation.com/africas-student-movements-history-sheds-light-on-modern-activism-111003.

Ismail, F. (2011). The Politics of Occupation. In M. Bailey & D. Freedman (eds), *The Assault on Universities: A manifesto for resistance* (pp. 123–131). London: Pluto Press.

Kalla, S. (2018). Do Not Criminalise Those Who Are Marginalised. Retrieved from www.dailymaverick.co.za/opinionista/2018-03-23-do-not-criminalise-those-who-are-marginalised/.

Kelley, R. D. G. (2018). Over the Rainbow: Third World Studies against the neoliberal turn. In A. Choudry & S. Vally (eds), *Reflections on Knowledge, Learning and Social Movements: History's schools* (pp. 223–236). New York: Routledge.

Kelsey, J. (2008). *Serving Whose Interests? The political economy of trade in services agreements.* Abingdon and New York: Routledge-Cavendish.

Lagnado, J. (2016). Towards a History of the Latin American Workers Association 2002–2012. In A. Choudry & M. Hlatshwayo (eds), *Just Work? Migrant workers struggles today* (pp. 106–128). London: Pluto Press.

Luckett, T. & Pontarelli, F. (2016, 4 March). #OutsourcingMustFall: Unity in Action in South African Universities. *The Brooklyn Rail.* Retrieved from https://brooklynrail.org/2016/03/field-notes/outsourcing-must-fall.

—— & Mzobe, D. (2016). #OutsourcingMustFall: The Role of Workers in the 2015 Protest Wave at South African Universities. *Global Labour Journal, 7*(1), 94.

Maharajh, R. (2018). Africa and the Fourth Industrial Revolution: The Need for 'Creative Destruction' Beyond Technological Change. *Perspectives Africa,* 3(December), 30–34.

Maira, S. (2019). Coming of Age under Surveillance: South Asian, Arab and Afghan American youth and post-9/11 activism. In A. Choudry (ed.), *Activists and the Surveillance State: Learning from repression* (pp. 79–96). London: Pluto Press.

Mandel, E. (1970, June). *The Changing Role of The Bourgeois University.* Speech delivered at Rijks Universiteit Leiden on the occasion of its 79th anniversary, June 1970. Retrieved from: www.marxists.org/archive/mandel/1970/06/university.htm.

Martinez, A. & Garcia, N. M. (2018, 28 September). #HuelgaUPR: The Kidnapping of the University of Puerto Rico, Students Activism, and the Era of Trump. *Frontiers in Education*. Retrieved from www.frontiersin.org/articles/10.3389/feduc.2018.00084/full.

Mirrlees, T. & Alvi, S. (2014). Managing with MOOCs: Taylorizing Academia, Deskilling Professors and Automating Higher Education. *Journal for Critical Education Policy Studies*, 12(2), 45–73.

Mojab, S. (2004). State-university Power Struggle at Times of Revolution and War in Iran. *International Higher Education*, 36, 11–13.

Moosa, F. (2019). Fees Must Fall Story As A Musical. Retrieved from www.thedailyvox.co.za/the-fees-must-fall-story-as-a-musical/.

Myers, M. (2017). *Student Revolt: Voices of the austerity generation*. London: Pluto Press.

Pauw, J. (2017). *The President's Keepers*. Cape Town: Tafelberg.

Pensado, J. M. (2015). *Rebel Mexico: Student unrest and authoritarian political culture during the long sixties*. Stanford, CA: Stanford University Press.

Quinlan, E., Quinlan, A., Fogel, C. & Taylor, E. (eds). (2017). *Sexual Violence at Canadian Universities: Activism, institutional responses, and strategies for change*. Waterloo, Ont.: Wilfrid Laurier University Press.

Rhodes Must Fall Oxford. (2018). *Rhodes Must Fall: The struggles to decolonise the racist heart of empire*. London: Zed Books.

Rodney, W. (2014). *The Groundings with My Brothers*. East Point, GA: Walter Rodney Press.

Salaita, S. (2014). Normatizing State Power: Uncritical ethical praxis and Zionism. In P. Chatterjee & S. Maira (eds), *The Imperial University: Academic repression and scholarly dissent* (pp. 217–236). Minneapolis, MN: University of Minnesota Press.

Scandrett, E. & Ballantyne, E. (2019). Public Sociology and Social Movements: Incorporation or a war of position? In M. Breeze, Y. Taylor & C. Costa (eds), *Time and Space in the Neoliberal University. Futures and fractures in higher education* (pp. 169–190). New York: Palgrave Macmillan.

Selwyn, N. (2013). *Distrusting Educational Technology: Critical questions for changing times*. New York: Routledge.

Sen, K. (2019, 7 June). My Mother was Wrongly Jailed for 'Waging War' on India: A Professor with Bad Knees, no Bed. *The Print*. Retrieved from https://theprint.in/opinion/my-mother-is-in-jail-for-waging-war-on-india-a-professor-with-bad-knees-and-no-bed/246808/.

Shivji, I. G. (2018). The Metamorphosis of the Revolutionary Intellectual. *Agrarian South: Journal of Political Economy, Centre for Agrarian Research and Education for South*, 7(3), 394–400.

—— (2005). Whither University. In S. Vally (ed.), Education as Market Fantasy or Education as a Public Good?, *Quarterly Review of Education and Training*, 12(1), 34–36.

Shumar, W. (1997). *College for Sale: A critique of the commodification of higher education*. London: Falmer.

Sian, K. P. (2019). *Navigating Institutional Racism in British Universities.* New York: Palgrave Macmillan.

Slaughter, S. & Leslie, L. L. (1997). *Academic Capitalism: Politics, policies, and the entrepreneurial university.* Baltimore, MD: Johns Hopkins University Press.

—— & Rhoades, G. (2004). *Academic Capitalism and the New Economy: Markets, state and higher education.* Baltimore, MD: Johns Hopkins University Press.

Solomon, C. & Palmieri, T. (eds). (2011). *Springtime: The new student rebellions.* London: Verso.

Sukarieh, M. & Tannock, S. (2015). *Youth Rising? The Politics of Youth in the Global Economy.* New York: Routledge.

—— (2018). The Global Securitisation of Youth. *Third World Quarterly,* 39(5), 854–870.

Tarlau, R. (2019). *Occupying Schools, Occupying Land: How the Landless Workers Movement Transformed Brazilian Education.* Oxford: Oxford University Press.

Thomas, K. (2018) Decolonisation Is Now: Photography and student-social movements in South Africa, *Visual Studies,* 33(1), 98–110.

Torres, C. & Schugurensky, D. (2002). The Political Economy of Higher Education in the Era of neoliberal globalization: Latin America in Comparative Perspective. *Higher Education,* 43(4), 429–455.

Toscano, A. (2011). The University as a Political Space. In M. Bailey & D. Freedman. *The Assault on Universities: A manifesto for resistance* (pp. 81–90). London: Pluto Press.

Vally, S. (2006). Resurgent Comparative Education in these Exigent Times. *Southern African Review of Education,* 11(1), 75–84.

——, Motala, E., Hlatshwayo, M. & Ngcwangu, S. (2019, 8 February). South African Students Are Protesting Again: Why it needn't be this way. *The Conversation.* Retrieved from https://theconversation.com/south-african-students-are-protesting-again-why-it-neednt-be-this-way-109964.

—— & Motala, E. (eds). (2014). *Education, Economy and Society.* Pretoria: UNISA Press.

Vrana, H. (ed.) (2017). *Anti-colonial Texts from Central American Student Movements 1929–1983.* Edinburgh: Edinburgh University Press.

Walker, R. (1990). *Ka Whawhai Tonu Matou – Struggle Without End.* Auckland: Penguin.

Weiss, M. L. & Aspinall, E. (eds). (2012). *Student Activism in Asia: Between protest and powerlessness.* Minneapolis, MN: University of Minnesota Press.

Wiewel, W. & Perry, D. C. (eds). (2008). *Global Universities and Urban Development: Case studies and analysis.* New York: Routledge.

Zamponi, L. (2018). *Social Movements, Memory and Media: Narrative in action in the Italian and Spanish student movements.* New York: Palgrave Macmillan.

Ziadah, R. & Hanieh, A. (2010). Collective Approaches to Activist Knowledge: Experiences of the new anti-apartheid movement in Toronto. In A. Choudry & D. Kapoor (eds), *Learning from the Ground Up: Global perspectives on social movements and knowledge production* (pp. 85–99). New York: Palgrave Macmillan.

2

The trajectory of the 2010 student movement in the UK

From student activism to strikes

Jamie Woodcock

The 2010 student movement in the United Kingdom (UK) was heralded as a return to campus activism, with large numbers of students taking part in occupations and demonstrations across the country. Although the tuition fee increases that they opposed were eventually passed, the movement almost brought down a government and exposed a generation of activists to the experience of mass movements. It brought together activists from previous movements, as well as students from both universities and further education colleges.

Students, by nature of their transitionary position, go on to new activities and occupations after their studies end. This means the trajectory of these activists, their experiences, and repertoires of struggle can become carried over and translated into other movements. This chapter argues that the key underpinning of the 2010 student movement was the earlier anti-war movement in 2003, the Palestine solidarity activism on campuses in 2008 and the financial crisis of 2008 following austerity programmes. This trajectory is followed for two reasons: first, these were important dynamics in shaping the events of 2010; second, I followed this trajectory of the movement in my own activism. I walked out of school in 2003 in protest at the invasion of Iraq, arrived at university towards the end of 2007 in time for the financial crisis and the Palestine solidarity movement, participated in the student movement of 2010, then later became involved in on and off-campus worker organising.

Despite much writing at the time about the birth of a new movement, its trajectory is only now starting to be documented (Cini, 2019; Myers, 2017a).[1] While there is a temptation to draw a clear line between the student movement and the rejuvenation of the Labour Party under Jeremy Corbyn's leadership – which, as Myers (2017b) and others have argued is worth drawing attention to – there is also a risk of missing the other processes and experiences learned from this moment.

In order to draw out these experiences, this chapter will draw on my own experience of this movement, taking my own 'engagement' (Burawoy, 1998, p. 5) and subjectivity as a starting point to reflect on the different moments of the student struggle, as well as the later connection with the labour movement. This took place in three related ways: first, students becoming academics and organising against casualisation and precarity; second, campus organising with cleaners; and third, students graduating and becoming active as trade unionists outside of the university. The chapter takes account of the 2010 movement, understanding it over a longer period of time in which the connections to other movements and events can be explored.

THE PRECEDING MOVEMENTS: STOP THE WAR AND PALESTINE SOLIDARITY

I was a school student in Oxford in 2003. At my school, like many across the country, we were outraged at the proposal of invading Iraq. I vaguely remember Tony Blair's election and a general feeling that things were going to get 'better' under a Labour government. However, things shifted rapidly once Blair began supporting George W. Bush in his calls for war. When the vote was passed in Parliament, I remember thinking that we had to do something to stop Britain going to war. We discussed the possibility of war in classrooms and the playground, asking friends' older siblings (some who were university students) what they planned to do. We heard the call for a school walkout and decided we would do the same. Some of us had been on protests before (although mostly taken by our leftie-liberal parents – my first was in a pushchair), but we had never organised anything ourselves. I remember whispered conversations and planning in advance, nervous about whether anyone would join.

When the day of the walkout came, we left school mid-morning. I was surprised at how many students followed us out of the buildings and towards the main gate. I vividly remember walking past a teacher who shouted at me: 'you can't leave! We'll put you in detention!' I waved my arms around, pointing at all the students now joining in, and responded: 'What? All of us?' and ran off grinning. We marched into the city centre to block roads and cause general chaos. As one leaflet at the time recounted: 'In Oxford 500 school kids walked out and took over the town centre, forcing an Army recruitment stall off the streets, trapping soldiers in their van for half an hour, and blocked the roads' (Marriot, 2009), while another went higher: '1000 blocked Oxford city centre including Carfax and bridges in the south' (Stop the War Coalition, 2003).

Like many others, I had my first taste of a mass movement with Stop the War. We marched – or mostly stood still given the size – along with an estimated 2 million other protestors (German & Murray, 2005) through London as part of 'the largest protest event in human history' (Walgrave & Rucht, 2010, p. xiii). Yet, despite our best efforts, the war went ahead. After ten years, the war led to the deaths of an estimated 1 million people (Physicians for Social Responsibility, 2015). Although we did not know this at the time, there was a feeling of failure and helplessness at seeing the 'shock and awe' of joint US and British military invading Iraq. We had tried to peacefully convince our government not to destroy another country, and they had not listened. This cynicism that followed for me slowly translated into fury at the government, but also became increasingly systemic as I started reading Marx. I finished school, worked boring jobs for a year, then headed off to university, convinced this would be an opportunity to put some of this into practice – with some interest in studying, too.

At the University of Manchester, I got involved with the growing Palestine solidarity movement in British universities. Some of those participating had been school students involved in the Stop the War organisation, while others were involved in Muslim organisations (with a significant crossover), and some were looking for a charitable cause. The students' union was a hub for these activities, as well as organising anti-fascist demonstrations, supporting a postal worker strike, and so on. In our local group, Action Palestine, we took part in educational events and stunts, as well as building connections with Palestinians in Gaza and the West Bank.

However, this changed in December 2008 after the Israel Defence Forces launched a two-week invasion of Gaza. The school students who had walked out over the invasion of Iraq, now joined with many new activists, once again saw the human tragedy of asymmetrical warfare. During the invasion 1,400 Palestinians were killed, with white phosphorus raining down on civilians trapped inside the Gaza Strip. The first action started at the School of Oriental and African Studies (SOAS) in London as students tried to stop a military exhibition, briefly occupying a building before forcing the event's cancellation. The news travelled fast through the Stop the War, Palestine solidarity, Socialist Worker Student societies, Amnesty groups and among other left-wing activists. Soon, students across the country were taking part, with occupations at 30 different universities. At the University of Manchester, we held a general meeting of the Students' Union to debate the issue, with over 1,000 students attending. From this meeting, we occupied buildings on the campus – first the management building, and then later a teaching building. The occupation lasted 31 days, becoming a hub for activism on campus. After escalating to blocking the Vice-Chancellor into his car park with upturned bins and setting off flares, the occupation won almost every demand – including the divestment of university funds from companies in breach of international laws, including those operating in Israel.

The occupation had become an accepted and successful tactic in the university. While the war on Gaza continued, students were able to express solidarity and win important concessions from local management. However, the university year had also started with the collapse of Lehman Brothers and the beginning of the 2008 financial crisis. While the campus occupations over Palestine were not explicitly anti-capitalist, students began to make the connection, with placards on the demonstration appearing with slogans like 'capitalism fails'. Moreover, the movement popularised anti-imperialist ideas and anti-authoritarian practices. This shocked many pre-existing groups like the national Stop the War Coalition, as well as the established Palestine Solidarity Campaign – which failed to support the students occupying over Gaza. As *The Independent* (Dugan, 2009) reported at the time:

> They are the iPod generation of students: politically apathetic, absorbed by selfish consumerism, dedicated to a few years of hedonism before they land

a lucrative job in the City. Not any more. A seismic change is taking place in British universities. Around the UK, thousands of students have occupied lecture theatres, offices and other buildings at more than 20 universities in sit-down protests. It seems that the spirit of 1968 has returned to the campus. While it was the situation in Gaza that triggered this mass protest, the beginnings of political enthusiasm have already spread to other issues.

One example of this is the G20 demonstration in April 2009 in London. Activists from these previous waves of struggle took their keffiyehs to a broad demonstration, ostensibly under the banner of 'March for Jobs, Justice and Climate'. The students I travelled down with from Manchester joined the anti-capitalist bloc 'G20 Meltdown' outside of the Bank of England. We were metres away from Ian Tomlinson (the newspaper seller who was not part of the demonstration) who was attacked and killed by the police (Lewis, 2009). The connections and experiences being developed in 2009 created the grounds for an 'anti-systemic movement' (Arrighi, Hopkins & Wallerstein, 1989) that would later follow. Students were waking up from a 'culture of silence' (Freire, 1970), while also finding a mass audience and milieu of activists that was being transformed through shared collective action. In the process, 'repertoires of contention' (Tarrow, 1998) were being developed. For example, the occupation was then used at SOAS against an immigration raid called by the university against its cleaners. These previous cycles of struggle also brought students into direct confrontation with university vice-chancellors and managers, something that would be quickly repeated in 2010.

THE 2010 STUDENT MOVEMENT

In May 2010, the Conservatives and Liberal Democrats successfully formed a coalition, ending the Labour government that had started with Tony Blair. While the new coalition began to propose wide-ranging changes to higher education, as well as the public sector more broadly, there was also a shift happening with the NUS (National Union of Students). This national organisation previously had very close ties to the Labour Party, even failing to put up any serious opposition to the introduction of tuition fees in 1998. As Dan Swain (2011, p. 98) has argued, the 'NUS's reluctance to challenge the Labour Party was a huge barrier to the movement', so it is 'no coincidence that its biggest mobilisation for decades came only once Labour was in opposition.' However, at the same time, two campaign groups were launched: the National Campaign Against Fees and Cuts (NCAFC) and the Education Activist Network (EAN) at the start of 2010. EAN (of which I was a founding member) started building solidarity with international campaigns and workers' struggles in the UK, while NCAFC organised on student-related issues.

It was not long before the lessons learned in the confrontations with university management in the previous year were being applied again. Lord Browne[2] outlined a proposal to increase tuition fees, and this was met with immediate protest from students. Again, universities were occupied, which quickly connected with each other to discuss tactics and strategies. Student assemblies were called, sending delegates across the country to decide on the way forward. From fighting local managers, students now started to coordinate a national campaign. The previous struggles were one part of a learning process that allowed the student movement to constitute itself as a national political actor for the first time.

Towards the end of the first term, the protests grew into national demonstrations. On 10 November, the NUS called a demonstration in London. We funded nine coaches from Manchester, bringing students down to take part. I remember handing out a marker pen on the coach for other protestors to take down the solicitor's number on their arm in case they were arrested. Many were surprised at this, saying they saw no need as the police would not cause any problems. Once we arrived on the demonstration, it was clear how large the movement was becoming: over 50,000 students filled the streets. We marched along the majority of the route, but took part in a breakaway that had been organised beforehand. As we turned off the agreed route, a NUS steward asked us to keep marching as there 'was nothing to see over there.' We caught a glimpse of the fires being started outside the Conservative Party headquarters.

This demonstration was a turning point. Students faced police brutality and the aggressive use of 'kettling' (the forming of a cordon around a protest and containing it within a limited space). However, on arrival at the headquarters, students surrounded and then occupied the building. The NUS president derided the 'violence' of the demonstrators, but this was a key victory for the movement. As an Egyptian comrade joked with me at the time: 'the students in London attacked the ruling party's headquarters before we did!' On the coach back from the demonstration, we argued about the student throwing a fire extinguisher from the roof (who would later be arrested), but the argument for writing solicitors' numbers down on our arms was no longer contentious.

This action created momentum for further demonstrations two weeks later, in which an estimated 132,000 students took part on what became called 'Day X.' Echoing the Iraq War protests, thousands of school and further education students walked out to join university students. In Manchester, students at a Catholic school had to scale walls to join our demonstration after their disciplinary teachers locked the front gates. These younger students would play a key role in the mobilisations, bringing energy and fury to the demonstrations. For example, at Bury College in Manchester, almost 1,000 students walked out. In London, 10,000 students marched and were kettled by the police. The head of the Metropolitan Police in London, Sir Paul Stephenson, announced to reporters: 'the game has changed, we are living in an era of mass protests' (quoted in Lewis, Taylor & Wintour, 2010).

By this point, there were 32 universities in occupation. These were organising centres, not raising demands like the Gaza occupations. Regular general assemblies were held, not only trying to build the student movement, but also inviting workers who worked on campus and outside of the universities. This was one of the ways that activists, particularly from EAN, tried to connect student militancy to the labour movement. In Manchester, we would leave the occupation daily to speak at trade union branches and trades councils – asking for support for our own struggle, but also trying to encourage them to take action. We wanted to see a response to the attacks they were facing, while also building towards our longer-term goal of coordinated action. In this context, EAN has helped to initiate coordination of occupations and campaigns. In its statement of intent, the coordination declared (EAN, 2010):

> Our fight for education is part of a wider fight against austerity which seeks to make ordinary people pay for a crisis not of our making. A victory

against tuition fees and to defend EMA would be victory for all those under attack. It's a fight that we can win, but not if we are left to fight alone ... We call on parents, workers and trade unionists to do everything in their power to join our resistance on the day of the vote in parliament, up to and including walking out to join our demonstration ... Visit our occupations and support every protest. We will return your solidarity in every way we can, starting with sending a delegation from this coordination to support the tube workers' strike. We are stronger if we fight together and we add our names to the call for a general strike. We stand in solidarity with our brothers and sisters fighting against austerity across the world.

On 9 December, the day of the vote in Parliament on tuition fees, the movement reached a turning point. There was a large demonstration in London's Parliament Square, which came under sustained attack from the police while the vote went ahead. Again, we brought coaches of students down from Manchester. From our contingent, a student had a collarbone broken by a police baton, while another had an arm broken. My friend Alfie Meadows was attacked by police at a cordon, needing emergency surgery to save his life – something the police tried to prevent by keeping him within the kettle (Gayle, 2018). The result of the vote was 323 MPs in favour and 302 against tripling the existing limit of tuition fees, allowing £9,000 in exceptional circumstances (which would rapidly become the norm). The Liberal Democrats, who had previously signed a pledge with the NUS not to raise fees, voted mainly in favour and could have changed the result.

We ended the demonstration kettled on Westminster Bridge in the freezing cold. The majority of our contingent missed the coaches back to Manchester. When we were finally let out of the kettle we had to walk single file through a line of police who photographed us, some of whom pushed or struck us with batons, and most verbally abused us. The learning process about the role of the police had come quite far by then. We tracked down our hospitalised or arrested friends, and arranged accommodation in the university occupations in central London, ending the day bruised and depressed. This protest was the crystallisation of a wider political mood in Britain. This had been shaped first by illegal wars, the greed of bankers, MPs' expenses scandals, many broken promises (first from Labour, then from the Liberal Democrats) and a worsening economic crisis. Despite the negative media coverage, polls showed that the majority of the public supported the students.

After this defeat, the movement diverted into local struggles on campuses, again fighting university managers. Attempts to organise demonstrations were lively, but never recaptured the intensity of 2010, particularly as the school and college students were not re-engaged. I served on the NUS National Executive Council the following year, watching the machinations of the Labour-dominated leadership, content to move back into lobbying the government. By 2012, the movement was a shadow of its former self. A demonstration was called on 21 November. The NUS planned for 10,000 students, but only 3–4,000 turned up. In a move to take even more energy out of the demonstration, the final rallying point was Kennington Park in South London – a place of no strategic or symbolic importance. The demonstration ended with speeches and the NUS president, Liam Burns, was 'pelted with eggs and fruit at the conclusion of the march' (Malik & Ratcliffe, 2012). Once again, echoing critiques made by David Widgery (1969, p. 119) following 1968, the NUS appeared to have 'all the passion of an ashtray.' There were arguments about the NUS being the problem, and that breaking away could be the solution. However, as Widgery (1969, p. 137) also argued, 'a real student movement will grow out of real struggle, not vice versa.' The student struggle was now at its lowest ebb.

BUILDING CONNECTIONS WITH THE LABOUR MOVEMENT

By 2012, many of the organisers of the movement had graduated from university. I had moved to London to start a PhD at Goldsmiths, while most of those I organised with at Manchester had moved onto new things too. Some organisers were elected into student union positions, the NUS structures, or started working for political parties or trade unions. In the UK, the window of being a student is usually three years (undergraduate), which can be extended to four (with a masters), or at the higher end seven years (with a PhD of three funded years). By doing a PhD, I stayed in the university far longer than many of the people I organised with. Many of the school and college students who protested in 2010 were excluded from university with the higher tuition fees. The state of higher education began to shift too, as many students had to take on one or more jobs to make ends meet while studying. The grants that I received while I was an undergraduate became few and far between. This was exacerbated by the wave of police repression which continued long after the demonstrations ended. However, many of the organisers from 2010 went on to be active in the labour movement.

For students like myself who went on to do PhDs, the university became a focus for labour organising. During this time, the traditional image of academic work had been eroded. As Gigi Roggero argues (2011, p. 22) 'unhitching itself from the traditional idea of working one's way up, or the passage toward tenure-track employment, precarity ceases in fact to designate a contingent phase in order to become a structural and permanent element of the corporatization of the university.' The reality of academic work fell well below the expectations of a generation of PhD students who became workers. While we had fought management as students, we became increasingly frustrated with the conditions of our work. By the end of the student movement, the majority of teaching staff in universities were now on precarious short-term contracts.

A group of PhD students, including me, pressured the NUS to organise a national survey of the pay and conditions of postgraduates that teach. The survey found that a third of the respondents were paid under the minimum wage, after taking into account the unpaid preparation time. Around another third had no employment contract for their teaching. Inspired by the workers' inquiry tradition, we launched a similar survey at Goldsmiths to start organising. We later won the best deal in the sector for casualised teaching staff. At SOAS, a survey was also used to start organising. During their campaign, which was led by organisers from 2010, they took unofficial industrial action to force concessions from their managers. Both of these, along with other anti-casualisation campaigns in universities, fed into organising with the UCU (University and College Union) that represents academic workers. There was national strike action of one-day strikes, ill-fated two-hour strikes, and the threat of a marking boycott in 2014.

In 2018, the union took 14 days of strike action across 64 universities against proposed pension cuts. Across different campuses, activists from the student movement could be found organising picket lines and pushing the union to go further: 42,000 workers took part in the action, with an estimated 575,000 teaching hours lost, affecting over a million students. As I have argued with others elsewhere (see Woodcock & Englert, 2018), the rank and file of the membership had little control over the direction, tactics or strategy of the dispute. Instead, this remained mainly in the hands of paid officials and the leadership of the union. As a response, with other activists who had previously been involved in the student movement, we started a workplace bulletin called *The University Worker*.[3] The bulletin was collaboratively written by rank and file activists and handed out at London universities – with copies sent to other cities and distributed online as a PDF file. It catalogued the dispute, sharing stories of the picket lines and proposing tactics and strategies to win.

By the third week of the strike, it was becoming clear that the leadership had diverged from the rank and file. There was an attempt to end the strike after the offer of a deal with no concessions, averted by an occupation and picket of the union's headquarters in London. Younger union members tapped pound coins on the windows of the union office, trying to have their voices heard in the votes about their pensions – and were met with warnings from officials that they would call the police if this continued. A petition was signed by over 10,000 members calling for the deal to be rejected. While the deal was voted down, the planned strike then ended just before the Easter holidays, pulling the momentum away from the struggle. A new deal was proposed, appointing a so-called 'joint expert panel' to spend a year reviewing the pension scheme. This was accepted by 64 per cent of the membership and no further strike action was called. This effectively froze the campaign, with the membership then expected to wait a year to find out the results. This was then followed by a union conference in which the paid staff organised a walkout over criticism of the general secretary, as well as the failure to win a strike ballot over pay. At the time of writing, the panel is still due to report back, with no progress having been made. While this has not ended in a victory, the mobilisation of the rank and file of the union at various points can also be traced back, in part, to activists who had come through the 2010 student movement (Woodcock & Englert, 2018).

A second example of this is activists who became involved in campus worker organising with cleaners. In addition to students, lecturers and administrators, a large number of cleaning, security and catering workers are employed on campus. From 2001 onwards, there were attempts to launch 'Justice for Cleaners' campaigns, in part modelled on the successes of 'Justice for Janitors' in the US. In London, these have centred around demands for a living wage. Citizens UK[4] was involved in setting the living wage, as well as some of the initial organising, building community union campaigns. The connection with student activists began in 2011, as they came into contact with workers on campus, as well as Citizens UK, UNISON and later the IWW (Industrial Workers of the World) (Kirkpatrick, 2014, p. 239). The organising became focused around the University of London Senate House, as well as SOAS, which is a central point for students in London. The workers eventually organised into the Independent Workers Union of Great Britain (IWGB) which led to the '3 Cosas' campaign. This was a fight by outsourced workers who were fighting for three areas of disparity between themselves and in-house workers: sick pay, holidays and pensions (the name 'tres cosas' – three areas – was taken from Spanish, the first language for many of the Latin American workers).

While the campaign has had a series of victories, helped by the support of student activists, it continues today at the time of writing. This involves a boycott of the University of London, with students (and those who used to be students) involved in pressuring organisations and speakers to pull out of events until the in-house agreement is made. This connection between the student and labour movement continues today. There are regular stalls hosted by students at universities in London, providing breakfast to cleaners and involving them in the campaign. Students who have gone through the experience of organising with cleaners on the campuses have then moved into other forms of labour organising after they have graduated.

The IWGB has grown from organising cleaners and university workers to foster care workers, electricians, couriers, food delivery platform workers, Uber and private hire drivers, security guards and most recently videogame workers. Across the union, those active in the student movement can be found organising, whether with Deliveroo and Uber drivers, or supporting new groups of workers to unionise. As well as the IWGB, some participants from 2010 have become active in other public sector and transport unions, continuing to put the tactics and strategies experimented with during the student movement to use in the new context of labour organising.

LEARNING FROM THE TRAJECTORY OF THE 2010 STUDENT MOVEMENT

Many lessons can be learned from the 2010 student movement, as well as the trajectory that it subsequently took. While my own path through these events was undoubtedly riddled with mistakes that could be learned from, there are also larger issues that can be drawn out. It is clear that there was a generation of activists who moved from anti-war protests to Palestine activism, learning from both to shape the 2010 student movement. Across these moments, they came into contact with new repertoires of contention, opposition and potential support. These different moments acted as learning processes that helped individuals to collectively grapple with the changing terrain of the student movement. At first, this was the introduction to mass movement politics and walkouts, then developing into direct confrontation and the seizing of space during occupations. These subjective factors shaped the emergence of (but certainly did not create) the student movement in 2010. For example, the widespread use of occupations provided the basis for the highly visible and strategically important occupation of the Conservative Party headquarters in 2010.

This is not to argue that it was just that generation of students who experienced these different moments in the run-up to 2010. The driving force of 2010 was the school and further education students, who had the most to lose from the raising of tuition fees and the removal of grants. The university students had already paid fees at the lower level, so were, in effect, fighting for the next generation – while also questioning the purpose of universities. The failure of 2010 could be felt in the rage of the London riots in 2011, channelled into a different form and cut off from the wider social movements. The failures – whether to 'stop' the Iraq War, the invasion of Gaza, the sell-out of the Liberal Democrats and tuition fees, or the continuing destruction of higher education – have also been points of divergence – at some points into rioting, depression and repression, or the movement into new terrains of struggle.

Participants in social movement networks engage in collective knowledge production and circulation (Juris, 2008). Thus, while the activists traced in this trajectory did not make up anywhere near the majority of the participants, they had developed experiences, skills, tactics and strategies that were widely shared within the movement.

Thinking this through as a participant myself, my intention is to contribute to the 'creative process of collective theorization and knowledge production carried out from inside social movements' (Juris & Khasnabish, 2013, p. 24). This has therefore been a contribution towards the 'collective wondering and wandering that is not afraid to admit that the question of how to move forward is always uncertain, difficult, and never resolved in easy answers that are eternally correct' (Shukaitis & Graeber, 2007, p. 11). While we may not have won, it is still useful to reflect on how these processes unfolded.

It is also an attempt to introduce another narrative to the trajectory of the student movement that has become popular today. This is not to discount that many activists have become involved in Corbyn's Labour Party, as Matt Myers (2017b) and others have argued, but to draw attention to another trajectory. The learning processes covered in this chapter do not automatically lead to involvement in the labour movement or workplace struggles. However, the role of activists who went through 2010 in the rejuvenation (both potential and actual) of the labour movement is worth tracing. Through these moments, student activists were changed by their attempts to change the world. That some now see the labour movement as a terrain of struggle from which the world can be changed is also important. The failures of Stop the War, international solidarity, students and higher education, the financial crisis and austerity and so on can be partly explained by the failure of the labour movement to move into action and confrontation. Through my own trajectory, this was a key lesson that I learned, and hopefully not one that is lost with those now organising within the Labour Party. While we were students, we fought to connect our struggle to the labour movement. Now part of the labour movement, those same connections need to be made, as well as to other struggles that emerge.

At the start of 2019, an international wave of school walkouts and protests started over outrage at climate change. I watched as students expressed their anger and were condemned in the media, by politicians – and in the UK, even criticised for trampling the grass outside of Parliament. That evening I had dinner with old comrades from the student movement who had followed the same trajectory outlined here. We reflected on whether their walkouts would be a similar transformative moment to the one that we started with. In the years to come, we concluded that we were sure it would be.

NOTES

1   I was interviewed for both publications cited here.
2   John Browne (Baron Browne of Madingley) a former CEO of BP, was appointed as the chair of the independent review into tuition fees.
3   See: https://notesfrombelow.org/tag/higher-education, the archive of the bulletins.
4   Citizens UK is a community organising group, with a membership of trade unions, religious groups and charities.

REFERENCES

[Date last accessed for all links: 30 May 2019]
Arrighi, G., Hopkins, T. K. & Wallerstein, I. (1989). *Anti-Systemic Movements.* London: Verso.
Burawoy, M. (1998). The Extended Case Method. *Sociological Theory,* 16 (1).
Cini, L. (2019). *The Contentious Politics of Higher Education: Struggles and power relations within Italian and English universities.* London: Routledge.
Dugan, E. (2009, 8 February). Students Are Revolting: The spirit of '68 is reawakening. *The Independent.* Retrieved from www.independent.co.uk/news/education/education-news/students-are-revolting-the-spirit-of-68-is-reawakening-1604043.html.
EAN. (2010). A Call to Workers. *Education Activist Network.* Retrieved from https://educationactivistnetwork.wordpress.com/about-us/28-nov-student-coordination/.
Freire, P. (1970). *Pedagogy of the Oppressed.* New York: Continuum.
Gayle, D. (2018, 15 October). London Police Force Must Act over Excessive Force Claim, says Court. *The Guardian.* Retrieved from www.theguardian.com/uk-news/2018/oct/15/alfie-meadows-london-police-force-must-act-over-officer-accused-of-excessive-force-says-court.
German, L. & Murray, A. (2005). *Stop the War: The story of Britain's biggest mass movement.* London: Bookmarks.
Juris, J. S. (2008). *Networking Futures.* Durham: Duke University Press.
—— & Khasnabish, A. (2013). *Insurgent Encounters.* London: Duke University Press.
Kirkpatrick, J. (2014). The IWW Cleaners Branch Union in the United Kingdom. In I. Ness (ed.), *New Forms of Worker Organization: The syndicalist and autonomist restoration of class struggle unionism* (pp. 233–257). Oakland, CA: PM Press.
Lewis, P. (2009, 7 April). Ian Tomlinson Death: Guardian video reveals police attack on man who died at G20 protest. *The Guardian.* Retrieved from www.theguardian.com/uk/2009/apr/07/ian-tomlinson-g20-death-video.

——, Taylor, M. & Wintour, P. (2010, 25 November). Student Protests: Met chief warns of new era of unrest. *The Guardian*. Retrieved from www.theguardian.com/education/2010/nov/25/student-protests-new-era-unrest.

Malik, S. & Ratcliffe, R. (2012, 21 November). Student March Ends in Eggs, Fruit and Anger. *The Guardian*. Retrieved from www.theguardian.com/education/2012/nov/21/student-march-eggs-anger.

Marriot, R. (2009). March 2003: Schoolkids against the Iraqi War [Blogpost]. Retrieved from https://libcom.org/history/march-2003-schoolkids-against-iraqi-war.

Myers, M. (2017a). *Student Revolt: Voices of the austerity generation*. London: Pluto Press.

—— (2017b). How 2017's Youthquake Started. *Vice*. Retrieved from www.vice.com/en_uk/article/ne7dmd/how-2017s-youthquake-started.

Physicians for Social Responsibility (2015). *Body Count: Casualty figures after 10 years of the 'War on Terror', Iraq, Afghanistan, Pakistan*. Washington DC.

Roggero, G. (2011). *The Production of Living Knowledge: The crisis of the university and the transformation of labor in Europe and North America*. Philadelphia, PA: Temple University Press.

Shukaitis, S. & Graeber, D. (2007). *Constituent Imagination*. Oakland, CA: AK Press.

Stop the War Coalition (2003). Mass Actions across the Country as War Breaks out [Online report]. Retrieved from www.labournet.net/ukunion/0303/stwtu2.html.

Swain, D. (2011). The Student Movement Today. *International Socialism*, 130, 95–112.

Tarrow, S. G. (1998). *Power in Movement: Social movements and contentious politics*. Cambridge: Cambridge University Press.

Walgrave, S. & Rucht, D. (2010). Introduction, *The World Says No to War: Demonstrations against the War on Iraq*. Minneapolis, MN: University of Minnesota Press.

Widgery, D. (1969). NUS – the Students' Muffler. In A. Cockburn & R. Blackburn (eds), *Student Power: Problems, diagnosis, action* (pp. 119–140). Harmondsworth: Penguin.

Woodcock, J. & Englert, S. (2018). Looking Back in Anger: The UCU strikes. *Notes from Below*, 3. Retrieved from https://notesfrombelow.org/article/looking-back-anger-ucu-strikes.

3

Insurgent subjects

Student politics, education and dissent in India

Prem Kumar Vijayan

Students are often perceived to be 'unruly subjects' (Boren, 2001). This chapter discusses these 'unruly subjects' as political subjects. It will frame this discussion around three deeply intertwined questions:

- What is entailed in this perception of the subject as 'unruly subject', i.e. how should we understand this phrase?
- What are the relations between the subject, *qua* subject, as this 'unruly subject', and as a 'political subject'?
- What are, or could be, the politics of this 'unruly subject'?

The elaboration of the rationale and logic for this framing is an attempt to constitute a theory of the student as a political subject. As theoretical propositions, therefore, they seek to make a global case of the discussion, and hence need to be tested for their explanatory power in empirical terms, continuously. I have sought to establish their explanatory power by elaborating their discursive logic, and analysing their political implications. Wherever possible, I have tried to illustrate them with instances from India.

STUDENTS AS 'UNRULY SUBJECTS'

My first proposition is that the perception of the student as 'unruly subject' is one reason why university campuses have historically been (or sought to be) isolated from other social spaces. The 'quarantining' of these 'unruly subjects' in enclosed college campuses and university towns seeks to ensure that their 'unruliness' does not seep into wider society (Dooley, 2001, p. 1368). It may be countered that this isolation is not in fact quarantine, but seclusion from distractions, with the intent to facilitate intellectual pursuits. But this does not square with the perception of the student as 'unruly subject'. The seclusion of such a subject then becomes a quarantining, regardless of intention. By extension, student politics too, is (sought to be) kept confined to campuses. However – and this is the second proposition – although thus confined, students and their politics remain affected by and susceptible to outside forces – cultural, social, political, but especially economic. Besides the funding and financing of educational and research programmes, external forces can also determine the kinds and contents of these programmes, along the lines of social capital, cultural prejudices and/or political affiliation – often through the control of funding itself.

Taken together, these two propositions recall the Gramscian-Althusserian contention that the primary objective of education (and any such ideological institutional apparatus), is to produce the subject as malleable, obedient and docile, as much as capable and productive (Althusser, 1995); and/or solicit their consent to 'subject' themselves to the larger hegemonic order – the field of power constituted by the articulations of these (ideological and repressive) state apparatuses with each other, and with civil society (Gramsci, 1971). 'Field of power' also recalls Foucault (1972) and Bourdieu (1984) in their analyses of education (Bang, 2014; Weininger & Lareau, 2018). They suggest that the entire structure and infrastructure of higher education (HE) is deliberately designed (or has historically evolved in design) to tame and subdue the generations of 'unruly subjects' who will pass through them. These subjects occasionally manage (or are allowed) to 'burst free'; but this is expected, tolerated, even encouraged (whether subtly or expressly) – the Foucaultian 'incitement'. It reminds us that this potential to 'burst free' requires a disciplinary edifice that can subdue it; or control it when it cannot be subdued; and quarantined so that, in any event, it causes minimum damage. This perception of the student is integral to the structuring of HE – not just as a form of, and means for, knowledge dissemination, but also to inculcate discipline, and produce 'disciplined', rather than 'unruly' subjects.

But of all the ways in which students' subjectivities could be conceptualised, why decide on 'unruliness' as the definitive characteristic? One common assumption is that it is part of being 'youthful': as youth, they are in a condition of temporal liminality, in transition from adolescence to adulthood (Dooley, 2001). But why that liminality should manifest as 'unruliness' is never examined; it is simply assumed to be 'natural'. This argument never explicates the specific rules that are 'violated' in this 'unruliness' (which literally means 'to not abide by the rules'). This allows for particular forms of conduct to be characterised as violative of a putative rule, which actually comes into being at that very moment, as precisely the proscription of that very form of conduct – a point we will return to later. Furthermore, students of 'vocational' and 'professional' courses are much less perceived as 'unruly', compared to 'generalist' courses in the sciences or arts – at least, in India. In these too, it is usually found more in liberal arts programmes than in the sciences (Pare, 2016). Finally, this is a deeply gendered argument.

ACCESS, EXCLUSION AND PREJUDICE IN HIGHER EDUCATION

Throughout world history, women have frequently had little or no access to HE opportunities. As such, they could not become students of the kind being discussed here – the educated 'unruly' ones. Even when they eventually gained access, starting in late nineteenth century Europe and America (King, 1981), rarely, if ever, were they conceived of *collectively* as 'unruly'. As the campaign *for* women's access to HE began to produce results, it quickly became one *against* these very institutions, for their gender-discriminatory practices. Access was more or less limited to the humanities, and some social sciences (Waltraud & Horwath, 2014). But for a long time, even they remained taught almost exclusively by men (Parker, 2015). Along with gender discrimination, women's access to HE was marked by the same exclusions and discriminations that demographically divide the male student populace – class, caste, race, religion, etc. HE did not produce the anticipated opportunities for women – at least, not immediately, not everywhere and certainly not in the same way for all women (Jacobs, 2002). This reveals that allowing women (or any marginalised and/or disempowered groups) access to

HE was never about providing them with new, more and better life opportunities.

The phenomenon referred to as 'allowing access to HE' is really a complex intersecting of multiple phenomena, or *modes of dominance*[1] – the intersecting masculine hegemonies of class, caste, race, religion, tribe, etc. Allowing or not allowing access to HE was thus about exercising not just gender dominance, but also caste, class, religious, etc. dominance. However, the systematic resistance to greater inclusiveness was, and is, unsustainable. Not only was women's demand for access legally sound, it very soon (especially during the two world wars) became evident that they could constitute a cheaper, yet equally skilled labour force in many industrial and commercial sectors. With intensifying economic globalisation, the creation of a cheaper labour force was possibly a major reason for increasing access to HE for women in less 'developed' countries (Tran-Nguyen, Zampetti & United Nations Conference on Trade and Development, 2004). But where increased access to HE occurred, it was massively overdetermined by a multiplicity of factors, and by extra-institutional social forces as much as by institutional ones. Perhaps that is one reason why the inclusion of marginalised groups has happened at a glacial pace.

The means of regulation of access are mostly techniques of exclusion disguised as stipulations of eligibility. In India, many HE institutions require students to take entrance examinations. They must first achieve a minimum percentage in their secondary school 'board' exams.[2] These exams are usually for admission to STEM courses – Science, Technology, Engineering, Mathematics (and in India, we can substitute 'Medicine' for Mathematics). Students from lower income families – who are also historically mostly lower-caste – tend to be excluded from these institutions, lacking the financial means and resources available to the upper-classes (mostly upper-castes), to compete effectively in these exams. Although the reservation system affords some compensatory access, it is often shoddily implemented, if at all.[3] Thus it effectively reinforces prejudice against the lower-classes and lower-castes as being inherently inferior and undeserving of access to HE.

This prejudice became starkly evident in 1989, in upper-caste reaction to the then Indian government's decision to implement the recommendations of the 'Mandal Commission[4] Report', which recommended that 27 per cent of all educational and employment vacancies in government institutions be reserved for Other Backward Castes (OBCs).[5] It immediately provoked nationwide upper-caste outrage. Since the majority of HE students then (and now) were upper-caste, it seemed as if the entire HE system was rising in protest. Perhaps for the first time in independent India, HE students mobilised along caste lines, nationwide, demanding that the move be reversed. They claimed that they would not get admission to HE institutions, and even if they did, would not get employment, because of reservations for OBCs, SCs and STs. Much of the resentment was articulated as a matter of 'merit' – i.e. that the lower-castes would get the benefits of education and employment despite being less 'meritorious' academically, than the upper-castes. Despite the high drama, culminating in a series of self-immolations, no government had the courage to overturn this decision. By the mid-1990s, the protests had faded away without impacting policy.

But they had a dramatic impact on the subsequent direction of student and national politics in India. These protests were arguably the first major, national open articulation of a right-wing sensibility and sentiment. They were a crucial part of the larger shift to the right in Indian politics and policies, that grew inexorably in the 1990s. As the economy shifted rightward, with the intensification of the drive to liberalise-privatise-globalise (LPG), employment opportunities in the expanding private sector opened up (Jakobsen, 2016, p. 256), while employment in government services declined by about 4 per cent between 1994 and 2012 (Khullar, 2015). Whatever advantage might have been gained by OBCs through reservation was – and continues to be – whittled away, with upper-caste interest shifting to the private sector – where reservations did not apply (Vijayan, 2012).

The 'Mandal agitation' also changed the fundamental dynamic of all subsequent student politics in India. It revealed the student populace to be deeply riven along caste lines, that quickly ramified into divisions along other lines too, especially religion and ethnicity. The phenomenal rise of the Akhil Bharatiya Vidyarthi Parishad (ABVP: All India Student Council), affiliated to the right-wing Bharatiya Janata Party (BJP: Indian People's Party) illustrates how subsequent student agitations were all marked by these evolving fissures. 'Between 2003 and 2013, the ABVP membership doubled to 22 lakh,[6] growing one lakh a year. In 2014, when the current government took power, the ABVP's membership jumped over nine lakh to reach 31.75 lakh' (Tiwary, 2016, n.p.).

There were two major contributory factors to this rise. First, in 2006, the OBC reservations proposed by the Mandal Commission were formally extended to HE, leading to large-scale ABVP-led protests. Although the agitation was unsuccessful, upper-caste students, who constituted the majority in most universities and colleges (and still do) (UGC, 2018, p. 15), rallied to the ABVP in large numbers. The ABVP seized the opportunity to indoctrinate them with its brand of religious 'nationalism'. Its first major success was in the 2008 agitation to have 'Three Hundred Ramayanas: Five Examples and Three Thoughts on Translation', an essay by renowned poet and scholar A. K. Ramanujam, removed from Delhi University's history syllabus, on the grounds that it hurt 'Hindu' sentiments. Since then, it has been actively involved in a series of agitations, mostly centred on questions of 'nationalism' (Ramachandran, 2017; Tiwary, 2016). Significantly, it has played little or no part in other major student agitations, dealing with other issues, such as the massive anti-rape protests of 2012–13; the anti-semester agitation[7] of 2011; and the 'Occupy UGC'[8] movement of 2015 (Dabral, 2018).

The second factor was the changing demographic of university campuses, after 2006. With OBC reservations, upper-caste numbers began falling below 50 per cent in many campuses (Ashraf, 2016). University and college campuses witnessed unprecedented clashes, mostly between the ABVP on one side, and left-wing and lower-caste student organisations on the other. The first major instance of this was when Prime Minister Narendra Modi visited Delhi University in 2013, as part of his election campaign, left-wing teachers' and students' organisations came together to protest, and were attacked by the ABVP as 'anti-nationals', with the open support of the police. By the time the Modi-led right-wing National Democratic Alliance (NDA) government took charge in 2014, the figure of the 'anti-national' had come to dominate political discourse. This polymorphously perverse bogeyman had to be named in all its forms – Islamic radicals, Naxalite-Maoists, Kashmiri militants, the 'pseudo-secular' leftist intelligentsia, most of the English media, Christian missionaries accused of conversion, etc. – and destroyed. Three clashes – the crackdown on 'seditious anti-nationals' in Jawaharlal Nehru University; the ABVP's harassment of Dalit (lower-caste) student, Rohith Vemula, leading to his suicide; and the harassment of the leftist woman president of the Allahabad University students' union, Richa Singh (Ashraf, 2016) – all in 2016, revealed their caste basis explicitly.

This factor has arguably intensified the push towards the privatisation of HE. Between 2001 and 2010, the HE sector doubled in size in India, but 63.2 per cent of that expansion was from private initiatives (Ashraf, 2016). Since the reservation policy is not applicable to these institutions, they are overwhelmingly upper-caste. This shows that exclusion from HE is structured and organised not only in institutional ways – e.g. through regulations and stipulations – but also through the organisation of social and economic conditions into obstacles that daunt the aspirations of the excluded. Denial of access is disguised by the seeming provision of access. Access is provided in a manner calibrated to exclude certain social groups, from disciplines and courses that feed certain 'power' sectors of employment – e.g. marginalised groups remain a minority in STEM courses, and hence in the science and technology sectors (as well as in the bureaucracy), which are top-heavy with upper-class, upper-caste (mainly male) employees (Gabriel & Vijayan, 2019; Mosse, 2018).

The opening of access to HE thus serves multiple purposes. It dangles the possibility of better life opportunities as incumbent on gaining access to HE. It then ensures that that access is highly controlled and regulated, institutionally, as well as rendered nearly inaccessible through the social and economic frameworks it is located in. HE's ostensible objectives have frequently been formulated as the improvement of the (student) self, and through that, of society at large: 'the interests and opportunities and demands of life are not limited to any few subjects one may elect to study. They cover the entire range of nature and of society. That is the best liberal education which best enables one to live a full life ...' (Ministry of Education, 1962, p. 103). But an increasingly prevalent understanding of late emphasises the role of education in 'the realization of the national goals ... [E]ducation should ... increase productivity, achieve social and national integration, accelerate the process of modernization and cultivate social, moral and spiritual values' (Ministry of Human Resource Development, 2013, p. 3). The focus has shifted to a more functionalist, even nationalist understanding of HE as necessary for economic productivity and national integration. Elsewhere, I had noted that the increasing private-corporate interest in HE in India (indeed, worldwide) is driven by:

> the need for 'surplus graduates and skilled workers' ... a readily available
> workforce at the service of commerce and industry, on a scale that ensures

the uninterrupted supply of labour. Such a situation inevitably favours employers over employees, serving to make and maintain the workforce as docile, internally divided by competitiveness over employment, and willing to be subjected to whatever passes for 'education' and 'skill-training' in the name of enhancing employability.

(Vijayan, 2016, p. 65–66)

HIGHER EDUCATION, THE POLITICS AND ECONOMICS OF KNOWLEDGE

This understanding constitutes the basis for my third proposition: that the project of HE – the pursuit and production of knowledge – has always been funded, shaped and decided by what will enhance nationalism, state-formation and economic productivity.

This is evident from history. One of the first major changes in the history of English education occurred in the 1660s, when 'Nonconformists began opening dissenting academies to teach law, medicine, commerce, engineering and the arts' (Gillard, 2018, n.p.). This period saw the rise of the English mercantile middle-class, and tremendous growth in literacy rates for both men and women. The changes in the political economy from the seventeenth through to the twentieth century – from being agriculture-driven to being driven by trade and then by industrial production, imperialism and colonial conquest – are markedly evident in the changes in the structure and curricula of HE in this period (Gillard, 2018; Mitch, n.d.). Changes in the structuring of HE allowed for the social and intellectual engineering of a new class, of its relations to power, and thereby of a new hegemonic order. This intensified over the next few centuries, as this class gradually morphed into an industrial capitalist one and eventually, into a class defined increasingly by finance-capitalism, by the end of the twentieth century.

However, as this new order began to consolidate, it encountered counter-hegemonic tendencies unleashed by its own dissenting academic institutions. Many debates around HE, from Matthew Arnold (Arnold, 1869) to Paulo Freire (Freire, 1970), engage almost obsessively with the political and economic challenges of opening educational institutions to the lower classes. Access to at least some aspects and forms of HE was deemed necessary, given the need for a workforce skilled in increasingly complex tasks, such as administration and management. Meanwhile, the nature of the education imparted, and the very disciplines into which this education was structured and organised, were all almost intractably configured by their historical roots in discourses of dissent and political liberty (Thompson, 2017). This dilemma is succinctly captured in the differentiation that gradually developed between 'liberal education' and 'vocational education' (Conway, 2010, p. 75). Further, the history of the development of this dilemma is mainly a masculine one, closely related to the emergence of the gendered history of the public-private divide. The education of upper- and middle-class women, increasingly confined to the private sphere, was decided by the genre of the 'conduct book' that emerged in the eighteenth century (Majewski, 2015, p. 9). This was clearly as much a means of exclusion from HE as the gendering of education itself (Davidoff, 2007, p. 15). In other words, HE was as much subject to the dynamics of this public-private divide as the economy and the organisation of social space. However, working-class and peasant women were not seen as needing even this limited access to education, until much later.

This sketch of the tangled relations that evolved historically – between the organisation of HE; that of gendered social spaces; the emergence of the discourse of rights; its centrality to the emergent understandings of 'democracy'; and the history of the formation of the nation-state in imperial Europe – reveals that the principle of exclusion that organises HE is resonant in each of these linked phenomena. This is true whether in the public-private divide and its gender hierarchies, or in the class hierarchies of this 'democracy', or in the intensification of national boundaries in the formation of nation-states. This brings me to my fourth proposition: that any implementation of this principle of exclusion is in itself a provocation to unrest, to desire not just inclusion but the right to be included. The principle of exclusion is premised on the perception of the excluded as *insurgent*. It incites a violence that is therefore inherent to this rights-based conception of 'democracy' (Vijayan, 2017). The moment of incitement to violence is, as Foucault argued, the moment of initiatives to contain it too – i.e. to represent this insurgency as requiring disciplinary measures – not just through corporal means, but institutional and discursive ones (Foucault, 1995). Unsurprisingly, those excluded are then torn between their urge to unrest, and the fear of discipline, and perhaps further exclusion.

Hence the perception of students' 'unruliness' is socially, not biologically, determined. Given the history of the gendering of social spaces, this unrest – potential or real – was inevitably masculinised (hence the easy slide into biological determinism as an explanation for 'unruliness'). Many patriarchal traditions articulate this 'unruliness' as the 'sowing-of-wild-oats' stage in the male subject's transition into adult masculinity. The resultant 'hegemonic masculinities' (Carrigan, Connell & Lee, 1985) are usually defined by success or failure at this violent transition. They manifest either as oppressor masculinities (enforcing discipline), or resistant masculinities (that resist that enforcement) or in transforming from the latter into the former.[9] Arguably, the last (i.e. transformation) is likely to happen only when the disciplinary/ enforcement actors (individuals, institutions, discourses, practices) are perceived to be too powerful to themselves be transformed (or removed) through resistance. The strength of this perception of greater power lies partly in its actual enforcement; but partly in continuously soliciting the subject's acquiescence to it – as Gramsci argued; or, in Althusserian terms, through the 'Repressive State Apparatus' (RSA) and the 'Ideological State Apparatus' (ISA).

A fundamental task of the ISA is to defuse the unrest by justifying the various forms of exclusion. Equally important is the need to induce in its subjects an absolute belief in, and unquestioning acceptance of, the sanctity, legitimacy, right and authority of the ISA and RSA, to administer the principle of exclusion, and manage and regulate the various instances of its application. The sites of application were – are – invariably located in demographies thought to require disciplining – women, children, the working class, peasants, the unemployed, people of colour, natives in the colonies – and of course, students. But by this logic, the student who gains access to HE should become a compliant subject, rather than an 'unruly' one, because the structure and organisation of HE is designed to ensure compliance. Access to HE is granted on the implicit condition that the student-subject accepts the absolute authority and rectitude of the knowledge imparted in these institutions, and of the institutions themselves. It is implicitly but pervasively linked to the acquisition of political and economic power, the exclusion from which renders these subjects insurgent in the very moment of exclusion. As significantly, the institutions and mechanisms of exclusion offer themselves as the means to tame those 'unruly subjects', and indeed, with their consent, compliance and obedience. How then can one explain the perception of the student as 'unruly' subject, once granted access to HE?

'UNRULY SUBJECTS' AND THE POLITICS OF STUDENT STRUGGLES

The answer lies in my fifth proposition: that the insurgency of this subject is never understood as completely erased. Only by continuously reminding the subject of the potential for insurgency, through the media, the continuous application of the principle of exclusion and of the putative threat that it poses to the discourse of exclusive rights that passes for 'democracy', can s/he not only gradually cease to see himself/ herself as an 'unruly' subject, but also begin to actively participate in the repression of that putative insurgency.

Thus the politics of the insurgency of this subject tends to be perceived in two ways: one, that this subject is easily amenable to becoming political, i.e. to organised politicisation, even 'radicalisation' (Ministry of Home Affairs, 2015); and two, that it is also easily amenable to adopting, and/or transforming into, a larger, more organised politics of regulated violence. The 'students' union' was perhaps the most insidious institutional mechanism that evolved for the latter. Within its 'safe space', 'unruliness' could play out as a competitive politics that acknowledged the student as a political subject, the student body as a legitimate political community, and thus the union as a legitimate political representative of that community. But the price that the students' union pays for its legitimate existence is that it must adhere to the rules for its existence laid out by the educational institution. This understanding of 'student union' is evident in the Lyngdoh Committee report,[10] which states that 'the aim of prescribing a system of elections is not only to provide for representation of student issues, but also to provide a base for young students to learn the basic fundamentals of representing others, as well as the principles of good governance' (Lyngdoh et al., 2006, p. 46). The report continues: 'The institution should organize leadership-training programs with the help of professional organizations so as to groom and instill in students leadership qualities' (Lyngdoh et al., 2006, p. 57). The union thus not only contains and regulates the 'unruliness'; through its alchemy, the (potentially) resistant-subject is morphed into the (potentially) oppressor-subject.

This understanding may seem somewhat counter-intuitive and dismissive of the political struggles that many student unions have engaged in, often successfully. Nevertheless, several scholars note this difference between institutionalised and non-institutionalised student politics, even if they do not necessarily interpret it in this way (Boren, 2001; Luescher-Mamashela, 2015; Milburn-Shaw & Walker, 2017). These two kinds of student politics (i.e. institutionalised and non-institutionalised – also distinguished sometimes as 'student organisation' versus 'student activism' or 'student movement') also can, often do, inform, colour and even determine the success or failure of each other's struggles. In fact, the successes of student unions noted above were arguably because of the synergy between them and the larger student movements.

Through the large-scale student participation in the political upheavals of nineteenth-century Europe, student unionisation began to constitute the basis of student activism, within and outside the university (Dooley, 2001, p. 1369). Further,

> Although students have been prominent in many revolutions and revolutionary movements, as well as other forms of contentious politics, student movements – social movements comprised wholly or mainly of students – are a distinctively modern phenomenon. Their emergence is predicated upon the existence in a society of a critical mass of students.
>
> (Rootes, 2013, p. 1453)

Here, Rootes refers to the prerequisite for mass, non-union, student political action, but does not clarify how we might understand the term 'critical'. If qualitatively, what would be the criteria, and terms of reference, of such criticality? If quantitatively, would it be a percentage of the student populace that is critical of a given society? Or the total student populace as a percentage of the total population of that society? What percentage, in either case, would constitute 'critical', and how? And perhaps most importantly (given that the entire HE system is closely linked to the larger systems of ISAs and RSAs, and works to enforce the principle of exclusion, as well as to thereby tame the insurgent subject) under what circumstances could such a critical mass (be allowed to) emerge in the first place?

The term 'mass' here registers a variable quantity because students constitute a transient population (e.g. Luescher-Mamashela, 2015, p. 43;

Rootes, 2013, p. 1456). In contrast to other kinds of social identities – race, ethnicity, gender, sexuality, nationality, class, caste – the student is an *institutionally produced* figure, i.e. determined by affiliation to an educational institution. The agency of the student, *qua* student, is defined, determined and circumscribed by the terms of institutional affiliation, which are decided by the institution. These include, but are not limited to, meeting the admission requirements, and submitting to stipulations like attendance, assessments and evaluations of academic performance, adherence to codes of conduct, disciplinary provisions, etc. Consequently, institutionally organised student politics – or student union politics – are frequently confined to issues related to these very institutional factors.

However, in many parts of the world, and certainly in India, students also organise – and/or get organised – in non-institutionally affiliated ways. This often takes shape as the student wings of larger political parties or other ideological-political formations. In India, several major pan-national student organisations are essentially the student wings of the national parties. Currently the three most high-profile outfits are (in order of decreasing influence and popular support): the ABVP; the 'National Students' Union of India' (NSUI), affiliated to the 'Indian National Congress (Indira)' (INC – referred to commonly as the 'Congress Party', or 'Cong-I'); and the 'All India Students' Association' (AISA), affiliated to the Communist Party of India (Marxist-Leninist) (CPI-ML). Several other student outfits are organised along ethnic, religious, caste or regional lines, such as the (now-banned) Students Islamic Movement of India (SIMI) and the Ambedkar Students' Association, for Dalit students.

None of these organisations have any real autonomy. These organisations are mainly just promissories of access to political power, that serve the same purpose as HE, in offering pathways to inclusion. The student as political subject is expected to comply with the requirements and stipulations of the student organisation, as well as its parent body. Students also organise around non-institutional, or non-campus issues, in ways that are not necessarily pre-planned. These may pertain to higher education in general; to larger social, cultural, political and/or economic issues; or could be in response to specific events, as with the 2012–13 mass protests against sexual violence (Bakshi, 2017). Such impromptu mobilisations have been the definitive hallmark of social movements in general – movements that remain insurgent, insofar as they refuse to be compliant and obedient. These kinds of student movements continue to emerge sporadically, but remain less effective and less influential. This is partly because of the increasing impact of corporate capitalist incursions into HE. Since the Report on a Policy Framework for Reforms in Education in 2000 (the Ambani-Birla Report) (Government of India, 2000), there has been an inexorable push towards privatising higher education. This report set the agenda for a series of further reports, policy initiatives and legislative measures. It has been matched by a series of similar private sector reports and documents urging privatisation as the panacea for higher education in the country (Vijayan, 2016). Several of these documents estimate the quantum of India's higher education market to be US$115 billion, over the next ten years (averaging about INR70,000 crores[11] per year). However, the gargantuan profits of this massive market can be harvested fully only if the state withdraws and permits freer private investment in this sector.

The other major HE policy change in India has been the drive to 'Indianise' the curriculum – which effectively means greater Sanskritisation and Hinduisation. These issues have been covered extensively elsewhere (Dayal & Hashmi, 2015; Gabriel, 2018; Vijayan, 2016). Suffice it to note that this dual-pronged approach to HE reform aims to ensure student compliance through the carrot of privatisation and the stick of Sanskritisation. As this process accelerates, the student as insurgent, 'unruly' subject is visibly disappearing, and the 'critical mass' that was referred to earlier seems to be becoming more and more difficult, if not impossible, to achieve, even in the sporadic forms of extra-institutional mobilisation mentioned earlier. If anything, this 'insurgency' is now openly, and with increasing acceptability, directed by outfits like the ABVP at the inclusive injunctions of the Indian constitution – to enforce secularism, socialism and democracy – in favour of an exclusivist, chauvinist politics.

CONCLUSION: TOWARDS A PROGRESSIVE STUDENT POLITICS

What then is the way ahead for a viable, progressive student politics? Given the genealogy of student politics as argued above, is such a politics even possible, as an effective political force – not just in India, but anywhere? Here, it may be salutary to recall the old Marxian dictum, that we make our own history, albeit not in circumstances of our own making. Perhaps the first task for any student political enterprise is to re-examine the identity 'student' – to see it, not as constituted by age or biology, class or gender, but as a particular element in a larger political-economic dynamic. It is to see, therefore, that not all student politics are necessarily either progressive or democratic, however much they may claim those qualities. It is to see that the terms 'progressive' and 'democratic' themselves need to be reviewed, given that they are increasingly defined by corporate and finance capitalist interests. It makes possible the building of mobilisations, alliances and consolidations in terms of the social relations within that political economy – i.e. in terms of other similarly situated elements – rather than relying on the possibility or hope of building a 'critical mass' of student insurgency. Finally, it is to embrace the idea of one's insurgency, even if it is recognisably a historically manipulated one, not as a form of guilt or debility, but as a force that can bring change – perhaps the only one that can, today.

NOTES

1 This phrase is theoretically elaborated in Vijayan, 2019.
2 E.g. the exams conducted by the Central Board of Secondary Education (CBSE), the Indian Certificate of Secondary Education (ICSE) or the various state boards, such as the Andhra Pradesh Board of Secondary Education.
3 This eventually reflects in the continuing low presence of lower-castes in government jobs (Gabriel & Vijayan, 2020 [forthcoming]).
4 Named after B. P. Mandal, the MP who headed the Commission.
5 Scheduled Castes (SCs) and Scheduled Tribes (STs), constitute the socially and economically weakest, most marginalised, sections of society in India. Together they constitute about 23 per cent of the population; along with the category Other Backward Castes (OBC), who constitute about 47 per cent of the population (Sachar, 2006: 7), the lower-castes comprise nearly 70 per cent of India's total population.
6 One lakh (written as 1,00,000) = One hundred thousand. So the numbers translate as 2,200,000 and 3,175,000.
7 Protests at Delhi University opposing the decision to replace the existing annual examination assessment with the bi-annual semester system.

8   Against the scrapping of fellowships for thousands of postgraduate students and the further commercialization of Indian higher education.

9   The converse is also possible but rare, and almost never forms as a hegemonic masculinity.

10 The short name for the 'Report of the Committee Constituted by Ministry of Human Resource Development, Government of India as per the Direction of the Hon'ble Supreme Court of India to frame Guidelines on Students' Union Elections in Colleges/Universities', published in 2006. The Committee was chaired by J. M. Lyngdoh, former Chief Election Commissioner of India.

11 1 crore = 10 million.

REFERENCES

[Date last accessed for all links, except where indicated: 18 July 2019]

Althusser, L. (1995). *On the Reproduction of Capitalism: Ideology and ideological state apparatuses.* London: Verso.

Arnold, M. (1869). *Culture and Anarchy.* (J. Garnett, ed.). Oxford: Oxford University Press.

Ashraf, A. (2016, 4 April). How Changes in the Reservation System in 2006 Sowed the Seeds for Today's Campus Tumult. *Scroll.in.* Retrieved from https://scroll.in/article/print/805919 (Accessed 31 August 2018).

Bakshi, G. (2017). The 'Nirbhaya' Movement: An Indian feminist revolution. *Gnovis Journal: Communication, Culture, and Technology, XVII*(2). Retrieved from www.gnovisjournal.org/2017/05/02/the-nirbhaya-movement-an-indian-feminist-revolution/.

Bang, L. (2014). Between the Cat and the Principle: An encounter between Foucault's and Bourdieu's conceptualisations of power. *Power and Education,* 6(1), 18–31. https://doi.org/10.2304/power.2014.6.1.18.

Boren, M. E. (2001). *Student Resistance: A history of the unruly subject.* New York: Routledge.

Bourdieu, P. (1984). *Homo Academicus.* (P. Collier, Trans.). Stanford, CA: Stanford University Press.

Carrigan, T., Connell, B. & Lee, J. (1985). Toward a New Sociology of Masculinity. *Theory and Society, 14*(5), 551–604. https://doi.org/10.1007/BF00160017.

Conway, D. (2010). *Liberal Education and the National Curriculum.* London: Civitas: Institute for the Study of Civil Society.

Dabral, N. (2018, February). Student Movements Across a Decade. *DU Beat.* Retrieved from dubeat.com/2018/02/student-movements-across-a-decade/.

Davidoff, L. (2007). Gender and the 'Great Divide': Public and private in British gender history. *Journal of Women's History, 15*(1), 11–27. https://doi.org/10.1353/jowh.2003.0020.

Dayal, J. & Hashmi, S. (2015). *365 Days: democracy and secularism under the Modi regime.* (J. Dayal & S. Hashmi, eds). New Delhi: Anhad.

Dooley, B. (2001). Student Movements. In *Encyclopedia of European Social History From 1350 to 2000, Vol 3* (Paperback, pp. 1368–1378). Charles Scribner's Sons. Retrieved from www.encyclopedia.com/international/ encyclopedias-almanacs-transcripts-and-maps/student-movements.

Foucault, M. (1972). *POWER/KNOWLEDGE: Selected interviews and other writings 1972–1977.* (C. Gordon, ed., C. Gordon, L. Marshall, J. Mepham & K. Soper, Trans.). New York: Pantheon.

—— (1995). *Discipline and Punish: The birth of the prison.* (A. Sheriden, Trans.). New York: Vintage.

Freire, P. (1970). *Pedagogy of the Oppressed.* (M. B. Ramos, Trans.) (2005, 30th ed.). New York: Continuum.

Gabriel, K. (2018). Turning Right, Losing Rights: An overview of educational reforms in the Modi regime. In J. Dayal, L. Dabiru & S. Hashmi (eds), *Dismantling India – A 4 Years Report* (pp. 60–65). New Delhi: Media House.

—— & Vijayan, P. K. (forthcoming, 2020). Whose State is it Anyway? Reservation, representation, caste, and power. In A. S. Rathore (ed.), *B.R. Ambedkar: The quest for justice.* New Delhi: Oxford University Press.

Gillard, D. (2018). Education in England: Timeline. Retrieved from www. educationengland.org.uk/history/print-timeline.html (Accessed 18 January 2019).

Government of India (2000). A Policy Framework for Reforms in Education. A Report submitted by special subject group on Policy Framework for Private Investment in Education, Health and Rural Development, Prime Minister's Council on Trade and Industry (Mukesh Ambani-Kumaramangalam Birla Report), New Delhi.

Gramsci, A. (1971). *Selections from the Prison Notebooks of Antonio Gramsci.* (Q. Hoare & G. N. Smith, eds & Trans.) (Paperback). New York: International Publishers. https://doi.org/10.1080/10286630902971603.

Jacobs, J. A. (2002). Gender Inequality and Higher Education. *Annual Review of Sociology,* 22(1), 153–185. https://doi.org/10.1146/annurev.soc.22.1.153.

Jakobsen, J. (2016). Disappearing Landlords and the Unmaking of Revolution: Maoist mobilization, the state and agrarian change in Northern Telangana. In A. Nilsen & K. Nielsen (eds), *Social Movements and the State in India* (pp. 239–268). London: Palgrave Macmillan. https://doi.org/10.1057/978-1-137-59133-3.

Khullar, V. (2015). *Vital Stats: Overview of central government employees* (PRS Legislative Research). New Delhi.

King, P. M. (1981). The Campaign for Higher Education for Women in 19th-Century Boston. *Proceedings of the Massachusetts Historical Society,* 93(1981), 59-79 CR-Copyright © 1981 Massachusetts Hi. https://doi. org/10.2307/25080888.

Luescher-Mamashela, T. M. (2015). Theorising Student Activism in and Beyond the 20th Century: The contribution of Philip G. Altbach. *Student Engagement in Europe: Society, Higher Education and Student Governance* (January 2015), 33–49.

Lyngdoh, J. M., Hasan, Z., Mehta, P. B., Prakash, V., Singh, I. P. & Dongaonkar, D. (2006). *Report of the Committee Constituted by Ministry of Human Resource Development, Government of India as per the Direction of the Hon'ble Supreme Court of India to frame Guidelines on Students' Union Elections in Colleges/ Universities.* New Delhi.

Majewski, E. K. (2015). *Breaking through Walls and Pages: Female reading and education in the 18th century British novel* (Master's thesis). Wake Forest University, North Carolina.

Milburn-Shaw, H. & Walker, D. (2017). The Politics of Student Engagement. *Politics, 37*(1), 52–66. https://doi.org/10.1177/0263395715626157.

Ministry of Education. (1962). *Report of the University Education Commission, 1948–1949.* Delhi. Retrieved from www.teindia.nic.in/Files/Reports/CCR/ Report of the University Education Commission.pdf.

Ministry of Home Affairs, G. of I. (2015, 19 January). Union Home Minister Shri Rajnath Singh Calls for Holistic Education. *Press Information Bureau, Government of India*, pp. 2–3. Retrieved from pib.nic.in/newsite/PrintRelease. aspx?relid=114786.

Ministry of Human Resource Development (MHRD). (2013). *Rashtriya Uchchatar Shiksha Abhiyan – National Higher Education Mission.* New Delhi.

Mitch, D. (n.d.). Education and Economic Growth in Historical Perspective. Retrieved from eh.net/encyclopedia/education-and-economic-growth-in-historical-perspective/ (Accessed 18 January 2019).

Mosse, D. (2018). Caste and Development: Contemporary perspectives on a structure of discrimination and advantage. *World Development, 110*, 422–436. https://doi.org/10.1016/j.worlddev.2018.06.003.

Pare, S. V. (2016). Why Are So Many Humanities Students Activists? Retrieved from www.huffingtonpost.in/shvetal-vyas-pare/why-are-so-many-arts-stud_ b_9434078.html (Accessed 12 January 2018).

Parker, P. (2015). The Historical Role of Women in Higher Education. *Administrative Issues Journal Education Practice and Research, 5*(1), 3–14. https://doi.org/10.5929/2015.5.1.1.

Ramachandran, S. K. (2017, 9 March). The Rise of ABVP and Why it Attracts the Youth. *The Hindustan Times.* Retrieved from www.hindustantimes. com/india-news/the-rise-of-abvp-and-why-it-attracts-the-youth/story-EINVYG4021aDovqD3f6IcK.html.

Rootes, C. (2013). Student Movements. In *The Wiley-Blackwell Encyclopedia of Social and Political Movements* (pp. 1453–1458). Oxford: Blackwell.

Sachar, R. (2006). *Social, Economic and Educational Status of the Muslim Community of India: A report. [Sachar Committee Report].* New Delhi.

Thompson, W. C. (2017). Liberalism in Education. In *Oxford Research Encyclopedia of Education* (Online, Vol. 1). Oxford: Oxford University Press. https://doi.org/10.1093/acrefore/9780190264093.013.49.

Tiwary, D. (2016, 24 February). JNU Row: Behind ABVP's confidence, govt and growth. *The Indian Express.* Retrieved from https://indianexpress.com/

article/india/india-news-india/jnu-protests-jnusu-behind-abvp-confidence-govt-and-growth-rohith-vemula/.

Tran-Nguyen, A.-N., Zampetti, A. B. & United Nations Conference on Trade and Development. (2004). *Trade and Gender: Opportunities and challenges for developing countries.* New York: United Nations.

University Grants Commission (UGC). (2018). *Higher Education: All India and states profile, 2017–18.* (P. Mittal, S. Chandra, & D. Rajput, eds). New Delhi: University Grants Commission. Retrieved from www.ugc.ac.in/pdfnews/ eUGC_HE AIS Profile.pdf.

Vijayan, P. K. (2012). *Making the Pitrubhumi: Masculine hegemony and the formation of the Hindu Nation.* Erasmus University, Rotterdam, The Netherlands. Retrieved from https://repub.eur.nl/pub/32246/.

—— (2016). Privatising Minds: New educational policies in India. In S. Gupta, J. Habjan & H. Tutek (eds), *Academic Labour, Unemployment and Global Higher Education: Neoliberal policies of funding and management* (pp. 57–78). London: Palgrave Macmillan.

—— (2017). The Violence of Democracy. *Kairos: A Journal of Critical Symposium,* 2(1), 83–99. https://doi.org/10.1057/9781137356642.0010.

—— (2019). *Gender and Hindu Nationalism: Understanding masculine hegemony.* New York: Routledge.

Waltraud, E. & Horwath, I. (2014). *Gender in Science and Technology: Interdisciplinary approaches.* (E. Waltraud & I. Horwath, eds). Bielefeld: Transcript Verlag.

Weininger, E. B. & Lareau, A. (2018). Pierre Bourdieu's Sociology of Education. In T. Medvetz & J. J. Sallaz (eds), *The Oxford Handbook of Pierre Bourdieu.* Oxford: Oxford University Press. https://doi.org/10.1093/ oxfordhb/9780199357192.013.11.

4

Neoliberalism, national security and academic knowledge production in Turkey

Gülden Özcan

Following the 2016 attempted military coup in Turkey, a massive purge was initiated against all opposition. Academics have also been targeted. Over 7,000 academics of all ranks were dismissed from public duty, and banned from leaving the country, while many others faced various rights violations and persecution. However, this was not an isolated case in Turkey's political history. After the 1980 military coup, a number of academics were dismissed, forced to retire or to resign, or had to flee the country after being accused of posing threats to 'national security'. This chapter aims to understand the recurrent purges in Turkish academe and map the major spaces of resistance of academics in both periods. In doing so, I will inquire about the possibilities and limitations of resistance among critical academics in both post-1980 and post-2016 periods by drawing on their experiences.

These two periods mark the turning points in the neoliberal restructuring of Turkey's higher education institutions, the initial phase after the 1980 coup, and the last phase of its consolidation after the 2016 attempted military coup. Comparing the ways in which critical academics as producers of dissident knowledge were labelled as 'threats to national security' and dislocated in massive numbers in these two periods enables us to better understand and theorise the operation of neoliberal authoritarianism in knowledge production processes not only in Turkey, but also in other neoliberal contexts. The chapter is divided into three parts. First, I will explore these significant turning points in the neoliberalisation process in Turkey and their significance for higher education. Second, I will discuss the case of dismissed academics in the name of securitisation of universities in both periods. Third, I will explore the fields of resistance and discuss the limits and possibilities of mobilisation.

NEOLIBERALISM AND ACADEMIA IN TURKEY

Much like Chile and Argentina, Turkey is an experimental case of neoliberal-authoritarianism, which was instituted under the three-year interim military regime following the 1980 military *coup d'état* (Ahmad, 1999; Klein, 2008). The interim military regime aimed to pacify all oppositional forces through civil-military joint action in the name of rebuilding and maintaining national security (Özcan, 2014) laying the groundwork for the articulation of neoliberal policies into the socio-political domain (Coşar & Özman, 2004). Between 1977 and 1980, the number of work days lost due to job actions and strikes was over twice those lost between 1973 and 1976 (Boratav, 2006, p. 146). Business owners began to openly demand the control and discipline of trade unions as well as the privatisation of state-owned enterprises. Two years before the coup, in 1978, a report by the Turkish Industry and Business Association (Türkiye Sanayiciler ve İşadamları Derneği – TÜSİAD) clearly stated the new paradigm:

> If the state tries to do everything, it ends up doing nothing ... If the state produces canned food, raises turkeys, makes shirts, opens grocery stores, the state then cannot find the required time and sources to perform its key function, that is protecting the nation's borders and maintaining the security of people and property.
>
> (quoted in Haspolat, 2012, p. 173, author's translation)

This three-year military regime was in a sense a counter-attack of capital while the military kept a vigilant eye on the labour market (Boratav, 2006, p. 148).

As part of the new political structure, the Council of Higher Education (Yüksek Öğretim Kurulu, YÖK) was established in 1981 as a constitutional organ under the military regime and worked towards centralising the university system. The YÖK became the main final decision-making body on the election of university presidents, deans, and the appointment of department chairs, also overseeing universities' internal affairs and deciding on the allocation of state funds (Coşar & Ergül, 2015, p. 110). The YÖK's control was justified in official discourse on the grounds that the previous system ensuring the autonomy of universities made it impossible to coordinate higher education institutions and ensure a viable system of instruction due to a high degree of politicisation (Coşar & Ergül, 2015, p. 105; Ulutürk & Dane, 2009). At a ceremony where universities presented General Kenan Evren (who led the 1980 military coup and remained as president until 1989 after transition to civilian rule) with an honorary doctorate in Law in 1983, he reassured university communities that the YÖK was a much-needed establishment:

> The council is not outside higher education; it is rather a part of it. This council, which has knowledge of the subjects related to the universities, took on the services of effective regulation, taking all kinds of initiatives for the improvement of the universities, for the best use of resources and especially the balanced distribution of faculty countrywide.
>
> (Kenan Evren'in Söylev ve Demeçleri, 1983, p. 159, author's translation)

Evren defined the universities of the pre-coup period as seedbeds of anarchy (Kenan Evren'in Söylev ve Demeçleri, 1982, pp. 101, 302).

The 1982 Constitution also opened the way to establish private universities for the first time. These universities receive state subsidies but depend heavily on tuition fees. In 1984, the YÖK's first president, Professor İhsan Doğramacı, became the founder of Bilkent University, the first private university in Turkey. Over time, the mentality of private universities has also spread throughout state universities. The YÖK has served to infuse a business mentality into universities via the practices of standardisation and the discourse of high efficiency, coupled with disciplinary regulations including bans on political activism on campuses (Coşar & Ergül, 2015, p. 111). It also facilitated the opening of universities to market-oriented research and the needs of neoliberal capitalism and imposed a market-friendly curriculum. Marxist economics professor Oya Köymen was dismissed from duty in 1983 after the YÖK's establishment, but returned to her post in 1990 following a successful lawsuit. She narrates her return to the Faculty of Economics seven years later:

> Everything was changed. In the textbooks, there was either no mention of Keynes, the founder of macroeconomics; or he could find a place in the footnotes. Classrooms with 50-student capacity started to hold 120 students. The buildings [on the campuses] were silent, because most of the faculty also had jobs outside the university. Economics was turned into an overwhelmingly mathematics-based discipline.
>
> (Quoted in Özen, 2002, p. 232, author's translation)

While curriculum development has increasingly been market-oriented, universities' primary objectives were redefined. They were expected to facilitate students' vocational skills, not critical or scientific thinking skills (Önal, 2012). The 1990s were the consolidation period of these neoliberal practices in higher education institutions. Those who were dismissed post-1980 were replaced by new hires who had no choice but to comply with the new system, as the consequences of non-compliance were severe.

The 2000s were the crisis phase of the post-1980 neoliberal restructuring process. The 2001 economic crisis, along with increasing conservatism, eased the way for the emergence of the Justice and Development Party (Adalet ve Kalkınma Partisi, AKP) with strong popular support. This process was also helped by the long-standing bans on left-wing political activism and union activism in the post-1980 period. In a sense, the AKP government stepped forward to complete the unfinished transition to neoliberalism in economic terms (Coşar, 2012). The AKP managed to get support from the capitalist class by promising to continue with International Monetary Fund/World Bank recovery plans. In line with global neoliberal policies, all forms of social solidarity were redefined and 'dissolved in favour of individualism, private property, personal responsibility, and family values' (Harvey, 2005, p. 23).

In higher education, the YÖK continued with increasingly neoliberal and authoritarian policies. The Bologna Process (BP), one of the sites where the YÖK's authoritarianism was matched with neoliberal requisites is exemplary in this respect. According to Coşar and Ergül (2015, p. 104), the BP in Turkey represents 'the fine-tuning between neoliberal educational policies and statist authoritarianism.' The BP aimed at comparability in the standards and quality of higher-education qualifications with Europe in the context of Turkey's candidacy to join the European Union. Turkey has been in the BP since 2001. The YÖK has facilitated the BP by making it compulsory for universities to take measures to adjust the higher education system to the European Credit Transfer System. In doing so, the Council used terms like shareholder/ stakeholder, competition-quality and strategy and directly laid the groundwork for course design according to free market dynamics and for opening university education to corporate control (Coşar & Ergül, 2015, p. 112). The number of private universities skyrocketed during the AKP's term: 64 new private universities opened – 14 of which were closed in the aftermath of the attempted 2016 coup. An increasing number of private universities and a growing student population did not reflect increasing resources for higher education. These expansions were made possible with the further precarisation of academic labour and unpaid overtime of those in relatively secure academic positions (Vatansever, 2018a, 2018b).

Immediately after the attempted 2016 coup, a state of emergency was declared, and a major purge of the alleged coup plotters in the name of national security was expanded to all kinds of opposition, including academics. The persecution of academics intensified as the authorities used the cover of the purge against the coup plotters to engage in extra-legal actions against Kurdish, unionised and left-wing academics. Fifteen private universities were closed, over 7,800 academics were dismissed, and large numbers have been persecuted with forced retirements, resignations, exile and other rights violations (Demokrasi İçin Birlik, 2017). The YÖK prepared the list of academics to be dismissed, on the recommendations of YÖK-appointed presidents of each university. The most striking group to be dismissed were those known as Academics for Peace, or Peace Academics. Academics for Peace drafted a peace statement calling on the Turkish government to end the violence in Kurdish provinces and resume the peace process in the face of increasing atrocities in the Kurdish cities in late 2015. The statement was also a call against the AKP's intensifying neoliberal-authoritarianism aimed at feeding the war economy. The statement quickly gathered 1,128 signatures from academics of diverse disciplines across the country. After the statement's release to the press on 11 January 2016, an intense campaign of intimidation against the signatories began, as President Erdoğan labelled the academics as 'traitors', accusing them of supporting terrorism:

> You pseudo-intellectuals; you are dark, and nothing beyond. You are not intellectuals at all. You are as dark and ignorant as that you have no idea of Southeast and East, even the whereabouts of these [regions]. But we know those places as we know the way to our home; the address of our home ... The masses, calling themselves academics blame the state. They do not suffice with this; and invite the foreigners to Turkey. This is called pro-mandate stance. The same mentality existed 100 years ago ... Today, we face the treason of the pseudo-intellectuals most of whom even are paid by the state, and carry state identity cards.
>
> (BBC News Türkçe, 2016)

Yet despite the defamation and harassment of signatories, the statement received over 1,000 additional signatures. Since then, signatories have faced arbitrary rights violations with an extraordinary range and degree of repression. These included disciplinary investigations, police interrogations, detentions and imprisonment, threats, mobbing, intimidation, bans on leaving the country, dismissals, suspensions from duty and cuts to their research funding. Persecution of the signatories intensified after the 2016 failed coup attempt. The two-year state of emergency that was announced after the attempted coup further epitomised the AKP government's repressive policies. This last 'cleansing' of the universities further helped transform higher education in Turkey while ensuring the docility of the remaining academics.

ACADEMIC INSECURITY IN THE ERA OF NATIONAL SECURITY

Regulation of the universities provides an exemplary case to understand the thread that links neoliberal authoritarianism to national security and to the state-controlled knowledge regimes. It has been well-documented how neoliberalism and militarisation of the universities goes hand-in-hand through the analogy of the military-industrial-academic complex (Giroux, 2007; Chatterjee & Maira 2014). Colonisation of the universities by the security forces had already occurred under the military regime in Turkey between 1980 and 1983. Major campuses were gated, and first the gendarmerie (military police, responsible for rural areas including Kurdish provinces), then private police were deployed at the gates to check identity documents of every individual entering the campus. Gündüz Vassaf, who resigned from his academic appointment to protest the dismissal of his colleagues after the YÖK's establishment, narrates: 'One day I went to visit my friends at the Middle East Technical University. An armed gendarmerie at the [campus] entrance blocked my way asking, "What business do you have here?" I replied asking, "What business do YOU have here?" He did a routine ID check. I moved on' (quoted in Özen, 2002, p. 178).

University students and academics were marked as threats to national security. After the 1980 military coup, the term 'national security' was expanded to define 'peace and security of society'. The new National Security Law defined the term as 'protecting and watching the constitutional order, national being, totality of the state as well as all its benefits including political, social, cultural and economic benefits and its contractual law against all kinds of internal and external threats' (quoted in Bayramoğlu, 2004, pp. 87–88, author's translation). The pacification of the universities in this period involved a war on diverse fronts. This ranged from curriculum to appointed presidents, from private security on campuses to harsh disciplinary practices against students and faculty including a new dress code and facial hair regulations (Köymen, 2007, p. 132). These measures in the name of national security culminated in the massive purge of academics. A group of academics, known as '1402'likler' (those subjected to Martial Law Act number 1402), were dismissed. The last clause of the second section of Act number 1402 suggested:

> Martial rule commanders may perform through relevant institutions and organs their demand to suspend or dismiss those public employees or local government employees working in their regions if they see that the work of these employees is objectionable to the general security, public security and public order or that the work they do is not beneficial to the public.
>
> (quoted in Köymen, 2008, p. 192)

Thousands of public employees were dismissed under this Act. Dismissals of faculty members were determined based on the recommendations from the YÖK-appointed university presidents as well as the then president of the YÖK, Doğramacı, and executed by the faculty deans. Those dismissed were given an infamous 'yellow envelope' in which a one-sentence letter read: 'It came to our attention that you are suspended from duty based on the last clause of the second section of Act number 1402 by the Martial Rule Commander's decision, dated XXX, numbered XXX' (Özen, 2002, p. 60). The letter omitted any words of respect or appreciation for their service. These yellow envelopes were often delivered by the faculty deans in the same manner the letter was written, as if it was a part of the routine military order-and-command chain. The recipients lost their right to work in the public sector.

The number of academics dismissed through these yellow envelopes has never been precisely determined as the dismissals were conducted individually. Reports from the authorities at the time misinformed the public about the numbers dismissed. The most thorough research done through a scan of the newspapers at the time reveals the names of 327 academics that were dismissed through the YÖK, and names of 861 academics who (voluntarily or involuntarily) resigned or retired because of the conditions. But the report itself, published by *Bilim ve Sanat* (*Journal of Science and Art*), explains that many names are missing. The actual number of those dismissed through the YÖK is at least more than twice the number quoted in the report (Köymen 2008, p. 194). Elimination of dissident academics paved the way for other aspects of neoliberal policies in Turkey's higher education sector in the post-1980 period, such as the mushrooming of private universities, an increase in project-based research, and business models of management (İnal & Akkaymak, 2012; Coşar & Ergül, 2015). The discourse of national security worked towards pacifying dissident voices. It created a securitised university environment, eliminating resistance.

Peace Academics who signed the 2016 Peace Declaration were also dismissed on the basis of claims about national security. This most recent cleansing of the universities occurred in a period where students, parents and to a certain extent, faculty members had forgotten the impacts of the 1980–1983 military regime on the universities. Until the early 2000s, the atrocities conducted under the military regime against politicised youth were still vividly present in collective memory, and youth were repeatedly urged to refrain from political involvement. The university youth of the 2000s did not receive as much advice to stay out of politics. It seemed as though the military regime had been successful in completely depoliticising the youth. But the Gezi Resistance,[1] starting in

June 2013, proved them wrong. Politicisation of university students was well underway with the emergence of the *Öğrenci Kolektifleri* (Student Collectives – ÖK) in 2006, and then the resurgence of the *Fikir Kulüpleri Federasyonu* (Federation of Debating Societies—FKF) in March 2013, a few months before the Gezi Resistance started. ÖK considers all Turkey's university students to be their members (Gencoglu & Yarkin, 2019). Their aim was defined on their website: 'ÖK first and foremost defends free education in the face of the marketisation of the universities … ÖK believes that education is a basic right and struggles for equal, free, scientific education in mother-tongue for all' (Öğrenci Kolektifleri, 2019). FKF, on the other hand, although reminiscent of the socialist student organisation of the 1960s with the same name, claims no ties with the previous organisation. It states its aim to be the struggle for 'the youth to voice their demands in a more organised, louder, and more effective manner' (Fikir Kulüpleri Federasyonu, 2019). Another example from the university campuses was the *Asistan Dayanışması* (Assistant Solidarity). Research assistants (mostly PhD students) were organised to stand up against the YÖK's new policies that risked precarisation of early career academic staff (Uğurlu, 2015). These and other student organisations worked to bring the masses together during the Gezi Resistance.

As in other crises, the crisis of the 2000s in Turkey meant significant changes in production, distribution and consumption. This meant further precarisation of the labour market, privatisation of state-owned enterprises, increasing household debts and further cuts to public services. Implementation of these changes required new security measures – again as in other crises. The Internal Security Package (2015)[2] was one of the most representative manifestations of the AKP's increasing authoritarian politics. The new laws were drafted right after the 2014 Kurdish protests in Turkey against the Islamic State's attack on the city of Kobane in Syria, near the Turkish border. During the protests, 35 were killed and many wounded as a result of police violence (BBC News Türkçe, 2014). New regulations aimed to prevent such protests. There was also reference to the Gezi Resistance as an instance of disrupting public security. The repressive package increased the powers of the police and gendarmerie on site, and equipped both with authority in intelligence services and discretionary powers. It further criminalised oppositional collective action of any kind (Coşar & Özcan, 2019, forthcoming).

The AKP's policies hinted at a new social order that required further security measures to pacify the social forces, including universities. The attempted coup in 2016 provided the justification for the government to cleanse universities of these dissident groups. In doing so, the AKP government followed in the footsteps of the post-1980 military regime. During the three-year military regime, along with economic adjustment programmes, societal consent to neoliberal policies was manufactured by civil-military joint action. In parallel, in the two-year state of emergency under the civilian AKP government (2016–2018), authoritarian measures were used to manufacture consent to the new social order.

RESISTANCE, LIMITS AND POSSIBILITIES

The 1982 Constitution that was written and ratified under military rule banned all kinds of political activities for groups and organisations that are not founded as political parties. Political parties were allowed only if they were approved by the National Security Council. Petitions were the only acceptable form of participation in social activism under martial law. Statements criticising military rule were banned, as were mass demonstrations. Military rule ended in 1983 with the election of a civilian government, but martial law was maintained, and the social order established under the military interim regime continued. In order to criticise this order, left-wing intellectuals came together following the lead of Aziz Nesin, a world-renowned socialist humourist and writer, and drafted a petition, entitled 'Observations and demands regarding the democratic order in Turkey', widely known as *Aydınlar Dilekçesi* (Petition of Intellectuals – 1984). In a short period of time, and despite the fear of being persecuted, 1,260 writers, artists, actors, journalists and lawyers signed the petition in the first round, and it was submitted to President Evren and Parliament. The petition focused on citizens' basic democratic rights and demanded an end to the rights violations without providing concrete cases, centring the text around more abstract concepts mainly to avoid disagreements among the possible signatories (Orman, 2005).

This was the first organised and effective resistance involving academics who were dismissed or who resigned after the foundation of the YÖK. As expected, government reaction was harsh. Evren denounced signatories as 'traitors'. In his public address, immediately after the petition was presented to him, he said:

> We saw many intellectuals. Many of them who engaged in acts of treason. There were some poets, they fled abroad. Weren't they intellectuals? There is no need to be an intellectual to rule this nation! The last Sultan [of the Ottoman Empire], Sultan Vahdettin, was an intellectual, too, but he handed our country over to the enemy.
>
> (Orman, 2005, p. 31)

The petition could not be shared with the broader public as its publication in newspapers was immediately censored. Only 59 among the first 1,260 signatories – those who supposedly led the petition – were tried for 'acting against the martial rule ban'. The trial lasted for a year and a half and resulted in the acquittals of all defendants (Orman, 2005, p. 32).

Ekmek ve Hak Dilekçesi (Bread and Rights Petition – 1986) was the second large attempt by intellectuals involving dismissed academics, again led by Nesin. The Petition of Intellectuals intentionally avoided any economic issues in order to emphasise civil rights. But two years later, it came to the attention of intellectuals that economic problems confronted all workers, farmers, civil servants, small entrepreneurs and students (Orman, 2005). So the main critiques in this petition concerned the Turkish economy's dependency on the IMF, the government's commitment to 'January 24 Decisions' (an economic restructuring package adopted before the 1980 coup, representing the Turkish economy's commitment to neoliberal policies) and privatisation of state-owned enterprises. This petition can be seen as a follow up to the Petition of Intellectuals, first as an anti-fascist, then as an anti-capitalist statement (Orman, 2005).

Another significant step in the resistance to the YÖK order at the universities was symbolised in the activities of the Ekin-BİLAR Incorporation, an initiative which Nesin also led. As mentioned above, the 1982 Constitution banned political activities of non-profit organisations, professional associations and charities. It was very difficult for a left-wing group to legally incorporate as a non-profit association. Nesin, by maintaining his sense of humour, suggested incorporating a for-profit joint stock company that would 'commodify' and 'sell' culture. Writers, artists and dismissed academics quickly came together as shareholders of a company they named Ekin A. Ş.

(Ekin means 'culture', and A. Ş. stands for joint stock company) and applied for incorporation on 9 October 1984 (Hafıza Kaydı, 2018). The application was denied. But they found another formula. In September 1985, they managed the transfer of the shares of another company to the Ekin A. Ş. executive board, and taking over the name of the company, BİLAR A. Ş. The company organised various arts and culture activities – but not without consequences. Throughout the year, people in the executive team were put on trial, and the venues they used for the activities were temporarily shut down by the governors. The then prime minister Turgut Özal criticised the company on the grounds that the group was misrepresenting their political activities as trade activities. Yalçın Küçük, a dismissed academic and one of the founders of Ekin-BİLAR A. Ş., commented on Özal's critique: 'the YÖK is selling diplomas, we are selling and making money out of science' (Cumhuriyet Daily, 1986). He was referring to the introduction of tuition fees to the public universities, and to the private universities both of which were initiated under the YÖK order. By late 1986, they initiated 'People's Universities' and began organising seminars, symposia and congresses. Various intellectuals including dismissed academics gave lectures in these seminars. The curriculum developed in these lectures offered an alternative to the YÖK-imposed curriculums at the universities (Özen, 2002). BİLAR A. Ş. was also in contact with universities in Germany, the Netherlands, Ireland, Denmark, Austria and England. Representatives of the company occasionally went abroad to talk about their alternative university experience (Hafıza Kaydı, 2018; Özen, 2002).

One of the major attempts that focused exclusively on 1402'likler (including academics, but also other public employees) came later in 1988. Founded in 1986, the Human Rights Association (İnsan Hakları Derneği, İHD) established a commission in 1988 for the victims of Martial Law Act number 1402, treating it as a human rights issue. This provided a strategic benefit for the victims, opening the door for a court case against the government. Organised efforts through the İHD made it possible to more accurately document the names, number and rights violations of the victims. It also enabled them to make the issue more visible internationally, leading to the European Parliament's condemnation of the practices based on Act number 1402 as human rights violations (Özen, 2002, p. 290). Joining forces, dismissed academics opened cases against the government, claiming that the decisions made under martial law by the commanders cannot apply during civilian rule. These court cases resulted in the return of dismissed academics to their universities starting in 1990.

While in the Petition of Intellectuals and in the Petition of Bread and Rights, issues of rights violations including the cases of dismissed academics were problematised around the new political regime and its economic policies, in this phase of the resistance, they approached the issues as human rights ones. This was mostly because it was the only possible option for reclaiming a space in the political realm. This is not to say things have been easy for the İHD. In the post-1980 period, the İHD was one of the rare organisations that made visible issues like the conditions of political prisoners and torture under arrest. Those involved in the association paid the price for doing so through endless trials, public intimidation and defamation campaigns. While this was one of the few options given the post-martial rule conditions, framing the issue as a human rights issue was limiting.

More recently, the mass dismissal of the Academics for Peace took place during state of emergency conditions. So far, resistance has been more structured than during the post-1980 period. One reason was that this time, dismissals were conducted through publicly announced lists of names published along with the decree-laws. Digital communication technologies made it easier to spread information. A key point of resistance has been *Dayanışma Akademileri* (Solidarity Academies, DA) formed in different cities. Claiming that higher education does not need a university campus, dismissed academics began teaching their courses in diverse venues. Some of these attempts have been more organised and consistent than others. DAs in smaller cities like Eskişehir, Kocaeli and Mersin have organised and continued their activities more effectively. In bigger cities, attempts have been more dispersed and diverse. It is too early to do a thorough analysis of the DAs' capacity for resistance, but there are a range of views on this question. Some argue for the high potential of 'commoning higher education' through the DAs (Erdem & Akın, 2019), while others claim that those who attend the lectures at DAs do so out of a show of solidarity rather than a pressing need to attend these lectures and learn about diverse perspectives as was the case in lectures of the BİLAR A. Ş. of the post-1980 period (Özkazanç, 2018). Similar to the post-1980 period, dismissed Peace Academics' resistance has mostly been limited to these off-campus courses, written statements, collaborative research projects and organising international petitions. Nevertheless, more creative ways of resistance are emerging in the diverse circles of academics among the signatories. In a way, academics are learning to be activists, which has not been their strong point (Choudry, 2015). Therefore, one could say that 'the Academics for Peace Initiative is a social movement in the making in Turkey' (Başer, Akgönül & Öztürk, 2017, p. 297).

Similar to the post-1980 period, the ruling authority aimed to divide the dissident academics in order to weaken resistance, by 'punishing' the same 'crime' differently for different academics. Signatories of the peace petition were subjected to disproportionate treatment. Some were dismissed from duty and had their passports cancelled, some were forced to retire, some did not have their contracts renewed while others continue to teach at their universities without facing any disruption. There is no precise information on how the list of academics being dismissed through the decree-laws were determined or what criteria were used (Altıparmak & Akdeniz, p. 2017).

The support that the dismissed Peace Academics received from international solidarity networks is not comparable to that received in the post-1980 period. Since the very beginning, the Scholars at Risk Network (SAR)[3] and Scholars Rescue Fund[4] have been very active in building international solidarity with dismissed or at-risk academics. Additionally, the German Federal Office officially supports the Philipp Schwartz Initiative of the Alexander von Humboldt Foundation to provide universities and research institutions in Germany with the means to host threatened foreign researchers for a period of 24 months on a fully funded research fellowship (Philipp Schwartz Initiative, 2019). In January 2017, the French Secretary of State for Higher Education and Research publicly announced a similar programme. The new programme, called PAUSE aims to host threatened international scholars in French higher education institutions for up to two years and with an individual support budget of €60,000 (Pause National Program, 2019). With the impact of these organisations, similar to the post-1980 period, the issue of dismissed academics has been framed around the topics of academic freedoms and human rights. Framing it in this way has its limits as the issue has been reduced to a legal question since the neoliberal-authoritarian nexus and pacification aims of the national security discourse are hidden.

CONCLUSION

Many intellectuals today argue that these are the darkest times for academic rights and freedoms in Turkey (see e.g. Erdem & Akın, 2019, p. 147). This chapter contests such a perspective which tends to do injustice to those who suffered immensely in previous years. This view also yearns for the 'good old days' ignoring the long history of discrimination against women, LGBTQ people, people with disabilities and Kurdish people in Turkish academia. Although it is true that anti-intellectualism is an identifying feature of neoliberal policy agendas, it is important to note that the anti-intellectualism of neoliberalism is built on state-led repression which aims to maintain the social order. Therefore, learning from past experience could not be possible by simply comparing today's suffering to that of the past. It would rather be possible through understanding the similarities and expanding the analysis beyond the rights discourse to include an analysis of the security apparatus.

Although academia has always been a contested space and contained the potential for the development of progressive areas of research, it has never been a safe haven for critical thinkers. Universities have always been under constant state surveillance and have been especially targeted after each *coup d'état* in Turkey. After the 1960 military coup, 147 critical academics were dismissed. Sociologist Ismail Besikçi, for a long time the only non-Kurdish academic studying Kurds in Turkey, was dismissed from his position after the military intervention in 1971. Between 1971 and 1999, he was in and out of prison eight times, spending 17 years in prison. To date, he has been subjected to police investigations and court cases just for researching Kurds. Another example is Pinar Selek, an anti-militarist feminist sociologist, writer of the most exhaustive history of the peace movement in the country, who has been prosecuted for over 15 years based on fabricated evidence in connection with an explosion in Istanbul in 1998. Although she has been tried and acquitted of all charges three times (in 2006, 2008 and 2011), she was sentenced to life imprisonment in 2013. Her crime was to research the Kurdistan Workers' Party (Partiya Karkerên Kurdistanê, PKK). Therefore, it is not a question of what is worse today, but rather a question of paying attention to what kind of pacification tactics and strategies the AKP inherited from the political culture of the past.

NOTES

1   This resistance initially contested the urban development plan for Istanbul's Taksim Gezi Park. The protests were sparked by outrage at the violent eviction of a sit-in at the park protesting the plan.

2   Passed by the Turkish Parliament in March 2015, these comprised two major "package laws" on national security and maintaining public order: 1) Polis Vazife ve Salâhiyet Kanunu, Jandarma Teşkilat, Görev ve Yetkileri Kanunu ile Bazi Kanunlarda Değişiklik Yapilmasina dair Kanun [Law on Amending the Police Powers and Duties Law, Law on the Gendarmerie's Organization, Duties and Authorities, and Some [Other] Laws], Law No. 6638, available on the Grand National Assembly of the Republic of Turkey website, at www.tbmm.gov.tr/kanunlar/k6638.html, archived at http://perma. cc/9NDU-HXY8. 2) Bazı Kanun ve Kanun Hükmünde Kararnamelerde Değişiklik Yapılması Hakkında Kanun [Law on Amendments to Some Laws and Decree Laws], Law No. 6639, 27 March 2015, RESMÎ GAZETE [OFFICIAL GAZETTE], No. 29327, 15 April 2015, www.resmigazete.gov.tr/ eskiler/2015/04/20150415-1.htm, archived at http://perma.cc/ML54- HQQX.

3   Established in 1999 and composed of an international network of institutions and individuals whose mission it is to protect scholars and promote academic freedom (SAR Network, 2019).

4   Founded in 2002 by the Institute of International Education trustees to make their efforts in protecting threatened scholars and students since 1919 more permanent (IIE-SRF, 2019). See also the October 4, 2019, Academics for Peace (2019) statement, following the acquittals of 329 academics by local courts after the Constitutional Court found that the rights of academics had been violated.

REFERENCES

Academics for Peace (2019). We request our unconditional reinstatement. Bianet. http://bianet.org/english/freedom-of-expression/213979-academics-for-peace-we-request-our-unconditional-reinstatement (Accessed 13 October 2019).

Ahmad, F. (1999). *Modern Türkiye'nin Oluşumu*. İstanbul: Kaynak Yayınları.

Altıparmak, K. & Akdeniz, Y. (2017). *Barış İçin Akademisyenler: Olağanüstü Zamanlarda Akademiyi Savunmak*. İstanbul: İletişim Yayınları.

Baser, B., Akgönül, S. & Öztürk, A. E. (2017). 'Academics for Peace' in Turkey: a case of criminalizing dissent and critical thought via counterterrorism policy. *Critical Studies on Terrorism*, 10(2), 274–296.

Bayramoğlu, A. (2004). Asker ve Siyaset. In A. İnsel and A. Bayramoğlu (eds). *Bir Zümre, Bir Parti: Türkiye'de Ordu* (pp. 59–118). Ankara: Birikim Yayınları.

BBC News Türkçe. (2014, 10 November). Kobani eylemlerinde ölenlerin sayısı 35'e yükseldi. Retrieved from www.bbc.com/turkce/haberler/2014/10/141010_kobani_eylem_olu_sayisi (Accessed 15 April 2019).

—— (2016, 12 January). Erdoğan: Sözde akademisyenlerin haddini bilmesi lazım. Retrieved from www.bbc.com/turkce/haberler/2016/01/160111_erdogan_akademisyen_aciklama (Accessed 15 April 2019).

Boratav, K. (2006). *Türkiye İktisat Tarihi 1908–2005*. Ankara: İmge Kitabevi.

Chatterjee, P. & Maira, S. (eds). (2014). *The Imperial University: Academic repression and scholarly dissent*. Minneapolis, MN: University of Minnesota Press.

Choudry, A. (2015). *Learning Activism: The intellectual life of contemporary social movements*. Toronto: University of Toronto Press.

Coşar, S. (2012). The AKP's Hold on Power: Neoliberalism meets the Turkish-Islamic synthesis. In S. Coşar & G. Yücesan-Özdemir (eds), *Silent Violence: Neoliberalism, Islamist politics and the AKP years in Turkey* (pp. 67–92). Ottawa: Red Quill Books.

—— & Ergül, H. (2015). Free-Marketization of Academia through Authoritarianism: The Bologna process in Turkey. *Alternate Routes: A Journal of Critical Social Research, 26*, 101–124.

—— & Özcan, G. (2019, forthcoming). Packaging Security under the AKP's Rule: Between the family and the state. Journal Article, under review.

—— & Özman, A. (2004). Centre-right Politics in Turkey after the November 2002 General Elections: Neo-liberalism with Muslim face. *Contemporary Politics, 10*(1), 57–74.

Cumhuriyet Daily (1986, 19 February). Nesin: Başbakan siyasetle kültürü birbirine karıştırıyor. Retrieved from www.cumhuriyetarsivi.com/katalog/192/sayfa/1986/2/19/7.xhtml (Accessed on 15 April 2019).

Demokrasi İçin Birlik. (2017). OHAL'in Birinci Yılında Demokrasi Enkaz Altında. Retrieved from http://sendika62.org/wpcontent/uploads/2017/07/dib_ohal_raporu_20temmuz2017.pdf (Accessed on 15 September 2017).

Erdem, E. & Akın, K. (2019). Emergent Repertoires of Resistance and Commoning in Higher Education: The Solidarity Academies movement in Turkey. *South Atlantic Quarterly, 118*(1), pp. 145–163.

Fikir Kulüpleri Federasyonu. (2019). Retrieved from https://fkf.org.tr/fikir-kulupleri-federasyonu-nedir/ (Accessed 15 April 2019).

Gencoglu, F. & Yarkin, D. B. (2019). The Student Movement in Turkey: A case study of the relationship between (re)politicization and democratization. *Journal of Youth Studies, 22, 5*, 658–677.

Giroux, H. A. (2007). *The University in Chains: Confronting the military-industrial-academic complex*. Boulder, CO: Paradigm Publishers.

Hafıza Kaydı. (2018). BİLAR A.Ş. Online Archive. Retrieved from www.hafizakaydi.org/5subat/bilar/hikaye (Accessed 15 April 2019).

Harvey, D. (2005). *A Brief History of Neoliberalism*. Oxford: Oxford University Press.

Haspolat, E. (2012). *Neoliberalizm ve Baskı Aygıtının Dönüşî mü: Türkiye'de Özel Güvenliğin Gelişimi*. Ankara: NotaBene Yayınları.

IIE-SRF. (2019). Retrieved from www.scholarrescuefund.org/about-us/our-history (Accessed 15 April 2019).

İnal, K. & Akkaymak, G. (eds). (2012). *Neoliberal Transformation of Education in Turkey: Political and ideological analysis of educational reforms in the age of the AKP*. New York: Palgrave MacMillan.

Kenan Evren'in Söylev ve Demeçleri. (1983). Ankara: TBMM Basımevi.

—— (1982). Ankara: Başbakanlık Basımevi.

Klein, N. (2008). *The Shock Doctrine: The rise of disaster capitalism*. Toronto: Vintage Canada.

Köymen, O. (2007). *Sermaye Birikirken: Osmanlı, Türkiye, Dünya*. İstanbul: Yordam Kitap.

—— (2008). *Kapitalizm ve Köylülük: Ağalar, Üretenler, Patronlar*. İstanbul: Yordam Kitap.

Öğrenci Kolektifleri. (2019). Retrieved from www.kolektifler4.net/sorularla-ogrenci-kolektifleri/ (Accessed 15 April 2019).

Orman, H. (2005). *Bindokuzyüzelli'den İkibinbeş'e Aydınlar, Bildirgeler, İlanlar*. İstanbul: Sanat ve Hayat.

Önal, N. E. (2012). The Marketization of Higher Education in Turkey. In K. İnal and G. Akkaymak (eds), *Neoliberal Transformation of Education in Turkey* (pp. 125–138). New York: Palgrave MacMillan.

Özcan, G. (2014). Revisiting National Security Discourse in Turkey with a View to Pacification: From military power to police power onto orchestration of labour power. *Moment Dergi*, 1(1), 37–55.

Özen, H. (2002). Entelektüelin Dramı: 12 Eylül'ün Cadı Kazanı. Ankara: İmge Kitabevi Yayınları.

Özkazanç, A. (2018). Interview with Hafıza Kaydı. Retrieved from www.hafizakaydi.org/5subat/bilar/taniklik (Accessed 15 April 2019).

Pause National Program. (2019). Retrieved from www.college-de-france.fr/site/programme-pause/index.htm (Accessed 15 April 2019).

Philipp Schwartz Initiative (2019). Retrieved from www.humboldt-foundation.de/web/philipp-schwartz-initiative-en.html (Accessed 15 April 2019).

SAR Network. (2019). Retrieved from www.scholarsatrisk.org/ (Accessed 15 April 2019).

Uğurlu, G. (2015). Emek Hareketinde Yeni Arayışlara Bir Örnek: Piyasalaşan Akademide Asistan Dayanışmaları. *Vira Verita E-Dergi*, (2), 45–64.

Ulutürk, S. & Dane, K. (2009). 1980 Sonrası Üniversite Bileşenleri, Örgütlenme ve Mücadele. Paper presented at the Karaburun Bilim Kongresi, Izmir, Turkey.

Vatansever, A. (2018a). Partners in Crime: The anti-intellectual complicity between the state and the universities in Turkey. *The Journal of Interrupted Studies*, 1(aop), 1–23.

—— (2018b). Academic Nomads. The Changing Conception of Academic Work under Precarious Conditions. *Cambio*, 8(15), 153–165.

5

Nous who? Racialisation and Québec student movement politics

rosalind hampton

The Québec student movement is widely recognised for its organising, militancy and successes in securing and protecting access to affordable post-secondary education. In 2012, the movement launched the longest and largest student strike in Canadian history, in response to the provincial government's plan to raise tuition fees by 75 per cent over five years. The strike lasted seven months, mobilising hundreds of thousands of students across Québec, who participated in hundreds of demonstrations, picket lines, disruptions and direct actions. Having first attempted to ignore and sidestep the student unions, the Liberal provincial government led by Jean Charest responded with draconian attempts to brutalise protesters into submission through violent militarised police interventions and the creation of unconstitutional laws designed to force an end to the strike. This galvanised broader public support for the strike, prompting neighbourhood assemblies and widespread nightly *casseroles* demonstrations.[1] Thousands of arrests were made, causing municipal courts to become backlogged, and millions of dollars were spent on police overtime hours – CDN $7.3 million between February and June by the Montreal police force alone (CBC News, 2013). Universities and CEGEPs lost at least $40 million (Lalonde & Dougherty, 2012).[2] The government was forced to call elections, and finally, was ousted from power. As he formally announced his resignation as the leader of the Parti libéral du Québec, Charest (2012) mobilised the language of Québec nationalism in his parting words:

Nous allons continuer à défier toutes les tendances et à réaliser les plus belles choses ensemble. Parce que nous sommes nous, les Québécois, un peuple de rêveurs, mais un peuple de bâtisseurs.[3]

This chapter critically reflects on the student movement in Québec to examine how it both challenges and reproduces dominant narratives and relations of settler colonialism. The phrase *nous, les Québécois* – also *nous Québécois* (we Québecers) or simply *nous autres* (us) – is an assertion of Québécois national identity intended to remind francophone Québecers who 'we' are, in relation to who is not 'us'. It is the internalised understanding of this Québec *nous* that keeps many English-speaking and racialised people from being seen – and seeing themselves – as 'real' Québécois.

In what follows, I discuss the imagined *nous* of Québec nationalism and how it has shaped the student movement, and how the movement is perceived and functions in Québec society. I begin by identifying key aspects and moments of the movement's early history, and an overview of the development of its politics and structures. I analyse how racialised social relations have impacted movement politics, and argue that the student movement must more intentionally address how white settler nationalism continues to limit its growth and potential. The participation of Indigenous, Black and other racialised student activists in the movement must be understood beyond liberal notions of inclusion. Racialised students and communities must be understood – and must understand themselves – as crucial actors in student movement politics, as they are in broader anti-colonial liberation struggles in Québec and Canada.

HISTORICAL HIGHLIGHTS

The Québec student movement was formed within the broader social context of the Quiet Revolution of the 1960s, and has contributed to and been shaped by debates regarding Québec national identity,[4] governance, autonomy and the role of the state. Until that time, Québec society had been dominated by the Catholic Church and elite business class, and oppressed by the authoritarianism and corruption of the government led by Maurice Duplessis for nearly two decades

(C. Bélanger, 2006; Levine, 1990). However, by 1960 a new francophone middle-class emerged from the universities and culture industries. A secular movement was formed to promote the economic and cultural interests of the broader population and make the Québécois *maîtres chez nous* (masters of our own house). Students were seen as 'the new nation-builders and guardians' of this revolutionary vision (Katz, 2015, p. 15), and universal access to education was understood as a key means to achieve it. As the state replaced the Church at the centre of modern Québec society, educational reform was prioritised and a powerful student movement developed alongside and in relation to increasingly militant nationalist, labour and feminist movements and organisations (P. Bélanger, 1984; Lacoursière, 2007; Lamarre, 2008; Milner & Milner, 1977).

The first student strike on record in Québec was a one-day walkout in 1958 by student associations of Université de Montréal (UdeM), McGill University, Université de Laval, Bishop's University, Sir George Williams University (SGWU) and the Université de Sherbrooke, followed by a three-month sit-in by three UdeM students at the office of Duplessis (AJP, 2012; Hébert, 2005). Years prior to the establishment of the Québec Ministry of Education in 1964, students at UdeM had already begun organising around the idea of student syndicalism. In 1961, the student association of the university, AGEUM,[5] created and adopted the *Charte de l'étudiant universitaire*, based on the 1947 *Charte de Grenoble* of the national union of students in France. The charter declared the rights and responsibilities of students as young intellectual workers with a critical role to play in society, and became the principles upon which the first Québec national student union was founded (P. Bélanger, 1984; Lamarre, 2008).

In 1963, the legal voting age in Québec was lowered to 18, further solidifying students' political power. Following a *journée syndicale* (union day) organised by AGEUM that year, the Union générale des étudiants du Québec (UGEQ) was formally established at a congress in November 1964 (P. Bélanger, 1984; Lamarre, 2008). UGEQ would be guided by student syndicalism, a 'healthy and positive nationalism', and an internationalist focus, in hopes of contributing to a new social order based on 'collaboration regardless of race, language or belief' (Lamarre, 2008, p. 55). The union officially promoted the 'abolition of all forms of imperialism, colonialism and discrimination', described itself as

Third Worldist, and took formal positions of support for the people of Vietnam and Black Americans fighting racial oppression (P. Bélanger, 1984; Lamarre, 2008; Mills, 2010).

Breaking any prior ties with the Canadian Union of Students (CUS) was required of any association joining UGEQ (P. Bélanger, 1984). UGEQ's founding principles strongly opposed the CUS corporatist structure that viewed 'the student as a passive consumer' receiving its services, rather than as an active citizen with rights and responsibilities (Favreau, 1974, p. 83). The significance of this class-based framing was underscored by resistance to joining UGEQ at McGill. As a founding institution of the Anglo-Canadian settler nation and a stronghold of Canadian and US imperialism and capital, McGill and the power it wielded had long been the target of Québec nationalist critique. In addition to concerns about separatism, McGill students expressed resistance to socialism, syndicalism, unconditional support for labour unions and to potentially jeopardising future professional private practice (Bereday, 1966). Due to persistent organising efforts by McGill student union activists, enough support was mobilised for a vote in favour of joining UGEQ at the beginning of 1967 (Bereday, 1966; Mills, 2010). Other anglophone institutions represented in the membership included SGWU, Loyola and Marianopolis Colleges (P. Bélanger, 1984; Lamarre, 2008). With tens of thousands of members, UGEQ launched a demand for free education for all, at all levels of Québec schooling.

By the mid-1960s, the movement was recognised as socialist and *indépendantiste* in orientation, and an institutionalised part of the Québec political landscape (Bereday, 1966). The first Québec general student strike followed in October 1968, just months after students and workers had taken over factories and universities in general strikes in France. Striking students in Québec demanded greater access to post-secondary education, financial aid and the overall democratisation of the universities. The strike lasted for several weeks and involved student takeovers at 15 of the province's 23 CEGEPs, the École des Beaux Arts, and several departments of UdeM. Political Science students at McGill also launched a ten-day strike during this time, promoting student syndicalism and asserting demands regarding the democratisation of their department and university (Andrew-Gee & Colizza, 2013; 'PoliSci', 1968; Reid, 1970). The students claimed and controlled a floor of the university for several days and won increases in student input and decision-making power. While this strike is rarely included in historical accounts of Québec student politics, it is a significant link in the overlapping events and issues that combined to build the power of the movement.[6] The strikes in France, Black Power and Black Campus movements in the US and anti-colonial movements in Africa and the Caribbean, were all sources of inspiration, knowledge and organising networks for overlapping groups of English- and French-speaking white student activists and Black international students from the Caribbean who were studying at SGWU and McGill.[7]

The 1968 strike led to a stronger student loans and bursaries system, a tuition freeze and the accelerated establishment of the Université du Québec à Montréal (P. Bélanger, 1984; Lacoursière, 2007). It was immediately followed at the beginning of 1969 by two additional major events at English universities in Montreal. The first of these events was a student protest and takeover of the computer centre at SGWU in response to the university's failure to adequately address allegations of anti-Black racism by a biology lecturer. The circumstances surrounding what happened at SGWU have been well documented elsewhere (Austin, 2013; Forsythe, 1971; Jacob & Shum, 2015; Martel, 2006). The protest ended in mass arrests, millions of dollars of property damage and reactions from individuals and institutions that revealed the virulent anti-Black racism within Québec and Canada. During the events, UGEQ issued a statement of support for the student activists. Unlike the CUS and several student associations, UGEQ did not lessen its support or condemn the activists after these events. In response to this position, the SGWU student association withdrew its membership from UGEQ, along with its $3,000 membership fees (P. Bélanger, 1984).

Weeks later, another major protest was held: *Opération McGill Français*, organised by a coalition of socialists at McGill, francophone student activists, Québec nationalists and radical labour unionists. Over 10,000 people marched on McGill's downtown campus demanding that the university become a pro-worker, francophone institution. The long-anticipated confrontation with the elite university signalled the arrival of a militant nationalist struggle in which student-worker solidarity was seen as essential (Bédard et al., 2001; P. Bélanger, 1984; Gray, 2004; Mills, 2010; Warren, 2008).

Since 1968, the student movement has repeatedly pressured governments into increasing financial aid and cancelling plans to increase tuition fees, escalating pressure tactics to the point of major general strikes in 1973, 1974, 1978, 1986, 1988, 1990, 1996, 2005, 2007 and 2012.[8] In the absence of the organisational base of a national (Québec) association in the early 1970s, the student movement did not participate in the historic Common Front strike of 1972 (Gray, 2004). The movement's institutionalised power became further entrenched in 1983, when the Lévesque government passed Law 32, allowing student associations to incorporate and collect mandatory membership dues. This has provided the associations with relatively stable funding and critical access to institutional resources.[9]

NATIONAL STUDENT ASSOCIATIONS

The political orientations and structures of the national associations shape their relationships with the state and with their members, as well as the potential and limits of their roles in the movement. Following UGEQ (1964–1969), the militant unions have been ANE(E)Q (1976–1994)[10] and ASSÉ (2001–2019).[11] ASSÉ further expanded its numbers and strengthened movement capacity through forming broader strike coalitions – CASSÉE (2005)[12] and CLASSE (2012),[13] leading to the largest, most combative mobilisations to date. The key strategy of the militant associations is to mobilise their base and build a *rapport de force* (balance of power) to pressure the government. They have spokespeople who are accountable to the general assembly and who are to communicate its decisions. These groups have consistently been dissolved by their membership when deemed to have become too bureaucratic or to have otherwise compromised their capacity for direct democracy (ASSÉ, 2019; P. Bélanger, 1984; Lamarre, 2008).

In the 1980s, less combative, corporate style federations were also established: the RAEU (1981–1986),[14] and FEUQ (1989–present),[15] and their CEGEP counterparts, FAECQ (1982–1987)[16] and FECQ (1990–present).[17] These organisations engage in lobbying and emphasise collaboration with governments. They are run in a more hierarchical fashion, concentrating power in their executives rather than in the general assembly (Lacoursière, 2007; Martin, 2013; Raza, 2012).[18] The FEUQ and FECQ dominated student movement politics throughout the second half of the 1990s. During this time, a coalition of radical student groups formed the MDE (1995–2000),[19] keeping the radical wing of the movement alive through direct action and ongoing demands for free education. The anarcho-syndicalist politics of ASSÉ subsequently renewed the militancy of the movement for its fight against neoliberal capitalism (Martin, 2013), re-situating it in relation to interlocking social issues and struggles across local and international contexts.

QUÉBEC NATIONALISM AND INDEPENDENCE

The student movement has been profoundly linked to Québec nationalism as a structure and ideology, and consequently shares the limits of a nationalism that derives its authority from settler colonialism and white hegemony. Below I discuss how nationalism and partisan politics have shaped the student movement and compromised its commitments. In doing so, I am arguing for a more heterogeneous and critical *nous* that is in good relation with Indigenous land and Peoples, and is defined through engagement with one another rather than by the state. Instead of avoiding issues of racialisation and racism, this calls for deep and critical race-class analysis and strategy. It calls for the abandonment of a politics of white settler entitlement, white citizenship and of all politics in which the enfranchisement of one section of the population requires the debasement of another (Olson, 2004).

The movement of the late 1960s had a formal principle of no political party affiliation, despite several members who identified as *indépendantistes* (Hébert, 2005; Lamarre, 2008). However, as René Lévesque's Parti Québécois (PQ) gained popularity, students provided an important base of support. As early as 1970, students had organised electoral support for the party, and the PQ received 40 per cent of the student vote (P. Bélanger, 1984, pp. 58–59). Several formerly high-profile student activists became elected members of the party,[20] while the PQ leadership increasingly spoke exclusively to francophone Québec (Lemoine, 1974). The relationship between the movement and the PQ was formalised in the lead-up to the 1980 referendum on Québec independence when ANÉ(É)Q adopted an official position in favour of a 'yes' vote in the referendum. This position was rigorously debated; students were aware that an official 'yes' position on the referendum amounted to a 'yes' vote in favour of the PQ as the representatives of

Québec's independence (P. Bélanger, 1984). Certainly, this support was not irrelevant in the subsequent passing of Law 32 to further secure the student movement's institutionalisation. Despite the 'no' vote in the 1980 referendum, the student movement became further aligned with the PQ, straining political affiliations between and within student associations along lines of linguistic and nationalist affiliations for years to come.

As the PQ's leadership has changed, the nationalism it promotes has become more explicitly racist and anti-immigrant (Bellefeuille, 2016). In 2012, its leadership successfully exploited the historical relationship between the movement and the PQ of Lévesque in its campaign rhetoric, promise to stop the proposed tuition hike, and in the candidacy of former FECQ president Léo Bureau-Blouin (Akher, 2013; Nadeau-Dubois, 2015). Having won the fall 2012 election by a minority vote, the PQ subsequently reneged on campaign promises, and in 2013 implemented an annual 3 per cent tuition fee increase framed as an 'indexation' to inflation. This back-pedalling, the rebranding and reassertion of some of the very same neoliberal policies of their Liberal predecessors and the racism of their proposed 'Charter of Québec values', all contributed to the failure of the PQ to form a majority government.[21] In a spring 2014 election, the Liberal party was reinstated.

White nationalism lives on in Québec, both similar to and arguably distinct from that of the rest of Canada. Issues of pervasive, institutionalised racism—and the inability to effectively address, confront and eliminate it—continue to undermine the potential breadth and reach of the student movement. The 2018 election of the right-wing *Coalition Avenir Québec* (CAQ) only underscores the volatility and divisiveness of Québec's particular politics of settler nationalism. With ties to far-right organisations hardly concealed, the CAQ promptly rebranded and resubmitted the PQ's Charter as Bill 21, *An Act Respecting the Laicity of the State* (Veilleux-LePage & Archambault, 2019). It was passed into law in 2019.

RACE AND RACIALISATION IN QUÉBEC

Concepts and relations of race have profoundly shaped identity and politics in Québec. English and French colonisers saw themselves as two distinct founding 'races' of what became Canada, and following the British conquest of New France in 1760, the social, economic and cultural domination of French Canadians relied upon characterising them as not-quite-white. As with other colonised peoples, this involved denigrating them as ignorant, lazy, unskilled, uncivilised and less than fully human (Scott, 2015).

The Quiet Revolution subsequently mobilised around this racialism, as Québécois nationalists drew inspiration from anti-colonial movements elsewhere. In the late 1950s, Québécois politician and journalist André Laurendeau famously characterised then Premier Duplessis as a *roi nègre* in a series of editorials in the newspaper *Le Devoir*. According to Laurendeau, Duplessis' reign offered an example of a British colonial practice common in Africa. The practice entailed appointing a native leader (or 'Negro king'), willing to collaborate with and protect the colonisers' interests in exchange for a position of power (C. Bélanger, 2006; Laurendeau, 1958). A decade later, Pierre Vallières furthered this discourse and popularised the idea of the Québécois as *nègres blancs d'Amérique* in his eponymous autobiographical manifesto. Inspired by the Black Power movement, Vallières (1968) drew comparison between the domination of the Québécois in Canada and of Black people in the United States, while denying the presence of Black people and anti-Black racism in Québec.

These appropriations of '*nègre*', remain embedded in Québec nationalist discourses, and despite being inspired by Black anti-colonial writers and activists, the premise underlying them has never been anti-racist (Austin, 2013; Cornellier, 2017). To the contrary, in declaring themselves *nègres*, the Québécois mobilised anti-Black racism in order to assert their whiteness and colonial entitlement to its benefits (Scott, 2015). Through appropriating the struggle of racialised, colonised others, French settlers re-imagined themselves as the 'native' population of Québec who faced foreign invasions of the British colonisers and American capitalists, and were subsequently 'decolonised' within the context of global anti-colonial struggles in the 1960s (Bellefeuille, 2016; Cornellier, 2017).

The new/ *nous* Québécois are thus defined as the 'sons' of a society in which the French preceded and once outnumbered the British, and in which the French-speaking white male was the 'central citizen' (Levesque, 1968, p. 20). This identity relies both on claims to a French (white, homogenous [*pure laine*]) racial ancestry and colonial entitlement, as well as on remembering the historical injustice of having been transformed by British domination into the colonised 'native' and (white) '*negre*'.[22] Modern Québécois identity thus rests on erasing the historical presence and experiences of Indigenous and Black people in New France/Québec, which destabilise this salient national narrative and dissolve the Québécois sense of self (Cornellier, 2017).

Crucial to the student movement as an institution developed to uphold the modern Québec nation, this 'refusal to relate with the other that I am (not)' forecloses the possibility for coalitional politics (Cornellier, 2017, p. 53). In keeping with dominant assumptions of Québec and Canadian settler nationalisms, 'the students' of the Québec student movement are always already assumed to be white descendants of European settlers. As the quintessential citizen of Québec, the French-speaking, white, young adult male is the assumed central subject of Québec student political organising and activism.

RACIALISED STUDENTS AND LOCAL COMMUNITIES IN 2012

Stronger critiques of the racialised nature of capitalism and of settler nationalism are necessary for the movement's growth and progression. The dominant perception of the student movement within Québec remains that it belongs to the (white, francophone) youth of *nous Québécois*, fulfilling their commitment to defend education as a bedrock of society and vehicle for the social advancement of the Québec people and nation. Consequently, Indigenous, Black and other racialised students, especially those who are English-speaking, are not necessarily perceived as part of the movement and its politics. As one young Black undergraduate explained to me early during the 2012 strike, she would have liked 'to support *them*', but did not want to miss her classes. As a Black anglophone woman, it did not occur to this student that she was part of the Québec student *nous*.

The mobilisation of symbols and rhetoric of Quiet Revolution-era nationalism in 2012 made it more difficult for non-white and non-francophone students and communities to identify with and support the movement, challenging racialised student activists to defend our participation. The situation escalated to a more public discourse when a small group of protesters made the decision to wear blackface at a national demonstration in Montreal. Five or six white youth dressed in suits and ties with their faces painted black, arrived with an enormous papier-mâché head meant to represent Premier Charest, which they pulled through the streets.[23] The performance mobilised old notions of the Québécois as *nègres* and imagined Charest, like Duplessis before him, as a *roi nègre*. The group was confronted by several other protesters and told that their performance and the concepts it relied on were racist. However, ultimately, they did march in the demonstration. I was present at the demonstration, and certainly was not the only racialised student among the hundreds of thousands of people who marched that day. Nor was I the only one who did not see the performance until photographs of it appeared in the news and social media, prompting responses and igniting important conversations and debates about race and racism in the movement and in Québec more broadly (Cooper, 2012; hampton, 2012; Morgan, 2012).

For myself and others organising with Students of Colour Montreal (SoCM),[24] this incident and its aftermath highlighted our roles as organisers, activists and members of multiple communities. Supporting one another and being knowledgeable and involved in the strike were our first objectives. This meant discussing and debating the strike in groups outside of academia and the activist communities adjacent to the universities. Several of us organised with multiple groups, an ongoing tradition of collaboration between racialised students, white leftists and anarchists in and around universities in Montreal since the 1960s. Members of SoCM contributed valuable input and analyses towards shaping discourses both within and about the movement (Ferrer, Hussain, Lee & Palacios, 2014; 'Gallery of voices', 2012; hampton, 2012; hampton, Luxion & Swain, 2014; Palacios, hampton, Ferrer, Moses & Lee, 2013; Thorburn, 2012). Reanimating principles that the movement itself has repeatedly claimed, members of SoCM prepared a motion that the CLASSE Congress adopt a formal position of anti-racism and anti-colonialism, to be reflected in all its public communications.[25]

The organised and visible participation of racialised students and community groups in the 2012 movement helps shape how the strike is remembered today, eight years later.[26] In addition to its near-expansion into a wider social struggle, it is frequently noted that the 2012 mobilisation saw a significantly increased participation of anglophone students, as well as of racialised and newer immigrant students. This is not disputed, and can be interpreted as a 'natural' outcome of changing demographics and an increasing number of racialised students attending universities in Québec.[27] The participation of racialised students in the movement can persuade others to join as they see themselves and their concerns represented, while the participation of racialised students has significant implications for expanding the reach of the movement across communities and sectors of Québec society. Racialised students often come to academia with important community networks, relationships and organising experience, as well as valuable knowledge and critical analysis of local and international contexts (Barlow, 1991; Ferguson, 2017).

CLASSE spokesperson Gabriel Nadeau-Dubois' book about the 2012 strike is instructive for how he, as the (expected) white, male representative of Québec's student movement and future, encountered the (unexpected) presence and participation of racialised students. For example, in the second chapter, titled 'A Generation No One Was Counting On', Nadeau-Dubois (2015) reflects on a crucial general assembly and early strike vote at a CEGEP. The last speakers at the mic prior to a vote can sway it in either direction. Nadeau-Dubois recounts that one of the last students to speak 'was a young black man dressed head to foot in classic hip hop style: low-slung trousers, baseball cap, gold chain around his neck – the works'. Nadeau-Dubois continues,

> At first glance, he hardly looked like your average activist, and he did not sport the red square that would identify him as pro-strike. Instinctively – our thinking is cunningly tainted by prejudice – I was afraid what he might say. But I was mistaken.

(p. 23)

He goes on to recount in some detail the student's strong and passionate argument in favour of the strike, which caused the assembly to erupt into applause. The vote went in favour of the strike by a large majority.

The reflection is remarkable in its naming of Blackness and of how racial bias shapes perception. Here I note the significant limits of 'recognition', and that Nadeau-Dubois does not offer significant analysis of racism in the movement, or of how racial hierarchy shapes access to education and structures Québec society. The young Black man can easily be understood as an opening punctum in a narrative otherwise dominated by white, francophone, predominantly male protagonists until the conclusion of the book, when Nadeau-Dubois describes edifying exchanges with an Indigenous Idle No More activist, and with a young Lebanese student. At the same time, in bookending his story of 2012 with racialised Québecois, Nadeau-Dubois (2015) gestures to change, to another *nous*, to 'another Quebec [that] has been on the march for some time now' (p. 128).[28]

To build the potential of the student movement is to expand entry points into it and into coalition with it; to learn, adapt and change in order to broaden and deepen our praxis. This requires letting go of some of the ideas and ways of doing things – and not doing things – that we may be attached to. It means knowing and growing our distinct and overlapping histories, and dismantling the social hierarchies and divisions that organise society. Cross-sector movement building requires understanding the other as being like us *and* different from us. It calls for knowledge of the histories and struggles of others and how they are both distinct from *and* related to our own. I have been thinking about this here, attempting to tell a story of the student movement that accounts for and is accountable to all members of Québec society today.

CONCLUSION: THE WORLD ENDED IN 2012

As I walked up Boulevard Saint Laurent in Montreal in December 2018, I came across what appeared to be relatively new graffiti: 'THE WORLD ENDED IN 2012.' I stopped in my tracks, excitement sweeping over me as I immediately recalled the many times I had walked under that very overpass with hundreds and thousands of others on night demonstrations. The radical hope of collectively moving through the streets with so many people is the feeling of we, of *nous*, defiant, practicing fearlessness in the face of state violence. I took a picture. I read the message again and again and tried to sort out what it was telling me, how it made me feel. I did not think for a moment that the phrase was intended to signal a negative loss.

There is a powerful depth of learning in social action, in studying the ruling relations of racial capitalism while a capitalist crisis exposes them and the fault lines in the social organisation they maintain. Such embodied learning exceeds the duration of a mobilisation, regardless of its political outcomes. The knowledge and cumulative, affective resonance of participation in the movement forges new relationships with words like solidarity and *autogestion*: they become imbued with a holistic knowing that another world is possible. That is the meaning I ultimately make of that message I encountered on the street: a reminder that the world as we know it can end, can have ended in 2012, can end again, because we know another world is possible.

Figure 5.1 Graffiti on Boulevard St. Laurent in Montreal.
Photo by the author, 3 December 2018.

NOTES

1 Popular protest involving banging pots and pans, inspired by *cacerolazo* in several South American countries.

2 Established in Québec in 1967, Collèges d'Enseignement Général et Professionnel (CEGEPs) are post-secondary institutions offering two-year pre-university programmes and three-year career-oriented programmes.

3 'We will continue to defeat all the tendencies and realize the most beautiful things together. Because we are we, the Québecois, a people of dreamers, but a people of builders.' All translations from French texts in this chapter are mine.

4 Québec-level politics and institutions are referred to as the 'national', while those of Canada are referred to as 'federal', reflective of the histories and politics of Québec discussed here.

5 Association générale des étudiants de l'Université de Montréal.

6 Similarly underrepresented in movement histories, McGill student activists took over floors of the institution's administration building twice during the 2011–12 school year (hampton, Luxion & Swain, 2014; Hurley, 2014).

7 For example, Austin (2013) calls attention to an October 1968 article about the uprising in France by Caribbean student activist Franklyn Harvey, in which Harvey identifies the French political action committees as a new form of political organisation signalling the emergence of a new social order. Harvey was both immersed in the study of Caribbean radical political thought, and writing from within a Québec context of militant student syndicalism, student-labour movement organising and the emergence of numerous citizens committees. *Comités d'action politique* would indeed form essential roles in the upcoming social upheaval and Common Front strike in Québec during the early 1970s (P. Bélanger, 1984; Dion & De Sève, 1974; Mills, 2010).

8 Sources vary slightly regarding how many strikes have been launched, depending on their size and duration.

9 Much has been written about the structure, creation and dissolution of Québec student associations, and the detailed contexts, conditions and timelines of various strikes. On Québec student movement history in general, see P. Bélanger (1984), Lacoursière (2007) and Raza (2012); on student activism and cross-sector organising in 1960's Montreal, Mills (2010) and Roussopoulos (1974); on the 2012 strike, Collectif de débrayage (2013), Collectif dix novembre (2014), Nadeau-Dubois (2015) on anarchist perspectives on the 2012 strike, Akher (2013) and SubMedia (2013).

10 Association nationale des étudiants (et étudiantes) du Québec.

11 Association pour une solidarité syndicale étudiante.

12 Coalition de l'ASSÉ élargie.

13 Coalition large de l'Association pour une solidarité syndicale étudiante.

14 Regroupement des associations étudiantes universitaires.

15 Féderation étudiante universitaire du Québec (initially called Féderation des étudiants et étudiantes du Québec).

16 Féderation des associations étudiantes collégiales du Québec.

17 Féderation étudiante collégiale du Québec.

18 See Cox (2012) and Martin (2013) regarding dynamics between the Federations and the ASSÉ and its coalitions.

19 Mouvement pour le droit à l'éducation.

20 For example, Bernard Landry was AGEUM president in 1961 and one of the UGEQ's co-founders; Claude Charron and Louise Harel (and Gilles Duceppe of the future Bloc Québécois), held executive positions in UGEQ from the mid-to-late 1960s (Lacoursière, 2007).

21 On the white nationalism promoted by the PQ during this time see hampton & Hartman (2019), Mugabo (2016) and Nadeau & Helly (2016).

22 On the significance of the Québécois nationalist imperative to remember suffering, see Cornellier (2017).

23 A photograph of this performance accompanies Morgan's (2012) article.

24 SoCM was formed in January 2012 by a group of students committed to participating in the movement, challenging white settler nationalism and ensuring that racialised students and communities would be seen and heard.

25 The SoCM Motion for CLASSE Congress passed by overwhelming majority on 5 May 2012 and can be viewed here: https://geographyonstrike.files. wordpress.com/2012/04/socmmotionforclasse-doc.pdf.

26 Participating community groups included (but certainly were not limited to) South Asian Women's Community Centre, Solidarity Across Borders, Immigrant Workers' Centre, Women of Diverse Origins, Dignidad Migrante, Montréal Nord Républik and Tadamon.

27 The percentage of Québec's population identified as 'visible minorities' increased from 7 per cent in 2001 to 13 per cent in 2016 when for the first time the census counted over a million visible minorities living in Québec (Statistics Canada, 2017).

28 Nadeau-Dubois became an MNA and the co-spokesperson of the leftist political party, Québec Solidaire in 2017, and has insisted that Québec can retain a distinct cultural identity from the rest of Canada while defending diversity and fighting against racism (see Orr, 2018).

REFERENCES

[Date last accessed for all links: 18 July 2019]

AJP (Association des juristes progressistes) (2012, 21 March). La grève étudiante n'est pas un simple boycott: Historique et perspectives [blog post]. www. ajpquebec.org/la-greve-etudiante-nest-pas-un-simple-boycott-historique-et-perspectives/.

Akher (2013). Vivre de combat: A critique of (CL)ASSE, Retrieved from https://mtlcounterinfo.org/english-vivre-de-combat-a-critique-of-classe/.

Andrew-Gee, E. & Colizza, C. (2013). An Oral History of the 1968 Political Science Student Strike. *McGill Daily* (4 April), 22–25.

ASSÉ (2019, 29 April). Congrès annuel 2018–2019: Le memebres de l'ASSÉ votent en faveur de la dissolution. Retrieved from www.asse-solidarite.qc.ca/actualite/congres-annuel-2018-2019-les-membres-de-lasse-votent-en-faveur-de-la-dissolution/.

Austin, D. (2013). *Fear of a Black Nation: Race, sex and security in sixties Montreal.* Toronto: Between the Lines.

Barlow, A. (1991). The Student Movement of the 1960s and the Politics of Race. *Journal of Ethnic Studies, 19*(3), 1–22.

Bédard, É., Provart, J., Gray, S., Dostaler, G., Gagnon, C., Ryan, C., Bélanger, P. & Lamontagne, G. (2001). McGill Français: 30 ans après. *Cahiers QÉP 20*, www.mcgill.ca/qcst/fr/publications/cahiers-du-peq.

Bélanger, C. (2006). The Negro-king Theory [la théorie du roi nègre]. Events, Issues and Concepts of Quebec History. Retrieved from http://faculty.marianopolis.edu/c.belanger/quebechistory/events/nking.htm.

Bélanger, P. (1984). *Le movement étudiant Québécois: Son passé, ses revendications et ses luttes (1960–1983).* Montréal: ANEEQ.

Bellefeuille, C. (2016). La campagne référendaire de 1995: Un discours racialisé. *Cahiers d'histoire, 33*(2), 185–209.

Bereday, G. Z. F. (1966). Student Unrest on Four Continents: Montreal, Ibadan, Warsaw and Rangoon. *Comparative Education Review, 10*(2), 188–204.

CBC News (2012, 13 July). Quebec Student Protests Cost $7.3M in Police Overtime. Retrieved from www.cbc.ca/news/canada/montreal/quebec-student-protests-cost-7-3m-in-police-overtime-1.1291158.

Charest, J. (2012). La réplique: Démission de Jean Charest – 'Je rentre maintenant à la maison'. *Le Devoir* (6 September). Retrieved from www.ledevoir.com/opinion/idees/358537/je-rentre-maintenant-a-la-maison.

Collectif de débrayage (2013). *On s'en calisse: Histoire profane de la gréve printemps 2012, Québec.* Montréal: Sabotart & Paris: Entremonde.

Collectif dix novembre (2014). Introduction to *This Is Fucking Class War: Voices from the 2012 Québec student strike* (pp. 2–47). Retrieved from http://luxgoodcreative.com/classwar/home.html.

Cooper, C. (2012). These Symbols Come with Baggage. *Montreal Gazette* (21 April). Retrieved from www.montrealgazette.com/life/opinion+these+symbols+come+with+baggage/6494053/story.html.

Cornellier, B. (2017). The Struggle of Others: Pierre Vallières, Quebecois Settler Nationalism, and the N-Word Today. *Discourse, 39*(1), 31–66.

Cox, E. (2012). The (CL)ASSE is Ascendant: Quebec student movement realigns in wake of strike. *Rabble.ca* (24 November), Retrieved from http://rabble.ca/blogs/bloggers/ethan-cox/2012/11/classe-ascendent-quebec-student-movement-realigns-wake-strike.

Dion, L. & De Sève, M. (1974). Quebec: Interest groups and the search for an alternative political system. *The Annals of the American Academy of Political and Social Science*, 413(1), 124–144.

Favreau, R. (1974). Union Générale des Étudiants du Québec. In D. I. Roussopoulos (ed.), *Québec and Radical Social Change* (pp. 82–90). Montreal: Black Rose Books.

Ferguson, R. A. (2017). *We Demand: The university and student protests*. Oakland, CA: University of California Press.

Ferrer, I., Hussain, F. N., Lee, E. O. J.,& Palacios, L. (2014). Building Solidarity: Searching for racial and migrant justice within the Québec student movement. In Collectif 10 novembre (eds), *This is Fucking Class War: Voices from the 2012 Québec student strike*. Retrieved from http://thisisclasswar.info/ferrer.html.

Forsythe, D. (ed.) (1971). *Let the Niggers Burn: The Sir George Williams University affair and its Caribbean aftermath*. Montreal: Our Generation Press.

'Gallery of voices and images from the Maple Spring'. (2012). *TOPIA: Canadian Journal of Cultural Studies* (28), 219–244.

Gray, S. (2004). The Greatest Canadian Shit-Disturber. *Canadian Dimension*, 38(6). Retrieved from https://canadiandimension.com/articles/view/stan-gray-the-greatest-canadian-shit-disturber.

hampton, R. (2012). Race, Racism and the Québec Student Movement. *New Socialist* (8 July). Retrieved from http://newsocialist.org/race-racism-and-the-quebec-student-movement/.

—— & Hartman, M. (2019). Whose Values; Who's Valued? Race and racialization in Québec. *Journal of Critical Race Inquiry*, 6(1), 1–31.

——, Luxion, M. & Swain, M. (2014). Finding Space in the Student Movement for Both/and Identities. In Collectif dix novembre (eds), *This is Fucking Class War: Voices from the 2012 Québec student strike* (pp. 188–202). Retrieved from http://luxgoodcreative.com/classwar/home.html.

Hébert, K. (2005). From Tomorrow's Elite to Young Intellectual Workers: The search for identity among Montreal university students, 1900–58. In T. Myers & B. Bradbury (eds), *Negotiating Identities in 19th and 20th Century Montreal* (pp. 202–231), Vancouver: UBC Press.

Hurley, A. (2014). In Anticipate of Unleashed Professoriate. In Collectif dix novembre (eds), *This is Fucking Class War: Voices from the 2012 Québec student strike* (pp. 246–255). Retrieved from http://luxgoodcreative.com/classwar/home.html.

Jacob, S. [Production] and Shum, M. [Direction] (2015). *Ninth Floor* [Film]. Montreal: National Film Board of Canada.

Katz, S. (2015). *Generation Rising: The time of the Québec student spring*. Halifax & Winnipeg: Fernwood.

Lacoursière, B. (2007). *Le mouvement étudiant au Québec de 1983 à 2006*. Montreal: Sabotart.

Lalonde, M. & Dougherty, K. (2012). UQAM Claims Student Protests Cost it $20 Million. *Montreal Gazette* (31 October). Retrieved from www.montrealgazette.com/news/uqam+claims+student+protests+cost+million/7477200/story.html.

Lamarre, J. (2008). 'Au service des étudiants et de la nation': L'internationalisation de l'Union générale des étudiants du Québec (1964–1969). *Bulletin d'histoire politique*, 16(2), 53–73.

Laurendeau, A. (1958). Maurice Duplessis à l'Assemblée nationale: la théorie du roi nègre. *Le Devoir* (Nov. 18). Retrieved from https://web.archive.org/web/20070114062826/http://www.ledevoir.com/histoire/90ans/90_duples.html.

Lemoine, B. R. (1974). Recent Elections in Québec: 1966 and 1970. In D. I. Roussopoulos (ed.), *Québec and Radical Social Change* (pp. 135–164). Montreal: Black Rose Books

Lévesque, R. (1968). *Option Québec*. Paris: R. Laffont.

Levine, M. V. (1990) *The Reconquest of Montreal: Language policy and social change in a bilingual city*. Philadelphia: Temple University Press.

Martel, M. (2006). 'S'ils veulent faire la revolution, qu'ils aillent la faire chez eux à leurs risques et périls. Nos anarchistes maisons sont suffisants': Occupation et repression à Sir George Williams. *Bulletin d'histoire politique*, 15(1), 163–177.

Martin, E. (2013). Le printemps contre l'hégémonie: La mobilisation étudiante de 2012 et le blocage institutionnel de la société québécoise. *Recherches sociographiques*, 54(3), 419–450.

Milner, H. & Milner, S. H. (1977). *The Decolonization of Quebec: An analysis of left-wing nationalism*. Toronto: McClelland and Stewart.

Morgan, A. (2012). Le grève et les minorités. *Huffington Post Québec* (27 March). Retrieved from https://quebec.huffingtonpost.ca/anthony-morgan/greve-etudiante-minorites_b_1383521.html.

Mugabo, D. (2016). On Rocks and Hard Places: A reflection on antiblackness in organizing against Islamophobia. *Critical Ethnic Studies Journal*, 2(2), 159-183.

Nadeau, F. & Helly, D. (2016). Une extrême droite en émergence? Les pages Facebook pour la Charte des valeurs québécoises. *Recherches Sociographiques*, 57(2–3), 505–521.

Nadeau-Dubois, G. (2015). *In Defiance*. Toronto: Between the Lines Press.

Olson, J. (2004). *The Abolition of White Democracy*. Minneapolis: University of Minnesota Press.

Orr, R. (2018). Pardon my French: Nadeau-Dubois's passionate defence of diversity. *Montreal Gazette* (2 April). Retrieved from https://montrealgazette.com/opinion/columnists/pardon-my-french-nadeau-duboiss-passionate-defence-of-diversity.

Palacios, L., hampton, R., Ferrer, I., Moses, E. & Lee, E. (2013). Learning in Social Action: Students of color and the Québec student movement. *Journal of Curriculum Theorizing*, 29(2), 6–25.

'PoliSci Association Issues Manifesto' (1968). *McGill Daily* (1 October), 3.

Raza, J. (2012). The History of the Quebec Student Movement and Combative Unionism. *Libcom.org* (8 December). Retrieved from https://libcom.org/history/history-quebec-student-movement-combative-unionism.

Reid, B. [director, producer] (1970). *Occupation* [film]. Montreal: National Film Board of Canada. Retrieved from www.nfb.ca/film/occupation/.

Roussopoulos, D. I. (ed.). (1974). *Québec and Radical Social Change.* Montreal: Black Rose Books.

Scott, C. (2016). How French Canadians Became White Folks, or Doing Things with Race in Quebec. *Ethnic and Racial Studies, 39*(7), 1280–1297.

Statistics Canada (2017). *Focus on Geography Series, 2016 Census.* Statistics Canada Catalogue no. 98-404-X2016001. Ottawa, Ontario. Data products, 2016 Census.

SubMedia [prod.] (2013). *Street Politics 101* [film]. Retrieved from https://sub.media/video/street-politics-101/.

Thorburn, É. (2012). Squarely in the Red: Dispatches from the 2012 Québec student strike. *Upping the Anti*, (14), 107–121.

Vallières, P. (1968) *Nègres blancs d'Amérique.* Montreal: Parti Pris.

Veilleux-LePage, Y. D. & Archambault, E. (2019, 2 May). La CAQ, La Meute and Bill 21. Retrieved www.opendemocracy.net/en/la-caq-la-meute-and-bill-21/.

Warren, J. P. (2008). L'Opération McGill français. Une page méconnue de l'histoire de la gauche nationaliste. *Bulletin d'historie politique, 16*(2), 97–115.

6

Learning from Chile's student movement

Youth organising and neoliberal reaction

Javier Campos-Martínez and
Dayana Olavarría

This chapter describes some of the milestones of the Chilean students' struggle for education since 2006. After briefly sketching the neoliberal takeover of Chile under the Pinochet dictatorship, and the maintenance of free-market policies by subsequent governments, we summarise over ten years of student mobilisations against market rule in the education system. We address two waves of student mobilisations, the 'Penguin Revolution' of 2006 and the 'Chilean Spring' of 2011, in more detail. We discuss the conditions that contributed to their gestation, student organising strategies and demands, as well as the unravelling of the conflicts. We conclude by noting the current feminist wave of activism in higher education, which has inherited some of the organisational structures and practices of protest exercised by students in previous years.

In the first section, we introduce the 'Penguin Revolution', when secondary students took over and occupied their school buildings and were able to achieve what is arguably one of the first victories against neoliberalism in years. They managed to bring an end to one of the most important laws inherited from Pinochet's dictatorship, The Organic Constitutional Law of Education (Law no. 18.962 (referred to by its Spanish acronym, LOCE)). An important feature of the 2006 mobilisation was the self-organisation strategies used by students to promote participation and engagement. In this struggle, students paid attention to the process by which their demands were built and radical participation in student assemblies became a strategy to expose the injustices of the neoliberal model and to generate alternatives to its hegemony.

In the second section, we introduce the Chilean Spring of 2011, which in part was a continuation of the 2006 struggle. In 2011, university and secondary students took up public space again in a new wave of resistance to market-based neoliberal policies in education. These demonstrations questioned the political class, denouncing the falsity of the doctrine of meritocracy, and challenging the market-based common sense that dominated the educational landscape. Along with traditional mobilisation strategies, students used art, performance, social media and other creative means to communicate their message. The 2011 movement won support from across Chilean society, and its demands shaped the political agenda over the following years. Finally, we introduce aspects of the current feminist movement that pushes the progressive agenda of social change in Chile. This movement is partially grounded in secondary and university student activism and continues to denounce the effects of neoliberalism on everyday life.

CHILE'S NEOLIBERAL TAKEOVER

The current status of Chile's education system results from a concerted plan implemented by civilians in alliance with the military during 17 years of dictatorship, and upheld by the post-dictatorship governments until now. This plan applied the principles of neoliberalism to the state and its institutions, relying primarily on the use of the military and the repression of opponents. Even after the dictatorship ended, these neoliberal principles were adopted and sustained by transitional governments. Neoliberalism advances a minimal role for the state and the centrality of the market in the economy and society. Neoliberalism imposes a common sense that pushes individuals to compete against each other to try to acquire wealth. Under market rule, the interests of the most affluent sectors of the country will almost always be guaranteed. The Chilean dictatorship imposed economic and cultural reforms that sought to restore the economic power of the dominant elite and to dismantle the social fabric that grounded the project of the progressive Popular Unity alliance of the early 1970s (Clark, 2017; Dezalay & Garth, 2002; Harvey, 2005; Morales & Rojas, 1986).

One of the first actions that the dictatorship took after the September 1973 coup concerning the education system was banning Chile's main teachers' union. In doing so, it disappeared, tortured, exiled and disenfranchised most of its leaders and militants. Teachers lost their status as state employees, their working conditions worsened and their employment benefits were attacked. The Pinochet regime changed the state's role in the administration of the public education system, as state schools were decentralised and transferred to the municipalities (city government). The school funding system also suffered important transformations. Funding went from being understood as a right, guaranteed in the national budget, to becoming something that was subject to the daily attendance of enrolled students. Neoliberal advocates claimed that the new funding system would force schools to compete against each other for enrolment and that this competition would drive the development of the educational system.

These reforms gained constitutional status on the last day of the dictatorship in March 1990 with the promulgation of the LOCE. In this law, the idea of education as a right was subsumed to the right of private actors to create their own educational projects, even if these did not guarantee students' rights to have an education. For example, a Catholic institution, by resorting to its private status, could refuse to accept students who were children of single mothers or non-traditional families. The implementation of this market logic allowed schools to choose students on the basis of criteria such as their abilities, religion and social/cultural background. The underfunded public system became the place where students rejected by other schools ended up. The result of this policy was the destruction of public education. At the beginning of the post-dictatorship era, almost 70 per cent of the students were enrolled in public institutions. But now, after 30 years of this policy, the public system only includes a third of the total number of students enrolled in schools. Between 1990 and 2015, over 1000 public schools have closed, while more than 3000 private voucher schools have been created.

Market-based reforms also transformed Chile's higher education landscape. Until the 1973 coup, tertiary education was mostly provided by the state in public institutions. Under the dictatorship, private universities proliferated with almost no regulation or public oversight. Private universities have extended their reach across the country focusing primarily on students who could not meet the test-score cut-off nor afford the fees of public institutions. Most private universities are owned by conservative groups within the Catholic Church or by for-profit companies such as Laureate Education, Inc. (Mönckeberg, 2013). These higher education institutions target low-income students who rely on loans. The project of accumulation by dispossession (Harvey, 2005) of the neoliberal elites operates through the indebtedness of young people and the transfer of funds from families to private education companies, which are also partially financed by the state. One of the most salient effects of the privatisation policies is the almost perfect socio-economic segregation of the country, which can be seen geographically, as well as between the different educational institutions that constitute the system. A 2004 OECD report described the Chilean education system as 'influenced by an ideology that gives improper relevance to the market mechanism for enhancing teaching and learning', noting that it appears to be 'consciously structured by social classes' (OECD, 2004, p. 278). One of the victories of the neoliberal reform is to break the social bonds that made the emergence of solidarity across different social groups possible. In Chile, educational and housing segregation combine to keep people from different backgrounds apart.

CHILE IN 2006

By 2006, these reforms had positively impacted the lives and the wealth of the country's elites, a success grounded in a loss of basic rights and sacrifices for the general population. Following the Washington Consensus blueprint of free market economic policies, the dominant political debate during this time centred around proposing measures to secure economic growth. By then, the market ruled almost every aspect of people's lives – i.e. health, housing, pensions, basic services, public transportation and education (De la Barra, 2012; Garretón, 2012; Riesco, 2012). Everything was divided and segmented according to income. Moreover, years of economic growth did not translate into greater social justice; on the contrary, during this period, social inequality increased

(López, Figueroa & Gutiérrez, 2013). The elite enjoyed increased wealth and power, while common people saw their living standards decrease as their lives deteriorated and youth faced an uncertain future.

The cultural project promoted by the neoliberal reforms was also partially successful. Individualism and meritocracy were ideas that were accepted and normalised by society. The lack of social bonds amplified dehumanising narratives that constructed the 'other' (the marginalised) as an internal enemy that must be contained (Lechner, 2002). Conservatives capitalised on this fear by promoting a security agenda, which among other things made Chile a country with one of the largest prison populations in the region (Ramos & Guzman de Luigi, 2000). Under these conditions, Chileans abandoned the public space and retreated to their homes, while individualism, distrust and isolation became widespread. Citizenship was practiced in the shopping mall, as participating in the consumer society became one of the favourite activities of large segments of the population (Moulian, 2002).

As for education, low-income students often ended their education prematurely, either because they stopped studying in order to dedicate themselves to work, or because they entered the prison system via 'youth protection' institutions. The middle classes, who attended publicly funded but privately owned schools, had more choices. They could attend public or private universities, but in most cases, in order to do so, they would still need to borrow their tuition money from banks. In many cases, after graduating, students struggled to repay these loans and entered into a cycle of debt. The pessimism in the population was almost proportional to the degree of social segregation, and the possibilities that young people envisioned for their future were very insecure.

THE 2006 PENGUIN REVOLT

The 'Penguin Revolt' erupted during the first semester of 2006. The nickname 'penguin' referred to the classic black and white uniforms that secondary school students wore. Students claimed this nickname as a political identity, creating a sense of collective struggle that gained support and forced the Bachelet government to shift the direction of its political agenda and address the students' concerns. The 2006 movement was incremental and mobilised secondary and higher education students.

The first protests started in April 2006 and related to the price of the students' public transportation fares, which disproportionally impacted students from low-income backgrounds. Under the market-driven school choice model, students commute to attend the 'best' schools they can, which were often far away from their neighbourhoods. Once the protests started to escalate, students added a demand to secure universal access to the standardised university admission examination (Domedel & Lillo, 2008).

Between 26 April and 19 May that year, several demonstrations were savagely repressed by the police. On May Day, labour movement rallies were filled with secondary education students and thousands were detained in Chile's major cities. On 19 May, students from two traditional public high schools took over and occupied their school buildings in downtown Santiago pressurising the government to address what were now demands for systemic changes to the education system. Students questioned the high degree of segregation in the educational system, the constitutional law inherited from the dictatorship, and the differences in quality, resources and support between public and private institutions (Bellei & Cabalin, 2013; Domedel & Lillo, 2008; Stromquist & Sanyal, 2013). In May 2006, the movement quickly began to gain strength. Each day, schools joined the mobilisation, as students in these schools self-organised in assemblies. On many occasions, students pressured their school administration to provide space for discussion and reflection about students' demands. All student assemblies sent speakers to participate in coordination meetings at the local and national levels. These speakers then returned to the school and presented the main issues discussed locally, regionally or nationally. This dialogue contributed to expanding critical awareness about the need for deep systemic changes to achieve an education system that promotes social justice (Cornejo, González, Sánchez, Sobarzo, & the Opech Collective, 2012; Domedel & Lillo, 2008).

The students' final demands of this period could be grouped into four areas (Bellei & Cabalin, 2013). These were: 1) Demand for a free and quality education, denouncing the class-based segregation of the state's financing system for education. 2) Defence of public education. Students denounced the decrease of state funding for public institutions in favour of the private sector, and the consequent deterioration of public education. 3) Rejection of profit in the education system. Students questioned the business and the profits of private entities using public funds. 4) The elimination of discriminatory practices of selection for admission. The students denounced selective admission practices especially in subsidised schools receiving state money such as screening tests, evaluations in preschool education, disclosure of family income and family interviews (Bellei & Cabalin, 2013).

After months of conflict, the government announced that it would review some of the student petitions. The official proposal was to create a presidential advisory board to draft a report that would guide the agenda of educational reforms to address student concerns. Almost 80 advisors comprised this board, including representatives from conservative think-tanks, teachers' unions, the church, the coalition government, industry and the private sector, NGOs, higher education institutions and secondary and higher education students. Students were suspicious about the board's composition, as they found that conservative interests were over-represented (Domedel & Lillo, 2008). Despite these misgivings, they decided to send some representatives to participate in this board. Along with participants from unions and other social organisations, student representatives on the advisory board did not agree with the final report and did not sign or subscribe to its final content. Finally, Chile's president committed to present a series of reforms to Congress, including reform of the LOCE, which would put an end to for-profit education institutions.

The 'penguins' took Chilean society by surprise and became one of the largest civil demonstrations of post-dictatorship governments (Domedel & Lillo, 2008; Bellei & Cabalin, 2013). The movement unleashed a deep debate about the neoliberal model and its consequences of inequality, strongly questioning the false promise of meritocracy and demanding structural changes in the system. But as the movement successfully captured public attention, the political elite responded with different strategies aiming to co-opt its discourse and neutralise its demands such as the creation of presidential advisory councils or the inclusion of moderate student leaders in state-funded positions (Cornejo et al., 2012). The ruling elite was able to repurpose student demands towards a new generation of neoliberal reforms. The demand for free education was met by a grant programme (OPECH, 2016), the demand for quality education opened the door to a new public management system (Fardella & Sisto, 2013), and a new unregulated education market grew to technically assist the recently regulated non-profit schools

(Assaél et al., 2012). Paradoxically, the neoliberal reforms opposed by the student movement intensified their reach and sophistication. For Cristián Cabalin (Mönckeberg, 2013), one of the Chilean academics who has explored the student movement in depth, 'when the educational discussion is technified it is also emptied of content and the demands of the students further limited, precisely because students demand a reformulation of the system' (p. 175).

CHILE IN 2011

The second wave of neoliberal reforms, which intensified after the Penguin Revolt, continued to deepen the education crisis. These reforms intended to further regulate the market and make public institutions more efficient by introducing private logics into their routines and management practices. After the Penguin Revolt, the traditional parties who controlled the state during the first 20 years of post-dictatorship governments suffered internal and external ruptures. It became evident to a wide portion of the population that the leadership of the progressive parties was compromised by private interests and that changing things from the inside would be an impossible task. The internal division within the liberal progressive front facilitated a conservative emergence and takeover of the state by the right. Yet, paradoxically, most of their actions in education simply continued and reinforced the reforms started during the previous government.

By 2010, Chile's educational system remained as segregated as it was in 2006, particularly along class lines. The promise of education as an engine for social mobility and individual progress vanished and the need for structural changes started to gain traction and enter the mainstream conversation in Chile. The experience of the 2006 mobilisations showed that an organised movement had the capacity to influence political debate and to undermine the dictatorship's legacy in educational institutions. On the other hand, it also showed the limitations of a strategy for social change that is purely sustained by grassroots groups, without links to the political world (Domedel & Lillo, 2008). The spark of the Chilean Spring in 2011 was ignited by broad social unrest which arose from the failure of the government to respond to social inequality and the deepening of neoliberal reforms since the dictatorship.

THE CHILEAN SPRING

At the beginning of 2011, two citizen uprisings, one with a regional character, the other, environmentalist, epitomised the unrest in society. These demonstrations were the first expression of the energy that would be released later that year in the streets. In one of Chile's southernmost cities, Punta Arenas, the citizens' assembly, backed by the general population, blocked the main access to the city in response to the arbitrary increase in the price of natural gas. This was not the first time that Punta Arenas had rallied against the government. During the dictatorship, the city had opposed Pinochet's policies during a historic demonstration, the *Puntarenazo* (Figueroa, 2012). Meanwhile, the environmental movement rallied thousands in the streets in Santiago for several weeks to oppose the construction of a hydroelectric plant in the Aysen district. The wide range of support against the dam also signalled a more profound discomfort among the people about how profit had become a priority over sustainability and life. In March, the start of Chile's academic year, students from a private Santiago university occupied their campus, after they discovered that members of the university board were planning to sell it to Laureate (Figueroa, 2012; Mönckeberg, 2013). This uprising was the first struggle that included students from private and public universities in solidarity and pursuing a common agenda – to put an end to profit in education. Other demands that students raised at this time related to the governance of universities, and educational access for traditionally marginalised groups, especially for economic reasons (Bellei, Cabalin & Orellana, 2014). In addition, students from different universities demanded better conditions for studying.

The students managed to place their problems on the national agenda. In this process, they used three types of strategies: rallies, building occupations and performances. CONFECH (the Confederation of Chilean Students) decided to implement an escalating plan of public demonstrations. During 2011, the marches increased in numbers and intensity through months of mobilisation. By May, they mobilised almost 400,000 people in Santiago and a million across the country. These marches were attended not only by students, but also by their families and teachers (Figueroa, 2012). The students awoke a generation silenced by fear during the dictatorship. The building occupations, or 'tomas', were direct actions decided inside each university by an assembly of students drawn from every part of the campus. The occupations had many purposes, such as creating space protected from the pressures of the school schedule to analyse, organise and sustain the student mobilisations. Inside the occupations, students also planned actions to win public opinion over to their demands.

In conjunction with the marches, and as a political response to the government and conservative media efforts to criminalise the movement, students devised creative and performative ways to transmit their ideas to the public and to conquer the common sense of the nation (Bellei et al., 2014). For example, students prepared flash mob actions to graphically display the impact of neoliberalism in education and their lives. One of them represented students as zombies, and choreographed Michael Jackson's song *Thriller*, protesting the role of the market in education. Some signs used in this action read 'buried in debt', alluding to the bleak future that students anticipated under the current higher education funding system. Another group of students decided to run non-stop around Government House for 72 days – 1800 hours representing the number of millions of Chilean pesos needed to pay for free and quality education (Bellei et al., 2014; Figueroa, 2012). The cultural movement that accompanied the 2011 mobilisation was also a declaration of the identity of a generation born after the end of the dictatorship. These demonstrations captured media interest, which covered both the conflict and the leaders and spokespersons who represented the students' voices.

As the mobilisation progressed, state repression increased to the point of besieging the country's capital using riot police to prevent students from demonstrating. On 4 August 2011, thousands of students were detained as they tried to march to la Moneda in Santiago. Hundreds of them were wounded by the police and teargassed. Inspired by a group of parents who, outside a police barracks, protested against the arbitrary detention of their children by hitting a pot, student leaders called for a national demonstration asking people to make noise that day to show support for the students and to condemn the government repression. A large majority of Chileans supported the students and condemned the government's handling of the crisis. That night, people throughout the country showed their support for the student demands (Figueroa, 2012). By beating their saucepans on the streets, people positioned themselves politically, showing their ideas in their neighbourhoods and among their neighbours.

During the 2011 mobilisations, in part because of the self-education work inside the occupations, students deepened their analysis of the issues that impacted them. Bellei, Cabalin and Orellana (2014) summarised the students' demands in five points: 1) Egalitarian access to higher education institutions for all; 2) A stronger public higher education system, where state-owned universities have more resources to advance the public good; 3) State control and oversight of the development and expansion of private education providers in higher education; 4) Effectively ending profit schemes in higher education; 5) More participation and shared governance of education institutions. Concurrently, students refined their arguments and characterisation of the roots of the problems facing them. For example, starting from this reflection, the students identified the Constitution, imposed during the military dictatorship, as a problem requiring substantive modification. They also identified the very close relationship between the operators of the for-profit universities and the members of political parties with access to government. Among their actions, they exposed the reason behind the government's lack of enforcement of the law, which prohibits the use of higher education institutions as a means to profit: traditional political elites were actively implicated in the education business (Mönckeberg, 2013).

Although the government did not give in to the pressure for structural changes in the education system, students managed to take more control of the government's reform agenda and gain citizen support for their demands that now constitute a new hegemony. These are important movement victories. The years following 2011 kept students mobilised, and each subsequent year saw one or two marches that recalled the validity of the students' positions. Finally, Michelle Bachelet proposed a government programme to incorporate the students' ideas. A group of student leaders was invited to participate in the design of higher education policy and some of its members were invited to be part of the education ministry. Some high-profile student leaders entered parliament either because their party joined the governing coalition, or because the coalition parties allowed the election of a student leader by withdrawing their candidates from the district where the student leader was running.

The Bachelet government reforms seemed to address the problems posed by students, but did not address the systemic inequality at the root of these problems. For example, financial aid was implemented, but consisted of a scholarship that benefits those who are in the top quintiles of the population. Options for the rest of the population are based on individual indebtedness. Another example was legislation passed to prevent schools from selecting their students in order to promote inclusion and to avoid school segregation. Yet this was accompanied by an increase in public resources transferred to the private sector, with the justification that the state must replace the contribution traditionally made by families to maintain the level of education provided by the establishment and safeguard academic freedom.

CHILE IN 2018: THE FEMINIST WAVE

Chile's feminist movement in higher education is grounded in the work of student organisations created during the 2011 struggle. It is in the context of the student movement that criticism grew about the patriarchal, sexist and heteronormative character of traditional education. This critique also extended to the student organisations and their leadership. One of the first steps in positioning the feminist agenda within the student movement was the creation of Secretariats (*vocalías*) of Gender and Sexuality. The first Secretariat of Gender and Sexuality was established in the Faculty of Philosophy and Humanities at the University of Chile during 2011, along with other feminist collectives of the University of Chile under CONFECH's wing, and in 2014 the first General Secretariat of Gender (SESEGEN) was created at the University of Chile. Subsequently, throughout the country, different universities replicated this example and began to found their own Secretariats of Gender and Sexuality. In parallel, other feminist organisations decided to maintain their distance and independence from the student representatives and created gender and sexuality commissions within their universities. These are constituted as a feminist force independent of the federations, just as the *vocalías* are defined as self-convened and self-representing organisations.

In 2016, the University Feminist Coordinating Committee (COFEU) emerged from a gender commission of CONFECH. Its objective has been to organise the work of the Secretariats or the Commissions at the national level and it has adopted a model of horizontal organisation and a system of rotating spokespeople. The COFEU also decided to establish itself as an independent organisation of CONFECH. The COFEU's mandate is to work against gender violence, fight for feminist education, the visibility of diverse sexualities, sexual and reproductive rights, the improvement of working conditions and the depatriarchalisation of their classmates. Likewise, these feminist organisations have questioned the way that previous student movements maintained patriarchal logics in their organisational structures, and point out the political influence that parties have over student federations and the patriarchal legacy they bring with them. The COFEU is an autonomous organisation independent of the student federations.

This feminist movement's focus is more localised – developing demands at each university which focus on improvements within these institutions and contexts. The work of the Secretariats and Commissions responded to an almost non-existent institutional response on allegations of abuse and gender violence reported by students. In fact, in November 2017, only seven out of 60 universities had designed and published their protocols to address sexual harassment (Muñoz-García, Follegati & Jackson, 2018). Another phase of the feminist movement in higher education started at Austral University with a feminist strike on 17 April 2018, producing a snowball effect as women across Chile began to self-organise and protest. By 22 May that year, CONFECH reported that 29 universities had participated in strikes or occupied buildings supporting the demands of the feminist movement.

Within the universities there were women's caucuses, which were crucial for raising demands because they were safe spaces for women to talk about their experiences and recognise the violence in higher education institutions. The movement also saw the development of a men's caucus, creating different meetings and dialogues around gender issues, as well as establishing an inter-group assembly. The feminist movement in higher education in Chile makes it clear that this wave was led by women in contrast to the previous student mobilizations.

The feminist wave was also able to illustrate how patriarchal culture manifested within higher education institutions. Examples include the lack of offices responsible to protect and condemn sexual harassment and gender violence, the lack of a legal framework or justice programmes to address incidents of harassment and discrimination, the lack of victim support, the lack of systems of accountability related to issues of gender and sexuality and the blatant discrimination against women and unequal distribution of opportunities between men and women. Thus the student demands respond to a particular aspect of the institutions, understanding patriarchy as a pervasive issue that affects the whole community. The demands included specific training for staff, faculty, and students and increased diversity of courses, to promote deep cultural change within the institutions. Students have requested concrete actions from the administration for gender equality, such as support for feminist student organisations, the development of a legal framework and organisational structure to implement sexual harassment protocols, and the creation of a position within the administration to advocate for and support survivors. Students have also requested the creation of infrastructure and services for childcare, the improvement of work conditions for women workers providing the cleaning services at the university, the establishment of gender and sexuality diversity policy and the development of programmes on preventing sexual harassment and the hiring of specialised staff to deal with sexual misconduct on university campuses.

Finally, the demand for a non-sexist education joined other emblematic petitions of Chile's recent student activism, like free public education. The power of the feminist movement lies in questioning institutional culture and practices. The 2011 student movement appealed to a material and individual improvement, like the need for a free, quality higher education system. However, the feminist movement is committed to transforming society, seeking improvements in the material conditions of women's lives but understanding that it is also necessary to bring about cultural change.

CONCLUSION

This chapter attempts to summarise some of the most notable features of Chilean secondary and university student organisation in recent years. It presented three waves in the continuing student movement that started in 2006 and was led by the first generation of youth born during post-dictatorship governments – the first generation entirely raised during democracy. One of this generation's biggest achievements was uniting different social actors who opposed the market-oriented, highly privatised, culturally individualistic and authoritarian framework shaping the educational system. Students were some of the first social actors that placed the question about the fairness of the neoliberal system into the mainstream social conversation, creating a new hegemony: a counter-hegemony. This was able to influence political agendas, although not always with the necessary depth to make changes that go beyond the cosmetic.

The difficulties in implementing deep transformations in the system have also been a constant. Although the movements have enjoyed broad social support, the neoliberal governments have managed to reduce the students' demands to technical issues and responded to them in ways that do not challenge the system's structural injustices. Students have shifted their organising strategies as they need to respond to the post-dictatorship neoliberal state's reaction (Cornejo et al., 2012). All the strategies used by students have proven to have strengths and vulnerabilities. One of the victories is that they won broad support of the wider population, encouraging many to take public positions and repoliticising Chilean social life. But the politicisation of society is not enough within the framework of a neoliberal institutionality that is designed to maintain the status quo. Jaime Guzman, one of the great ideologues behind the institutional application of neoliberalism, referring to the constitution designed and approved during the dictatorship, explained:

> The Constitution must ensure that if the adversaries come to govern, they are constrained to follow an action not so different from what we would have done, because – minding the metaphor – the range of alternatives that the playing field imposes on those who play in it is small enough to be extremely difficult to do otherwise.
>
> (Guzman, 1979, p. 19)

The students have verified the effectiveness of the design of the neoliberal constitution in action. Every time they have risen up, their movements have been co-opted by the establishment and/or met with reforms that, instead of challenging the foundations of the neoliberal system, contribute to improving its design. Neoliberalism has shown an incredible ability to adapt to the shape of the social context in which it develops. In Chile, it adapted to student mobilisations by refining its ways of exploiting people and continuing to execute its mandate of restoring the power of economic elites.

The generation of students born in the post-dictatorship era has managed to generate massive popular responses to the readjustments and the attempts at shutting down the debate implemented by the neoliberal governments. They experimented with different forms of organisation and self-government. Student activists have used technology to produce knowledge and inform citizens about their causes, and have gained broader support for these. Despite these gains, the neoliberal re-accommodation looks darker than ever. This generation of students, many of them under 30, will have to face the alliance between neoliberal and ultra-conservative interests, as well as the global emergence of nationalist populism combined with the global increase in economic and social tensions. The greatest challenge of this generation will be to unite to prevent the ultra-conservative right from taking charge of the social debate and the state. In their future struggles, students will have to use what they have learned to make some decisions about their strategies. This means choosing between pushing an agenda with radical actions or dialogue within the system; that is, a choice between helping the system to re-accommodate or changing it fundamentally. It also requires grappling with how to do this in a context where the discourses of intolerance and hatred occupy increasing social space.

REFERENCES

[Date last accessed for all links: 30 May 2019]

Agacino, R. (2013). Movilizaciones estudiantiles en Chile: Anticipando el futuro. *Educação Em Revista*, 14(1), 7–20. Retrieved from www.bjis.unesp.br/revistas/index.php/educacaoemrevista/article/download/3294/2552.

Assaél, J., Contreras, P., Corbalán, F., Palma, E., Campos, J., Sisto, V. & Redondo, J. (2012). Ley SEP en escuelas municipales emergentes: ¿cambios en la identidad docente? *Paulo Freire. Revista Pedagogía Crítica*, 11(11), 219–228. Retrieved from http://bibliotecadigital.academia.cl/bitstream/handle/123456789/1963/219-228.pdf?sequence=1.

Bellei, C. (2013). El 'fin de lucro' como política educacional. *Centro de Estudios de Políticas Públicas En Educación*, 85–114.

Bellei, C. & Cabalin, C. (2013). Chilean Student Movements: Sustained struggle to transform a market-oriented educational system. *Current Issues in Comparative Education, 15*(2), 108–123. Retrieved from: https://files.eric. ed.gov/fulltext/EJ1016193.pdf.

Bellei, C., Cabalin, C. & Orellana, V. (2014). The 2011 Chilean Student Movement Against Neoliberal Educational Policies. *Studies in Higher Education, 39*(3), 426–440. http://doi.org/10.1080/03075079.2014.896179.

Cabalin, C. (2012). Neoliberal Education and Student Movements in Chile: Inequalities and malaise. *Policy Futures in Education,* 10(2), 219–228. http:// doi.org/10.2304/pfie.2012.10.2.219.

Cabalin, C.,& Bellei, C. (2013). Chilean Student Movements: Sustained struggle to transform a market-oriented educational system. *Current Issues in Comparative Education, 15*(2), 108–123. https://doi.org/10.1080/01436597.2016.1268906.

Clark, T. D. (2017). Rethinking Chile's 'Chicago Boys': Neoliberal technocrats or revolutionary vanguard? *Third World Quarterly, 38*(6), 1350–1365. https://doi. org/10.1080/01436597.2016.1268906.

Cornejo, R., González, J., Sánchez, R., Sobarzo, M. & the Opech Collective. (2012). The Struggle for Education and the Neoliberal Reaction. In X. De la Barra (ed.), *Neoliberalism's Fractured Showcase: Another Chile Is Possible* (pp. 151–177). Chicago, IL: Haymarket Books.

De la Barra, X. (ed.). (2012). *Neoliberalism's Fractured Showcase: Another Chile Is Possible.* Chicago, IL: Haymarket Books.

Dezalay, Y. & Garth, B. G. (2002). *The Internationalization of Palace Wars: Lawyers, Economists, and the Contest to Transform Latin American States.* Chicago, IL: University of Chicago Press.

Domedel, A. & Lillo, M. P. (2008). *El Mayo de los Pingüinos.* Chile: Ediciones Radio Universidad de Chile.

Fardella, C. & Sisto, V. (2013). El despliegue de nuevas formas de control en la profesión docente. *Estudios de Biopolítica, 2*(7), 133–146.

Figueroa, F. (2012). *Llegamos para quedarnos: Crónicas de la revuelta estudiantil.* Santiago de Chile: LOM Ediciones.

Garretón, R. (2012). Chile: Perpetual transition under the shadow of Pinochet. In X. De la Barra (ed.), *Neoliberalism's Fractured Showcase: Another Chile Is Possible* (pp. 73–92). Chicago, IL: Haymarket Books.

Guzman, J. (1979, December). El camino político. *Revista Realidad, 1*(7), 13–23. Retrieved from https://archivojaimeguzman.cl/uploads/r/archivo-jaime-guzman-e-3/5/e/5/5e5a5eee5a4517203e32d80fc661c712275e0858b0d9d26ec7c689c52bb56968/RR.1.7.01.pdf.

Harvey, D. (2005). *A Brief History of Neoliberalism.* Oxford & New York: Oxford University Press.

Lechner, N. (2002). *Las Sombras del Mañana. La Dimensión Subjetiva de la Política.* Santiago de Chile: Lom Ediciones.

López, R., Figueroa, E. & Gutiérrez, P. (2013). La 'parte del León': Nuevas estimaciones de la participación de los súper ricos en el ingreso de Chile. *Serie Documentos de Trabajo, 379,* 1–32. Retrieved from www.researchgate. net/profile/Eugenio_Figueroa2/publication/237154183_La_Parte_del_

Leon_Nuevas_Estimaciones_de_la_Participacion_de_los_Super_Ricos_
en_el_Ingreso_de_Chile/links/0046351b9ef23df1cf000000/La-Parte-del-
Leon-Nuevas-Estimaciones-de-la-Participacion-de-los-Super-Ricos-en-el-
Ingreso-de-Chile.pdf.

Mönckeberg, M. O. (2013). *Con fines de lucro: La escandalosa historia de
las Universidades Privadas en Chile.* Santiago de Chile: Random House
Mondadori.

Morales, E. & Rojas, S. (1986). *Relocalización Socio-Espacial de la Pobreza.
Politítica Estatal y Presión Popular, 1979–1985* (Documento de Trabajo No.
280). Santiago de Chile: Facultad Latinoamericana de Ciencias Sociales
(FLACSO).

Moulian, T. (1997). *Chile Actual anatomía de un Mito.* Santiago de Chile: Lom
Ediciones.

Muñoz-García, A. L., Follegati, L. & Jackson, L. (2018, May). *Protocolos de acoso
sexual en universidades chilenas: Una deuda pendiente.* CEPPE Policy Briefs,
No. 20, CEPPE UC.

OECD. (2004). *Revisión de políticas nacionales de educación.* Santiago, CL:
Organización para la Cooperación y el Desarrollo Económico.

OPECH (2016). Minuta sobre gratuidad en educación superior 2016. Retrieved
from: www.opech.cl/wp/wp-content/uploads/2016/05/Minuta-sobre-Gratuidad-
en-Educaci%C3%B3n-Superior-OPECH.pdf.

Ramos, M. & Guzman de Luigi, J. (2000). *La Guerra y la Paz Ciudadana.*
Santiago de Chile: Lom Ediciones.

Riesco, M. (2012). Neoliberalism, a Counter-revolution in Chile. In X. De la
Barra (ed.), *Neoliberalism's Fractured Showcase: Another Chile Is Possible* (pp.
14–45). Chicago, IL: Haymarket Books.

Robertson, S. L., Mundy, K., Verger, A. & Menashy, F. (2012). An Introduction
to Public Private Partnerships and Education Governance. In S. L. Robertson,
K. Mundy, A. Verger & F. Menashy (eds), *Public Private Partnerships in
Education: New actors and modes of governance in a globalizing world* (pp.
1–17). Northampton, MA: Edward Elgar Publishing.

Simbuerger, E. & Neary, M. (2014). Free Education! A 'Live' Report on the Chilean
Student Movement 2011–2014 – Reform or Revolution? [A Political Sociology
for Action]. *Journal for Critical Education Policy Studies, 13*(2), 150–196. Retrieved
from www.jceps.com/wp-content/uploads/2015/10/5-13-2-5.pdf.

Stromquist, N. & Sanyal, A. (2013). Student Resistance to Neoliberalism in Chile.
International Studies in Sociology of Education, 23(2), 152–178. https://doi.org/1
0.1080/09620214.2013.790662.

7

Resisting the US corporate university
Palestine, Zionism and campus politics
Rabab Ibrahim Abdulhadi and Saliem
Shehadeh

In recent years, the Israel lobby industry has intensified its campaign to censure, silence and discredit campus dissent, especially advocacy for justice in/for Palestine. Zionist groups attempt to punish Palestine advocacy through a wide array of tactics including passing legislation to criminalise the movement for Boycott, Divestment and Sanctions (BDS), pushing for judicial reinterpretation that would criminalise other channels of support such as charitable donations to Palestinian NGOs and smearing Palestine advocates as anti-Semitic. It is a new McCarthyism. San Francisco State University (SFSU) has been a major site for this campaign, with the objective to bully and smear faculty, discipline student activism and dismantle the Arab and Muslim Ethnicities and Diasporas (AMED) Studies programme whose pedagogy, scholarship and public engagement unambiguously insists on framing justice for/in Palestine as part of the indivisibility of justice. This chapter historicises and contextualises current campus conditions, enabling us to understand the waves of campus repression and assault on free speech and efforts to fight back. We discuss the political economy of the Israel lobby and the interconnected dynamics of the corporatisation of this public university. Concluding with lessons for social movement organising against the criminalisation of campus activism, we present three cases of campus mobilisation to resist the nexus of the corporatisation and Zionisation of SFSU.

On 23 February 2018, SFSU President Leslie Wong sent an email to 30,000 students, faculty, staff and donors legitimising Zionism from the highest office of the university, declaring, 'Let me be clear: Zionists are welcome on our campus' (Wong 2018). Wong's statement was neither spontaneous nor did it come out of nowhere. Rather, it was the latest sign of the neoliberal transformation of SFSU from a campus with 50 years of an avowedly social justice mission to one with an intimate relationship with Zionism. While the university administration allowed other right-wing expressions, such as Nazism, under the pretext of protecting speech, it has denied similar protections to campus advocates of justice for/in Palestine, in effect weaponising free speech in order to silence the dissenting voices of those supporting Palestinian rights. The more SFSU accepted funding from Zionists and other right-wing donors, the more it engaged in a systematic campaign of silencing, harassment and retaliation.

ENLISTING RACISM, ORIENTALISM AND ISLAMOPHOBIA

Today a number of well-funded organisations whose mission is to salvage Israel's badly damaged public image have launched a vicious campaign in the US academy to silence scholarship, pedagogy and advocacy for justice in/for Palestine. Israel lobby groups have twisted faculty and student calls for justice by labelling them anti-Semitic, enlisted Islamophobic 'war on terror' rhetoric and increasingly demanded that university administrations adopt policies that police dissent, including narrower student conduct charges and accusations against faculty during hiring and promotion processes.

The Israel lobby organisations that have more overtly engaged in such harassment and bullying include: The AMCHA Initiative (founded in 2011), The David Horowitz Freedom Center (founded in 1988), Campus Watch (founded in 2002), Middle East Forum (founded in 1990), Canary Mission (founded in 2014), Hillel International (founded in 1923), the David Project (founded in 2002) and the Lawfare Project (founded in 2010). These organisations became more active after September 11, 2001, and increasingly following the warning signs by the Reut Institute of the expanding base of their 'delegitimization network' following Israel's brutal war against Gaza in 2008–2009 (The Reut Institute, 2010). Their work seeks to advance hegemonic discourses that support Israel's colonialism, racism and occupation (or apartheid). This is especially true as US public support for Israel declined with its escalating anti-Palestinian assaults. This lobby network receives support from organisations whose wide-ranging scope has brought them into campus politics such as: the Simon Wiesenthal Center (founded in 1977), Stand With US (founded in 2001), the Zionist Organization of America (founded in 1897), the Brandeis Center (founded in 2012), the Anti-Defamation League (founded in 1913), the Jewish Federations of North America (founded in 1935) and its public relations wing, the Jewish Community Relations Councils (founded in 1944). While each organisation employs different tactics, some deploying more aggressive language and imagery than others, they seem to share a basic commitment to silencing Palestine advocacy.

White supremacist nationalist organisations and individuals, well-connected with the current US political establishment and who formally endorse and/or support Zionism, including Christian Zionists, work closely with the Israel lobby industry. Their xenophobia stretches far and targets non-white people, LGBTQI people, environmental and feminist groups and the working class. These right-wing groups are leaders of the Islamophobia industry. Their work includes overt hate speech such as Pamela Geller's *Stop the Islamization of America*. The Southern Poverty Law Center, for example, has characterised many of these organisations as hate groups and classified their leaders as the driving force behind anti-Muslim, anti-immigrant and anti-Black racist movements (Southern Poverty Law Center, 2019, see webpage 'Anti-Muslim'). The webpage of the Christian Zionist organisation, Christians United for Israel, boasts of being 'the largest pro-Israel grassroots organization in the United States' (Christians United for Israel, 2019, see homepage). The work of such organisations is deeply embedded in US Evangelicalism that embraces Zionism as an integral part of its teaching.

Funding for these organisations ranges from localised small-scale Zionist donors to multimillion-dollar donations from mega-millionaires and billionaires, such as Sheldon Adelson, Haim Saban and Paul Singer. Organisations such as the Jewish Federations of North America have adopted a standard approach by channelling donations to a wide array of Zionist Jewish organisations, including those operating on university campuses. In explaining their impact on campuses, we have identified several structural factors that contribute to their efficacy including labour, campus connections, professionalisation, coercive donations and the legal harassment of Palestine advocates.

ZIONIST CAMPUS CONNECTIONS

The extensive funding that Zionist organisations receive enables them to hire full-time staff. This is reflected in a complex organisational model with a staff that includes a board of directors, advisors, regional directors, project directors, analysts, editors, public relations specialists, assistants, interns, general members, as well as volunteers. These human resources allow these organisations to hire campus liaison officers, bring students, faculty and administrators onto their payroll to collect intelligence about everyday campus developments, hire lawyers to file lawsuits, and develop website coders to build online platforms. By contrast, most Palestine-centred campus organising is done by volunteer students, faculty and staff out of their own commitment for justice in/for Palestine rather than as a paid job. But that also affects their capacity for consistent messaging, media impact and tracking ever-changing campus rules that shrink the public space for counter-hegemonic organising.

A key organising strategy of well-funded Israel lobby organisations is to establish strong connections to campus administrators and student groups to normalise support for Israel as part of the campus status quo politics. Zionist organisations have a skilled lobbying cadre that inundates administrators with letter writing campaigns and regular meetings with donors and political pressure groups. For example, Hillel, the Jewish fraternity AEPi and The Israel on Campus Coalition operate as a conduit for other Zionist organisations that target youth. The David Project, an Israel lobby group well-known for instructing students on how to bring charges against professors that teach Palestine, was once a strategic partner with Hillel and has now fully been absorbed within Hillel. Birthright Israel is another programme that uses Zionist campus organisations as a foothold to recruit students by offering free trips to Israel that act as a propaganda tool for Israeli colonial and racist policies. The Jewish Community Relations Council (JCRC) has turned itself into 'the go-to' liaison with political and civic leaders, including campus administrators and officials (JCRC, 2019, see 'Public Affairs' webpage). The Lawfare Project, specialising in legal bullying, pursued the same strategy when it filed a Federal lawsuit against SFSU and several staff and administrators. A co-author of this chapter (Abdulhadi) was the only Palestinian, Arab and Muslim faculty member who was targeted for frivolous litigation while being smeared for similar false allegations. Lawfare Executive Director Brooke Goldstein defined the goals of this legal harassment to 'Make the enemy pay' and exacting 'massive punishments' for critics of Israel (Abunimah, 2016). After 14 months of continuous attacks, Lawfare was dealt a monumental defeat when Federal Judge Orrick dismissed the lawsuit with prejudice, meaning that they cannot file it again. In his written opinion, Orrick stated that being anti-Zionist and supporting Palestinian resistance does not make Abdulhadi anti-Semitic (*Mandel v. Board of Trustees*, 2018, p. 29). Lawfare then resorted to another tactic in their war of attrition against their grassroots opponents. They filed another lawsuit against SFSU, in the California State Court, and did not name Abdulhadi nor any of the student and faculty organisers who could have had the legal standing to defend more rigorously than the university's corporate lawyers. Both lawsuits attempt to silence Palestine campus advocacy by falsely accusing critics of Israel of anti-Semitism.

CORPORATISING AND THE PROFESSIONAL INSTITUTIONALISATION

The professionalisation of Zionist organisations has come to define the bloated managerial class of the neoliberal economy spanning across the public sector, semi-private civil service organisations and NGOs. The interconnected network provides a platform to train new mobile administrative professionals. SF Hillel, at the forefront of attacking this chapter's co-authors, the AMED Studies programme and campus activism, is a prime example. Oliver Benn, SF Hillel's Executive Director, began his career as a lawyer and then became an entrepreneur who participated in the metropolitan council for the JCRC and the Jewish Community Federation Board (SF Hillel, n.d., see Webpage 'Our Professional Team'). The employment trajectory of the current Associate Executive Director, Rachel Ralston, highlights the resources of the Israel lobby networks of training new administrative professionals. Ralston worked her way up from being a student member of SF Hillel to becoming a high-level administrator after graduating from SFSU in 2011 (ibid.). University administrations are not exempt from this modus operandi. The highest-placed Zionist at SFSU, Jason Porth, was promoted to SFSU as Vice President in charge of several portfolios such as University Enterprises and the University Corporation. The latter oversees SFSU 'development' and construction plans and the internal expenditure of grants and contracts (Porth, 2019). Porth worked his way up from a disabilities labour attorney to the chief of staff for two SFSU presidents. He simultaneously doubled up for three years as the President of the Raoul Wallenberg Jewish Democratic Club (the Jewish club in the San Francisco Democratic Party) that 'has been a force on issues pertaining to Israel, in particular, fighting anti-Israel resolutions in the cities of San Francisco and Berkeley' (Raoul Wallenberg, 2019). Porth lobbied against a resolution submitted to the San Francisco Board of Supervisors (BOS) (city council) in 2010 condemning the attack on the Turkish ship *Mavi Marmara* attempting to end the blockade of Gaza. One of the co-authors of this chapter was among the speakers who urged the BOS to adopt the resolution on the basis of the indivisibility of justice. The resolution, submitted by a broad-based community coalition, was not tabled (Palevsky, 2010).

MOVING MONEY: THE POLITICS OF ZIONIST COERCIVE DONATIONS

Neoliberalism has had a direct negative impact on transparency and accountability. An emerging new public discourse justifies increasing reliance on student tuition, grants and donations, but how the funds are used is not disclosed. As a result, academic institutions increasingly hire more administrators and less faculty and staff who might belong to an employee union where they could negotiate a collective bargaining agreement, as is the case with SFSU. While tuition fees rise and neoliberalism becomes the lexicon of interaction, students are slowly transformed into consumers and the faculty as customer service. As the measure of a university's success is the size of its endowment, the relationship between the university and its private donors is transformed in favour of what the donors want, i.e. 'donor-driven' programmes. Indeed, the job description of the 2019 search for a new SFSU president emphasises the relationship with donors. The job advert's subheading of 'finances' exclusively focuses on the university's success in garnering donations and grants, even noting the largest donation of the previous year; a $25 million donation made by SFSU alumni George and Judy Marcus. George Marcus is an emeritus member of the California State University (CSU) Board of Trustees serving on the CSU Foundation's Board of Governors (San Francisco State University, n.d., see Webpage 'George and Judy Marcus Donate over $28 million to SF State'). The CSU/SFSU public relations strategy of aligning administrators with donors is so entrenched that they receive an honourable mention in the job description for the highest office at the university. Absent in this job description is any discussion of demanding public funds from California's legislature, reducing student tuition, providing affordable housing for out of town students, and hiring more faculty to respond to the needs of students on public loans to graduate more quickly.

Zionist organisations are not SFSU's largest donors. Their influence on campus, however, is quite substantial and stems from their ability to plug into the clientele model paved by the administration's increasing commitment to neoliberalism. Shared characteristics among these philanthropists are how they made their fortunes in 'land development', as real estate brokers or as CEOs of San Francisco's industries. The irony is not lost on SFSU students, faculty and staff who can barely afford rental or real estate costs in the San Francisco Bay Area that have caused student homelessness and hunger, massive indebtedness, and have pushed them out of their neighbourhoods in deliberate gentrification. The widening class divisions between donors and potential donors on the one hand, and students, staff and faculty, on the other, reflect the same logic that marginalises campus activists, students and faculty.

The Helen Diller Family Foundation is a prime example. Founded in 1999 by real estate tycoon and billionaire Sanford Diller and his wife Helen, the foundation made millions of dollars in tax-deductible donations to 'support education, science, and the arts largely in the Bay Area and also in Israel' (Inside Philanthropy, 2018, see Webpage 'The Helen Diller Family Donation'). In its 2016 tax filings, the Diller Foundation reported a $100,000 donation to The Central Fund of Israel listing the purpose as 'Canary Mission for Megamot Shalom'

(Nathan-Kazis, 2018). Canary Mission is a well-known shadowy website whose mission is to smear, harass and intimidate campus critics of Israel by publicising their personal information and other misinformation 'to damage the lives of activists' (Against Canary Mission, n.d., see Webpage What Is Canary Mission?). In an attempt to obfuscate the connections and funding source, The Central Fund of Israel transferred the funds to the Jewish Community Federation (JCF) of San Francisco who, in turn, distributed it to Canary Mission. Nathan-Kazis, a reporter for the Jewish newspaper *The Forward* exposed this collaboration between the organisations and noted that two staff members of the JCF sit on the Diller Foundation's board (Nathan-Kazis, 2018).

Furthermore, Jaclyn Safier, current president of the Diller Foundation and current CEO of the real estate group sits on the UC Berkeley Board of Visitors and the external advisory board for the chancellor of the university (University of California Berkeley, 2019, see Webpage 'Board of Visitors'). Safier also sits on the University of California, San Francisco's Board of Overseers as a distinguished director whose function is to raise money for the university ('About the UCSF', 2019). In May 2019, the Diller Foundation gave $5 million to UC Berkeley (UCB) to fund the Helen Diller Family Chair in Israel Studies (Pine, 2019). The first Chair of Israel Studies is on active duty in the Israeli army and advocates against BDS. We therefore should not expect any better at UCB.

For university administrators, the lessons from both the Diller Foundation as well as George Marcus are clear. Installing foundation directors on the university's board of directors not only increases the likelihood of the foundation's donation but also equally troubling is the influence Israel's supporters can and do exercise over university policies and treatment of faculty and students who advocate for justice in/for Palestine. In effect, this ensured a direct pipeline from the corporate boardroom to university boards that are populated with corporate representatives instead of educators. The tiered structure of California's higher education is made up of three different systems. In the California Community Colleges system, five out of the 14 members of the Board of Governors are experienced educators (California Community Colleges, 2019, see Webpage 'Board of Governors Members'). In the California State University system, the number on the Board of Trustees falls to 3 out of 17 (California State University, 2019, see Webpage 'Meet the Board of Trustees'). In the University of California, its Ph.D. granting system, only 2 out of 17 members of the Board of Regents have experience in higher education (University of California, 2019, see Webpage 'Board of Regents'). Most trustees and regents are comprised of corporate leaders, including CEOs, partners at mega law firms, foundation directors and policy analysts in non-adjacent fields. These boards reflect the economic structure of higher education that allows the private sector to exert more influence over the public sector and thus blur the lines between the two and allow corporations to exert undue influence over public education that is supposed to provide a public good for all. Thus, indirectly, it feeds into normalising the status quo of support for Israel irrespective of how flagrant its violations of Palestinian rights and international consensus.

A glaring example of the ever-expanding role of corporations and private donors at SFSU is evident in the Koret Foundation's 2016 $1.7 million donation to SFSU. The foundation sought to leverage its donation to the university to punish Palestinian student participants in a broad-based student protest on 6 April 2016, against Nir Barkat, the right-wing mayor of occupied Jerusalem (now a Knesset member), who was hosted on campus by SF Hillel with help from the JCRC. Barkat was visiting San Francisco on a private fundraising trip for AIPAC (the American Israel Public Affairs Committee) (Pine, 2017). The foundation's donation was part of a $50 million campaign Koret promised to twelve colleges in California (Asimov, 2016). As the Lawfare lawsuit against SFSU and Abdulhadi noted, the Koret Foundation had 'pledged to give a $1.7 million gift to SFSU, but had held back because of concerns about anti-Jewish animus on campus, especially after the shut-down of Mayor Barkat's speech and *the lack of sufficient response from SFSU following the event*' [emphasis added] (*Mandel v. Board of Trustees*, 2017, p. 43). The 'lack of sufficient response from SFSU' refers to SFSU's disciplinary process. Nearly four pages of the lawsuit describe what Lawfare alleges to be student protestors' violations. The lawsuit claims that 'no actions were taken by SFSU against the disruptive students, no disciplinary charges were ever filed, and no sanctions ever imposed against GUPS … or any other individuals responsible for committing these acknowledged violations' (*Mandel*, 2017, p. 30). The lawsuit further reveals that at a meeting with Jewish faculty members regarding the Koret Foundation, President Wong said that 'in his entire career he had never had a donor invoke "political reasons" to withhold a gift' (*Mandel*, 2017, p. 40).

Not unlike the rest of the Lawfare lawsuit, this was a misrepresentation of the disciplinary process. Sanctions were imposed on GUPS, the only organisation singled out for charges. GUPS leaders were placed on oral notice that any future demonstrations taken by GUPS or its members would be met with strict disciplinary punishment. The effect was that of a gag order imposed by the Koret Foundation on Palestinian students through donations to SFSU. The business-as-usual response of SFSU betrayed the corporatisation of SFSU and its submission to Zionist pressure. While the university hired an independent law firm to investigate what had transpired during the Barkat affair, nonetheless SFSU found and fired Osvaldo Del Valle, the Director of Student Conduct, who had carried out the prosecution of the Palestinian students. Del Valle was asked by his supervisor, Luoluo Hong, Vice President of Student Affairs, to submit his resignation. The independent investigator's report vindicated GUPS and other student protesters and made it clear that neither Palestinian students nor any other student protesters engaged in violence nor had exhibited any anti-Semitic actions or discourses. Nonetheless, in their first statement following the filing of the Lawfare lawsuit, SFSU referred to the protest as 'ugly reminders [of] anti-Semitism' (SF State News, 2017). Despite SFSU's misrepresentation of the truth, the Koret Foundation rescinded its donation.

ALLEGATIONS AND INVESTIGATIONS

To silence advocates for justice in/for Palestine, Zionist organisations rely on legal harassment tactics by filing discrimination charges. Allegations range from violations of campus policy to accusations of treason and collaboration with terrorists. There is a wide spectrum of views among Zionist groups. Some, like Hillel, have condemned the use of violent images by the David Horowitz Freedom Center (DHFC) and dismissed Horowitz's actions as those of an extremist. However, the logic of a narrative that associates Palestine advocacy with criminality and hatred of Jews constitutes a racialised discourse that is rooted in Islamophobia that permeates Zionist groups. Hillel students falsely alleged that Palestinian students physically threatened them despite lack of any evidence. Hillel students claimed that Palestinian students came to the protest of Barkat's campus visit with shielded knives and that they had 'readjusted their head coverings in a threatening manner' according to the Lawfare lawsuit against SFSU and Abdulhadi (*Mandel v. Board of Trustees*, 2017, pp. 3, 33). In 2014, Hillel students accused the GUPS President of planning to kill Israelis. This resulted in his suspension for one year and investigations by the SF Police Department, the FBI's Joint Terrorism Task Force and the Israeli Consulate. Soon after, AMCHA and its associates alleged that the GUPS advisor (Abdulhadi) inspired the student following her 2014 trip to Palestine. AMCHA then falsely accused Abdulhadi of misusing public funds to support terrorist activities by meeting with Leila Khaled and Sheikh Raed Salah. SFSU then re-audited Abdulhadi's trip to Palestine and Jordan twice and proceeded to investigate her international travel for the previous five years in response to AMCHA's rejection of the outcome of the two new audits.

Though these various audits vindicated Dr Abdulhadi, the university's redundant investigation lent credibility to the smearing of her reputation. This represents a key tenet of Islamophobia, anti-Arab and anti-Palestinian racism. Such racialisation has legitimised the surveillance and interrogation of Muslims, and those perceived to be Muslim, on a mass scale. At the centre of it is the constant Zionist use of terms such as 'exposure', misuse, anti-Semitism or terrorism. This messaging implies that the targeted individuals are intrinsically predisposed to such illicit behaviour and hide behind an academic facade in US cities and universities. The language shared equally by Zionist organisations and neoliberal university administrations portrays Palestine advocates as deviant. Palestine Legal, a legal group that defends students, reported that between 2014 and 2018 it responded to 1247 incidents of suppression of Palestinian advocacy work and 318 that required legal intervention across 68 campuses (Palestine Legal, 2019). Spending their time defending their standing at and reputation outside the university, students and faculty experience anxiety and lose irreplaceable time to study for exams, join clubs, read books, take up internships, find jobs, write and publish, construct lesson plans, attend conferences, enjoy stimulating conversations with friends and colleagues and engage in other activities related to the academy.

RESPONDING TO BULLYING AND McCARTHYISM:
ORGANISING FOR AN INDIVISIBLE SENSE OF JUSTICE

Organising at SFSU for the survival and growth of GUPS and AMED has been a lesson in collaboration and building a broad-based community of justice. A camaraderie has developed at SFSU between anti-racist and anti-colonial faculty and student organisations who lead what have become known as the Historical Orgs. The naming goes back to 1968/69 – the longest student strike in the history of the US student movement, led by the Third World Liberation Front, initiated by the Black Student Union mostly made up of the Black Panther Party. Student groups that had not been established at that time but were now organising in the spirit and according to the principles of the coalition are given honorary status by the Historical Orgs. A measure of acknowledgement can be seen in the murals of various struggles that adorn the Cesar Chavez Student Center. These Historical Orgs also mark historical events such as the Sabra and Shatila massacre of Palestinian refugees and displaced Lebanese following the Israeli invasion of Lebanon. These historic events receive funding from the student government and are able to access a designated funding pool for such purposes. Ebbs and flows characterise coalition work among Historical Orgs and their allies depending on how experienced student leaders are and how hostile the campus environment is in any given semester. The extent of hostility is characterised by the degree to which the administration enforces disciplinary mechanisms against students and faculty and the strength or weakness of faculty resistance to such coercive methods and shrinking academic public space. This usually correlates with the intensity of Zionist and other right-wing attacks and private donors' intervention in university affairs. The larger coalition of historical and honorary organisations include *Movimiento Estudiantil Chicanx de Aztlán* (MEChA), League of Filipino Students, Student Kouncil of Intertribal Nations, Black Student Union, Pacific Islander Club, Muslim Student Association, Muslim Women Student Association, African Student Association, JUSTICE, Students for Quality Education, Black n' Brown Liberation Coalition, Ethnic Studies Student Organization, and students minoring in Arab and Muslim Ethnicities and Diasporas Studies academic programmes.

TASERS: THE BATTLE OVER CAMPUS 'GUN CONTROL'

A major battle that tested the faculty-student-staff coalition of justice was a year-long confrontation with the administration over what the students defined as wrong governance. The first confrontation emerged against the use of electroshock weapons (tasers) as 'standard issued' weapons for the University Police Department (UPD). The issue arose in 2013 over a collective bargaining agreement (CBA) between the California State University (CSU) system, to which SFSU belongs, and the State University Police Association, a union representing all of the CSU campus police departments (Miller, 2013). A major point of the CBA stipulated that University police would be permitted to carry tasers at all CSU campuses but that CSU would defer the decision on whether these would be distributed at individual campuses to each campus president (Barba, 2015). While 17 campuses had already issued tasers to their UPD by that time, SFSU did not participate (Middlemiss, 2014; Rodriguez, 2013). To guarantee that the SFSU President would not change his mind, SFSU Historical and honorary Student Orgs formed a new coalition called *Students Against Police Brutality*. Students organised rallies, demonstrations and town halls and called attention to the dangers that tasers and an armed police force would entail. Students were reminded of the killing of Oscar Grant. On New Year's Day 2009, Grant, a 22-year-old Black man, was murdered in Oakland, California by a police officer, Johannes Mehserle. At his subsequent trial, the police officer's legal defence team argued that Mehserle mistook his gun for a taser. Massive protests and rallies were organised against police brutality and anti-Blackness and demanded justice for Oscar Grant and other victims of police brutality. Black-Palestinian solidarity was evident in these protests where posters carried the slogan 'Justice for Oscar Grant! Justice for Gaza! End Government Sponsored Murder in the Ghettos of Oakland and Palestine' (The Palestine Poster Project Archives, 2009). In February 2014, the SFSU student coalition was successful in pressuring President Wong to deny university police access to tasers on campus (Abu-Zaghibra, 2015). But the success was temporary. A new CBA between the police union and CSU in 2015 guaranteed all campus police access to tasers as 'standard issued' weapons as part of their equipment package (California State University, 2015, see 'Bargaining Agreement: Unit 8'). In fall 2015, students held more rallies outside the

Administration Building but by then the campaign had suffered a major defeat and could not be sustained.

'POURING RIGHTS'? EXCLUSIVE CONTRACTS TO COCA-COLA AND PEPSI MULTINATIONALS

But the student organising learning curve was not wasted. The energies and experiences gained by *Students Against Police Brutality* shifted to a new campaign to block a proposal to award an exclusive contract of soft drinks to either Coca-Cola Company or PepsiCo. Jointly launched by the University Administration and the University Corporation, the proposal was sanitised as 'pouring rights' to camouflage its true nature from the university community. Students and faculty saw this move as another manifestation of the intensification of the privatisation of their public university. Both the cafeteria and restaurants as well as the university bookstore were already privatised. Students and faculty also opposed this neoliberal policy that began to transform university governance that, along with rising tuition costs, alienated them from their university. Students and faculty were opposed, as a matter of principle, to the two beverage multinational corporations with their history of union busting, exploiting indigenous labour and resources, privatising access to public water sources, and their contribution to the global plastic waste crisis. They also criticised the companies for selling high sugar content beverages due to the adverse health effects of obesity and diabetes. Poor families and individuals (such as indebted and cash-starved college students) were especially vulnerable since soda is usually even cheaper than bottled water, a major issue when municipal water sources were unsafe to drink (Firger, 2017). Students, faculty and the faculty union, the SFSU chapter of the California Faculty Association (CFA), organised a sustained campaign in fall 2015 against 'pouring rights'. They rallied, held demonstrations, voiced opposition in town hall meetings and issued public statements. Finally, in late November 2015, President Wong announced the cancellation of the proposed contract, but lamented the loss of the $2 million signing fee and the $125,000 annual payment for the duration of the contract (Huehnergarth, 2015).

DEFEND AND ADVANCE ETHNIC STUDIES

Following the victory against Coca-Cola and Pepsi, students embarked on a new campaign to demand increased funding for the College of Ethnic Studies (CoES). At the time, the college had been denied funding for new tenure-track faculty hires for nearly a decade. As a result, the Administration restricted faculty hires to replacement upon retirement or resignation and relied on low paid adjunct lecturers for teaching. In late fall 2015, the College Dean got wind of the Administration plan to deny two faculty searches to fill vacancies in Africana Studies. The College news was shared by the Dean at an emergency CoES meeting attended by the students. Leaders of the Historical and honorary Student Orgs had come to consider CoES their academic home based on their commitment to anti-racist and anti-colonial curriculum. Going beyond the College's immediate needs for hiring new faculty in Africana Studies, students formed a coalition inspired by the 1968 student strike with elected leadership from the Historical Orgs, along with honorary groups and students with majors and minors and in graduate programmes in the College's various departments. They formulated a list of ten demands similar to those of the 1968 students. Their demands included the reinstatement of the two faculty lines for the AMED Studies programme along with administrative assistance and an operating budget; a new department for Pacific Islander Studies (PIS), changing Race and Resistance Studies from a programme to a department and more substantial funding for the rest of the College departments with increased staff, operating budgets and scholarship funds. After successive town halls, demonstrations, rallies and a hunger strike, the administration agreed to most demands but fell short on all the demands concerning AMED Studies. SFSU's President refused to fund any of the AMED needs. The Zionist pressure, including the Koret Foundation's decision to rescind its $1.7 million to SFSU, following the student protest of Barkat's visit, did the trick. CoES faculty who participated in the negotiations agreed to abandon AMED needs in favour of the other demands such as the departmentalisation of Race and Resistance Studies and the hiring of a fundraiser for the College – an add-on by the administration to the student demands.

RESISTING CORPORATISATION AND
ZIONISATION OF SFSU

As SFSU continues to deeply sink into neoliberal structures and corporatisation, students and faculty from marginalised backgrounds increasingly become the most susceptible and vulnerable facing a hostile campus environment. Not only is this public university reneging on its commitments to provide affordable education, but also its policies have almost rolled back the spirit of '68 and the student movement that has transformed US higher public and private education (Abdulhadi, 2017). Attempts to co-opt otherwise radical faculty have intensified, while the punishment of those who speak up has escalated (Abdulhadi, 2018). As we have seen in the campaign to shut down the AMED Studies programme to target and criminalise campus activism, including this chapter's co-authors, SFSU's social justice mission has slowly been eroded and replaced by the weaponising of free speech in favour of right-wing Zionists, Nazis and white supremacists.

In the face of such corporatisation, a tilt to the right and collusion with the Israel lobby, SFSU student, staff and faculty activists have continued to wage their struggle to reclaim SFSU's social justice mission.

In this context, framing Palestine as a question of justice rather than as an issue that only belongs to Palestinians, making Palestine visible becomes an organic part of the indivisibility of justice. Palestine as a topic of study and as a cause of justice can no longer be ignored, evaded or treated as a 'controversial issue' towards which scholars and students can choose to remain neutral to escape the cost Zionists have been exacting. While feigning 'neutrality' in the context of struggles for justice is definitely a career-building move for many academics, the complicity with white supremacy, Islamophobia and Zionism is rooted in ideological and intellectual commitments grounded in how authority and domination are centred, which can be seen in the ways in which the fear of challenging the oppressive status quo plays out.

Today, the combination of repeated Zionist attacks (for several years and in different forms) have succeeded in Zionising SFSU. Recruited to implement a right-wing and Zionist agenda while making it sound legitimate, bureaucrats are rewarded in different ways – a pay raise, a promotion etc. It sounds disturbingly familiar to those of us who have lived experiences of what domination does and how it works. In practice, this also meant strangling AMED Studies in order to shut it down. After cancelling tenure-track searches to accommodate Zionist pressure, defunding faculty lines, refusing to provide staff or an operating budget, the next logical step for a complicit administration has been to recruit lower-level administrators to force out the only remaining faculty member. Not unlike other structures of domination, those in power do not dirty their own hands, but rather, the foreman and the forewoman are assigned that task to camouflage the act.

As a result of this hostile campus environment, student activists and their faculty allies came up with a multi-pronged approach that combines a protracted view to counter their escalating marginalisation on campus. This consists of a social movement building strategy along with public criticism to shame university administrators, refusing to allow the university's Zionisation and privatisation to proceed in a business-as-usual fashion. Constantly monitoring and analysing the political economy of the university's corporatisation, campus activists have come to learn that they can, in fact, defeat such designs under the right conditions and with a well-organised campaign. For example, during the three years before this chapter was written, campus activists, directly and indirectly, prevented SFSU from bringing in $3.7 million in irresponsible and problematic funds: $2 million from beverage corporations and $1.7 million from a Zionist foundation.

Along these lines, the CFA's stance has also shifted towards a more organising-based approach, replacing the old 'business' model. The further radicalisation of the CFA also impacted the long-established pro-Israel status quo. The CFA has voted in favour of two resolutions against the silencing and bullying of Palestine advocacy, submitting these to the San Francisco Labor Council, that passed both unanimously with a few abstentions, including the past cautious CFA president who practised a policy of peaceful co-existence with the SFSU administration.

Despite the deepening retaliation against a co-author of this chapter by the University Provost, several groups reacted quite forcefully to President Wong's welcoming Zionists to campus. Not only did GUPS come out with a strong statement that was followed by equally forceful articulations by the Black Student Union, African Studies Association, Black Residents United in Housing and Black Business Association at SFSU; Jews Against Zionism. Community groups such as Jewish Voice for Peace-Bay Area, Palestinian Youth Movement, International Socialist

Organization-Northern California issued strong condemnations. On campus, the Department of Women and Gender Studies posted a scathing critique of President Wong. A new student group, Jews Against Zionism (JAZ) was formed in direct response and to make it clear that Zionists do not own Jewishness nor speak for Jewish Students at SFSU. Most recently, SFSU students led by JAZ blocked the rail lines of the MUNI public transportation system next to the University to protest SFSU's settlement with Lawfare in the California State Court. Although Lawfare sought to come in the window to accomplish what they failed to do through the door, students made it clear that corporatisation and Zionisation will not pass uncontested. Young students of all backgrounds were saying: Zionism does not speak for all Jews and our campus is not for sale.

REFERENCES

[Date last accessed for all links: 20 June 2019]

Abdulhadi, R. (2017, 14 July). The Spirit of '68 Lives On! Palestine Advocacy and the Indivisibility of Justice. *Mondoweiss.* Retrieved from https://mondoweiss.net/2017/07/palestine-advocacy-indivisibility/.

—— (2017, 7 August). Death by 10,000 Cuts: The Zionist campaign to silence Palestine at SFSU. *Mondoweiss.* Retrieved from https://mondoweiss.net/2018/08/zionist-campaign-palestine/.

Abunimah, A. (2016, 25 June). Israel Lawfare Group Plans 'Massive Punishments' for Activists. *The Electronic Intifada.* Retrieved from https://electronicintifada.net/blogs/ali-abunimah/israel-lawfare-group-plans-massive-punishments-activists.

Abu-Zaghibra, R. (2015, 2 September). Tasers Mandatory for Campus Police. *Golden Gate Xpress.*

Against Canary Mission. (n.d.). What Is Canary Mission? [Webpage] Retrieved from https://againstcanarymission.org/what-is-canary-mission/.

Asimov, N. (2016, 15 June). Koret Foundation to Give $50 million to 12 California Colleges. *SF Gate.* Retrieved from www.sfgate.com/bayarea/article/Koret-Foundation-to-give-50-million-to-12-Bay-8212675.php.

Barba, M. (2015, 3 September). SF State to Equip Campus Police with Tasers. *San Francisco Examiner.* Retrieved from www.sfexaminer.com/news/sf-state-to-equip-campus-police-with-tasers/.

California Community Colleges. (2019). Board of Governors Members [Webpage]. Retrieved from http://extranet.cccco.edu/SystemOperations/BoardofGovernors/Members.aspx.

California State University. (2015). Bargaining Agreement: Unit 8: State University Police Association – 24 March 2015–30 June 2018 [Webpage]. Retrieved from www2.calstate.edu/csu-system/faculty-staff/labor-and-employee-relations/ Pages/unit8-supa.aspx.

—— (2018, 1 November). San Francisco State University President Search. Retrieved from http://presidential-search.sfsu.edu.

—— (2019). Meet the Board of Trustees [Webpage]. Retrieved from www2. calstate.edu/csu-system/board-of-trustees/meet-the-board-of-trustees.

Christians United for Israel. (2019). Homepage [Webpage]. Retrieved from www.cufi.org/.

Duss, M., Taeb, Y., Gude, K. & Sofer, K. (2015). Fear, Inc. 2.0: The Islamophobia Network's efforts to manufacture hate in America [PDF file]. Center for American Progress. Retrieved from https://cdn.americanprogress.org/ wp-content/uploads/2015/02/FearInc-report2.11.pdf.

Firger, J. (2017, 4 May). Sugar-sweetened Beverages are Now Cheaper than Bottled Water in Many Countries. *Newsweek Magazine.* Retrieved from www.newsweek.com/sugar-sweetened-beverages-soda-cheaper-obesity-cancer-diabetes-594827.

Huehnergarth, N. F. (2015, 20 November). San Francisco State University Pouring Rights Contract Fizzles After Student Protests. *Forbes.* Retrieved from https://tinyurl.com/y5zwa3qr.

Inside Philanthropy. (2018, 19 December). The Helen Diller Family Donation [Webpage]. Retrieved from www.insidephilanthropy.com/fundraising-bay-area-grants/the-helen-diller-family-foundation-bay-area-grants.html.

International Jewish Anti-Zionist Network. (2015, March). The Business of Backlash [PDF file]. Retrieved from www.ijan.org/wp-content/uploads/2015/ 04/IJAN-Business-of-Backlash-full-report-web.pdf.

Jewish Community Relations Council. (2019). Public Affairs [Webpage]. Retrieved from https://jcrc.org/what-we-do/public-affairs/.

Mandel v. Board of Trustees, 3:17-CV-03511-WHO. (N.D. Cal., 2017). Revised 31 August 2017.

——, 17-CV-03511-WHO. (N.D. Cal., 2018). Filed 29 October 2018.

Middlemiss, J. (2014, 19 February). Students Search for Definitive Answer on Why Wong Said No to Tasers. *Golden Gate Xpress.*

Miller, J. (2013, 13 November). I Have a Pen and I Could Probably Kill You with It: Official absurdities and student brilliance abound in the opening salvos of the taser debate at SFSU. *San Francisco Bay View National Black Newspaper.*

Nathan-Kazis, J. (2018, 3 October). Revealed: Canary Mission blacklist is secretly bankrolled by major Jewish federation. *The Forward.* Retrieved from https:// tinyurl.com/y48se4la.

Palestine Legal. (2019, 23 January). Year-In-Review: Palestine Legal responded to 289 suppression incidents in 2018, over 1,200 in last 5 years [Webpage]. Retrieved from https://palestinelegal.org/news/2019/1/23/2018-report.

The Palestine Poster Project Archives. (2009). *Justice for Oscar Grant!– Justice for Gaza!* [Webpage]. Retrieved from www.palestineposterproject.org/poster/ justice-for-oscar-grant-justice-for-gaza.

Palevsky, S. (2010, 11 June). San Francisco, Richmond to consider resolutions condemning Israel. *The Jewish News of Northern California*. Retrieved from www.jweekly.com/2010/06/11/richmond-s-f-to-consider-resolutions-condemning-israel/.

Pew Research Center. (2019, 3 January). Faith on the Hill: The religious composition of the 116th Congress [Webpage]. Religion & Public Life Project. Retrieved from www.pewforum.org/2019/01/03/faith-on-the-hill-116/.

—— (2019). Religious Landscape Study [Webpage, database]. Retrieved from www.pewforum.org/religious-landscape-study/.

Pine, D. (2017, 7 April). SF State President Fires Back after Jerusalem Mayor Dust-up. *The Jewish News of Northern California*. Retrieved from www.jweekly.com/2017/04/07/sfsu-president-fires-back-after-jerusalem-mayor-dust-up/.

—— (2019, 2 May). A $5 million gift will create UC Berkeley's first endowed Israel Studies chair. *The Jewish News of Northern California*. Retrieved from www.jweekly.com/2019/05/02/7-million-in-gifts-to-create-uc-berkeleys-first-endowed-israel-studies-chair/.

Porth, J. [LinkedIn profile]. (2019). Jason Porth. Retrieved from www.linkedin.com/in/jason-porth-6902116.

Raoul Wallenberg Jewish Democratic Club [Facebook profile]. (2012). Retrieved from www.facebook.com/pg/SFRWJDC/about/?ref=page_internal.

The Reut Institute. (2010, March). Building a Political Firewall Against Israel's Delegitimization: Conceptual framework [PDF file]. Retrieved from http://reut-institute.org/Data/Uploads/PDFVer/20100310%20Delegitimacy%20Eng.pdf.

Rodriguez, J. F. (2013, 24 September). SFSU Police get Tasers. *San Francisco Bay Guardian*.

San Francisco State University. (n.d.). George and Judy Marcus Donate over $28 million to SF State [Webpage]. Retrieved from https://develop.sfsu.edu/Marcus-gift.

SF Hillel. (n.d.). Our Professional Team [Webpage]. Retrieved from www.sfhillel.org/staff-786568.html.

SF State News. (2017, 20 June). San Francisco State University Statement Disputing Lawsuit; Affirming commitment to continued comprehensive action to ensure a safe and welcoming campus for Jewish students. *SF State News*. Retrieved from https://tinyurl.com/y48h4mbn.

Southern Poverty Law Center. (2019). Anti-Muslim [Webpage]. Retrieved from www.splcenter.org/fighting-hate/extremist-files/ideology/anti-muslim.

University of California Berkeley [Office of the Chancellor]. (2019). Board of Visitors [Webpage]. Retrieved from https://chancellor.berkeley.edu/about-office/advisory-groups/board-visitors.

University of California San Francisco. (2019). About the UCSF Foundation; Giving to University of California San Francisco [Webpage]. Retrieved from https://giving.ucsf.edu/about.

University of California. (2019). Board of Regents [Webpage]. Retrieved from https://regents.universityofcalifornia.edu/about/members-and-advisors/index.html.

Wong, L. (2018, 23 February). Message from President Wong to SF State Community. *SF State News*. Retrieved from https://news.sfsu.edu/announcements/message-president-wong-sf-state-community.

8

The Palestinian student movement and the dialectic of Palestinian liberation and class struggles

Lena Meari and Rula Abu Duhou

In September 2016, the student movement at Birzeit University announced a strike against tuition fee increases, asserting the principle of 'education for all'. Student activists shut down the university for 28 days during which the different tendencies of the student movement organised various events and activities. Some of these resembled popular education activities in which students discussed the role of the student movement, its struggles, and the components of 'education for liberation' which they sought. The long strike evoked heated debates within the university and wider Palestinian society on socio-political issues and the type of society envisioned. Taking the student strike as a point of departure, this chapter outlines the formation, priorities, strategies and vision of Palestinian student activism from the 1950s until today.

We argue that the strike offers potential for student activism to transcend the post-Oslo impasse through forging a space for a unified struggle that links Palestinian national liberation with class struggle.

The current student movement in Palestinian universities emerged during the 1970s, and had been organically linked to the broader Palestinian national liberation struggle. It played a vital role, with other collective mass organisations, in mobilising young Palestinians for the struggle for liberation and resisting the occupation. The post-Oslo neoliberal transformations and their ramifications influenced all sectors and aspects of Palestinian society and had important consequences for the student movement. The chapter traces the pre- and post-Oslo student movement's formations and its dialectical relations with the wider Palestinian liberation struggle. It also considers the connection between the student movement and union struggles against neoliberal governance and its demands for radical institutional change. This chapter will identify the tensions in the student movement in all its phases and the different meanings and dynamics it produced contingent on the conditions in broader Palestinian society.

First, we trace the origins of the Palestinian student movement in the diaspora in the late 1950s and its development inside colonised Palestine with the establishment of the Palestinian universities during the 1970s. The student movement, similar to other Palestinian social movements, such as the women's movement, emerged in response to the Zionist settler-colonial project, and had been linked with the national liberation struggle, prioritising the national liberation of Palestine. However, this does not mean that the different parts of the student movement overlooked matters concerning the social and economic conditions of Palestinian students and raised demands related to them.

The second section discusses the post-Oslo transformations and their effects on the student movement, showing that the student movement had been enormously affected by the deterioration of the Palestinian liberation project and the prevalence of the economic, social and political neoliberal rationalities and material conditions. The division within the Palestinian political sphere between Fateh and Hamas, particularly since the student wings of both parties had competed throughout the last decade in student council elections, also impacted on the student movement.

The third section examines the space of activism within Birzeit, one of the leading Palestinian universities, as reflected in the student movement struggle against tuition fee increases, which constituted a major event at the level of the university and broader Palestinian society. Here we reflect on the proceedings of the strike and the debates it instigated, based on a detailed reading of statements and posts on the Facebook page of the student council at the time of the strike as well as conversations with student activists who were involved.

We contend that the social class features of the strike offered the possibility to overcome the ideological-political divisions among the students from different factions, leading them to form an alliance to confront the new post-Oslo material conditions that affected the liberation project and created class discrepancies within Palestinian society in the 1967 occupied territory. This possibility applies to other recent Palestinian union struggles, such as the Palestinian teachers' struggle, constituting an opportunity to revive the class struggle and link it to the liberation struggle.

THE PALESTINIAN STUDENT MOVEMENT: ORIGIN AND DEVELOPMENT

The student movement in the diaspora

The emergence of an organised widespread Palestinian student movement[1] preceded the establishment of the Palestinian Liberation Organisation (PLO).[2] Following the Nakba (catastrophe) of the Palestinian people in 1948 – when Zionist military groups occupied 78 per cent of Palestine, destroyed over 500 Palestinian villages, and expelled two thirds of the Palestinian people – Palestinians realised the need to form collective organisations and movements to resist the Zionist settler colonial project in Palestine. The Palestinian student movement was one of the first and most active movements. Throughout the 1950s, Palestinian (and other Arab) students at universities, specifically in Cairo, Damascus and Beirut, established student associations to raise awareness of the Palestinian cause and operate within and outside their campuses to mobilise the youth for the liberation struggle. Student activists represented diverse political positions, convictions and ideologies and were active in political movements and parties as well as in student unions. Through their activism, Palestinian students acquired political skills and leadership competences.[3] Thus, early student activism constituted an incubator for individual and collective revolutionary capacities and laid the foundations for Palestinian collective organisations. Palestinian activism had been inspired by the national sentiments prevalent in the Arab countries during the second half of the 1950s.

This activism was the nucleus for the establishment of one of the earliest Palestinian general unions, the General Union of Palestinian

Students (GUPS), which was formed in a students' conference in Cairo on 29 November 1959 (The Palestinian Revolution, n.d.).

Following the PLO's founding in 1964, GUPS became part of the many other representative popular organisations comprising the PLO such as the professional unions of teachers, engineers, journalists, as well as the Palestinian political parties, and gained representation in the Palestinian National Council – the PLO's legislative body. GUPS, like the other PLO institutions, was based outside Palestine and played an active role in fortifying Palestinian national identity and mobilising Palestinian youth. Many GUPS activists, particularly from the Palestinian National Liberation Movement (Fateh) and the Popular Front for the Liberation of Palestine (PFLP) engaged in vibrant university activism in Arab, Eastern European and Western countries. They organised Palestinian students and supported their studies, particularly the incoming students from occupied Palestine who benefitted from scholarships offered by the Soviet Union and Eastern European countries throughout the 1970s and 1980s.

Palestinian student activism had emerged as a response to the Zionist settler colonial project and was organically connected to the Palestinian national liberation struggle. In this, the student movement does not constitute an exception. All other Palestinian unions share this feature that is affected by the magnitude of the Zionist settler-colonial project. This project was, and still is supported by imperial Western powers which aim at eliminating the Palestinians, uprooting them and dividing the Middle East according to imperial interests. The 1950s and 1960s witnessed the emergence of Third World national liberation movements with their socialist vision, as well as the victory of the Cuban and Algerian revolutions, which inspired the Palestinian liberation movement. While the socialist commitment of the liberation movements gave rise to class-consciousness, particularly within the leftist parties comprising the PLO, national liberation constituted its priority. In this sense, GUPS' main goal had been preparing Arab youth for national liberation, and mobilising Palestinian students to engage in it. GUPS became the incubator and producer of political and military leaders and cadres for the Palestinian revolution (Twam, 2010). This was reflected in the vital role GUPS members played in confronting the 1982 Israeli invasion of Lebanon, when GUPS called on its student members to take part in the battle, and thousands of its members moved to Lebanon and resisted the invasion (Muhammad, 2000; Twam, 2010).

The student movement inside Palestine

Following the expansion of the Zionist settler-colonial project and the occupation of the remaining parts of Palestine in 1967 – the West Bank, Gaza Strip and East Jerusalem – GUPS began its activism by enrolling its members in the clandestine military groups inside the 1967 occupied territory. The student movement inside the 1967 occupied parts of Palestine[4] had been formally created with the establishment of the first Palestinian universities[5] in the 1970s. During the late 1970s and early 1980s, the student movement in Palestinian universities was one of the various emerging popular mass organisations which constituted a front of semi-legal organisations to the clandestine political fractions of the PLO in the 1967 occupied parts of Palestine (Taraki, 1989). The mass organisations in general, and the student movement in particular, focused on the mobilisation of the masses for confronting the occupation and brought tens of thousands of young people from diverse social groups into the Palestinian national liberation movement. This included the traditionally marginalised social class from urban and rural areas, as well as refugee camps into the political and institutional domains. Another factor for this inclusion was the increase in the number of Palestinian universities and the increase in the enrolment of Palestinian students in these universities, benefitting from the financial support that the PLO provided to universities which covered student fees. This financial support enabled poorer youth to join higher education institutions, hence influencing the diversification of the student movement and adding a popular character to the movement.

According to Salim Tamari (1991), the mass organisations generally adopted 'radical populism' challenging the structure and perspective of the traditional nationalist movement in the 1967 occupied territory, rejecting its elitist and nepotistic character through involving all sectors of the population in its organised political activities rather than making them the passive recipients of these activities. However, the marks of populism were evident in the amorphous overarching thrust of the movement and in its lack of a specific class perspective, as well as its hesitation to tackle issues about the position of women in Palestinian society and the status of women in the domestic sphere (Tamari, 1991; Taraki, 1989). The marginalisation of the 'woman question' within the student movement is reflected in the constant low representation of female students in student councils (Kuttab, 2000; MIFTAH, 2014). Nevertheless, the leftist parties in general and the leftist student blocs in particular, enabled relatively more female representation as reflected in the case of Maha Nassar, the first female student who headed the voluntary work committee of Birzeit's student council from 1973 to 1974 (Abu Duhou, 2009).

The student movement, like other mass organisations, was from its inception riven by factionalist divisions. Student organisations were one of the organisational popular arms of the PLO political parties. For instance, the student blocs 'al-Shabiba', 'jabhat al amal altulabi altakadumi' and 'kutlat al wihda', were linked to the main Palestinian political organisations Fateh, PFLP and DFLP respectively. According to Tamari (1991), the student movement's dual feature of factionalism and populism had transferred the rivalry of the parent political parties to the general student populations of the universities. Yet, paradoxically, during the 1980s, factionalism also constituted an effective mechanism for mass mobilisation by creating an institutional and organisational framework, and providing incentives to the individual to belong and to act within a familiar, and exclusive, concrete identity (Tamari, 1991). Ibrahim Makkawi (2004) concurs: 'Party identity could be viewed as a mediating level of identification linking between the personal identity (self) and collective identity (society) ... The political organisation provides them with the opportunity to examine and express their ideas about the national cause and their feelings of belonging' (p. 43).

Although the student movement in Palestinian universities emerged in opposition to the occupation, as part of the national liberation movement, not in opposition to Palestinian university administrations' policies and practices,[6] student activists engaged in union struggles and promoted students' interests and demands (Twam, 2010). In this regard, Gibril Muhammad (2012) provides multiple examples of union struggles waged by the student movement at Birzeit University, such as the success of Birzeit students in their struggle to transfer the management of the university's cafeteria to student control following a long strike in the late 1970s, in what was termed 'the nationalisation of the cafeteria'.[7] Successes also include the achievement of student representation in university councils. Besides the students' struggle to schedule university fees according to individuals' level of income, they achieved a subsidy from the university towards the costs of educational books. The student movement also cooperated with the union of employees at Palestinian universities and supported their struggles to improve their working conditions.

Moreover, the leftist student blocs at Palestinian universities perceived the dialectical relation between the nationalist and social class struggles and promoted the merging of these struggles. According to Wisam Rafidi (2016), this was reflected in the articles that appeared in the *Altaqadom Bulletin*, a monthly review published by the Progressive Student Work Front, the student organisation linked with the PFLP in Palestinian universities and colleges between 1984 and 1987. The bulletin gave space to the social class perspectives of the student movement by featuring writing on student union struggles about the curricula, overcrowding in university classes, freedom of speech in universities, solidarity with the struggles of the academic staff union, and against the oppressive practices of the university administration toward academics and students.

Despite the attempts mentioned above at merging class-unionist and national liberation struggles, particularly by the leftist student blocs, the student movement's main contribution had been its success in developing organisational structures and mobilisation tools, as well as in nurturing political national cadres. During the 1980s and early 1990s, the leadership of the different political parties originated from the cadres of the student movement involved in student union activism and struggle in all universities, especially at Birzeit where the student movement had matured. This had played a vital role in sustaining the Intifada (Palestinian popular uprising) which erupted in 1987. University students' active engagement in resisting the oppressive occupation forces increased during the Intifada, and as a result, the Israeli military governor[8] closed the universities, hoping that this would decrease the student movement's role in the struggle (Salameh, 2013). However, the return of the student activists to their localities charged the local rural areas with cadres experienced in organisational and political skills, who played a mobilising role among all political parties for the popular Intifada in rural areas. For instance, with the closure of the universities, the PFLP decided to dissolve the party's student organisation and join the rural popular organisations or build such organisations. This catalysed the struggle in the rural areas which are the bases for the Palestinian working class and which lacked the organisational and political structures to organise and defend itself against the occupation. Student activists played a critical role on this front (interview by the authors on 20 May 2019 with W. R. a PFLP activist during the Intifada).

POST-OSLO TRANSFORMATIONS

After the interruption of university student life during the Intifada because of the long period of university closures by the colonial authorities,[9] Palestinian students returned to their campuses amidst a new reality following the Oslo agreements. The signing of the Oslo agreements by the PLO's right-wing leadership and the subsequent transformation of the Palestinian liberation project into a state building project amid the continuation of Zionist settler-colonial expansion meant fundamental shifts that reached every aspect and sector of society. The establishment of the Palestinian Authority (PA), which was structurally bonded by the economic and security agreements with the Israeli colonial entity, and its dependence on the donor community and its conditionalities, distorted the Palestinian political sphere, and weakened the political parties, popular organisations and the unions that were previously organically linked to the liberation project. Gradually the PA replaced the PLO which since the mid-1960s had been the representative of the whole Palestinian people. Consequently, the PLO was turned into an empty institution and its components including the GUPS were paralysed. The accumulation of the post-Oslo transformations and the adoption of an all-encompassing neoliberal rationality steadily shifted Palestinian material conditions, political culture and sociality. It also transformed the values of collectivism, voluntarism and sacrifice into the values of individualism, self-interest and consumerism. These transformations led to the regression of the democratic popular mass organisations, including the student movement.

The economic policies of higher education institutions became mainly based on generating high student fees to cover costs, particularly after PLO support to universities ended.[10] Following the Oslo accords, the European Union played a major role in funding Palestinian higher education. This funding was conditioned on structural changes within the universities to increase ostensible 'effectiveness' and develop self-sustainability through different procedures. Given these conditions, in addition to the small portion of the PA budget allocated to education and the disinclination of the PA from transferring already allocated funds for higher education to universities, university administrations began to raise student fees to the degree that they cover 65 per cent of the costs today (Muhammad & Batta, 2019). The growing tendency of Palestinian higher education institutions toward privatisation was further encouraged by the World Bank and other funding agency policies (Salem, 2000). The ability of the poor to enrol in higher education had been affected, increasing the burden on students' families. Thus, a growing portion of students had to combine education with work in order to be able to pay their fees, affecting their involvement in student activism. This trend had also impacted on the living conditions of academics and employees of Palestinian higher education institutions and provoked union struggles aimed at improving members' living conditions.

Already weakened and deeply divided, these conditions produced a new negative reality for the student movement to confront. The divisions had been deepened by the weakening of the PLO and the political parties that composed it, particularly the leftist ones. Islamist parties (mainly Hamas) were strengthened as they obtained financial resources and continued to offer the choice to resist the occupation and settler-colonialism in relation to Fateh that constituted the ruling party. The context affected the student movement's formation and practices and limited its ability to organise and act at the national level (Ramadan, 2016; Youssef, 2011).

Although factionalism had typified the student movement since its inception, within the new post-Oslo reality, factionalism acquired a new signification and dynamic. The student blocs became mere recipients of directives, not active agents in strengthening and influencing their mother political parties. The latter, despite perceiving their student wings as a source of legitimacy, popularity and a thermometer for their presence in the street, did not provide the requisite support to nurture its cadres. In addition, the student movement faced new challenges such as the interference of the PA's security forces in universities and its continuous attempts to control the oppositional student blocs.

Within these new conditions, the student movement adopted the role of service provider to students, mainly in the election season, instead of defending students' interests against the structural changes of higher education institutions. That is, despite the shift of the focus of the student movement from mobilisation for the liberation struggle to focusing on students' everyday needs, a unionist-class perspective connected with the liberation struggle was missing.

THE STUDENT STRIKE AT BIRZEIT UNIVERSITY

The new conditions under the PA, its subjection to Oslo's security arrangements and economic protocols, as well as its dependence on funders' political agendas were apparent in its securitisation practices and social-economic policies. This had constrained Palestinian resistance prospects and increased economic gaps among Palestinians, bringing class issues to the fore. These issues formed the context of Birzeit's 2016 student strike.

Reflections on the chronology of the strike

In mid-August 2016, the Birzeit student council called for a protest against the administration's decision to raise tuition fees for current and new students. The protest, labelled 'the last chance', was announced on the student council's Facebook page under the hashtag 'will not pass'. This was the main slogan throughout the strike. All components of the student council and the student movement united in the struggle against the tuition raise and suspended lectures on that day from 12:00 to 13:30 to enable students to participate in the protest. One Birzeit student wrote on the student council's Facebook page, the main communication tool among the student body: 'my father worked very hard all his life to educate me, he does not sleep at nights worrying for not being able to get the money to pay my fees – and higher education should be free'. Another student wrote, 'education is not a business'.

These two posts reflect the sentiments that drove the strike. They expressed the students' position regarding two conflicting perspectives, specifically on higher education, and on societal matters in general: a social perspective held by the student movement that perceives higher education as a public resource that should be available to all, and a contrasting narrow economic perspective that perceives education as a commodity in accordance with a market logic.

Hundreds of students attended the protest that the student council called for on that day. The head of the student council directed his speech at the protest to the university administration saying: 'the solution for the financial crisis of the university should be through pressing the Palestinian government and demanding its support for the university instead of raising the tuition fees'.

The head of the student council's speech stated that the struggle of the student movement against the tuition fees increase did not just target the university's administration, but also the PA's economic policies of privatisation and its abstention from supporting higher education institutions. The student movement opposed the university administration's attempt to resolve its financial problems through the tuition increase, demanding instead that the PA allocate a greater portion of its budget to education. It is worth noting that 'the security sector consumes more of the PA's budget than the education, health, and agriculture sectors combined' (Tartir, 2017).

At the end of the protest, the head of the student council announced that the student movement would give the administration ten days until 25 August to cancel the decision regarding tuition fees. Meanwhile, the students formed a unified committee composed of representatives of the student council and all the student movement blocs to manage the crises.

Between mid-August to the end of September 2016, the student movement dedicated its activities to the struggle against the fees increase. It simultaneously focused on Palestinian political prisoners on hunger strike. The student movement organised multiple protests supporting the hunger strikers Malek Al Qadi, Muhammad and Mahmud Al Balbul, Ayad Al Harimi and Bilal Kayed who had been on hunger strike for 64 days. Additionally, the student council's Facebook page followed up and condemned several cases of student arrests by the Palestinian security forces such as the arrest and detention of the student council's head of the specialisation committee.

Hence, while waging the battle against the tuition increase – one with a class dimension – the student movement also engaged with one of the Palestinian national liberation struggle's main issues – that of political prisoners in the Israeli colonial prisons. At the same time, students raised their voices against the securitisation of everyday post-Oslo Palestinian life by the security forces. While engaging with class and political issues, they also insisted on continuing their battle to defend education for all.

At the end of the ten day deadline, the student council and the student movement held a press conference at the university and announced an open-ended strike until the cancellation of the tuition increase. The crisis management committee issued a statement declaring that the university gates would be closed to all except for the students and the administrators involved in the negotiation committee. The student movement representatives commandeered all the university's gates and began their open sit-in on the campus on 25 August 2016. They began negotiations with the administration's negotiation committee and announced all the developments to the students through their Facebook page, which was followed not only by the students but also by the university community, broader society and the media.

Soon after the beginning of the open strike, the Palestinian media began to cover the details of the crisis which turned into one of the most debated issues in the media and among Palestinian society. Students from different Palestinian universities arrived on campus to support the student strike. Representatives of the different students' clubs – an important component of the student movement (Twam, 2010) – expressed their support. Students' family members supported the students' right to strike, and some called for joining the students on campus. Heated debates occurred among faculty and administrators about the right of students to strike through shutting down the university. A few faculty members and employees organised to support the students and arrived at the campus individually and collectively to listen to the students and defend their right to strike.

The debates among the Birzeit University community led to serious engagements with the university's economic policies, administrative and financial practices, and educational approach. Two years later, these issues became the main matters raised and fought for by members of the union of academics and employees mainly by those who were involved in supporting the students' strike. That is, the eminence of the student strike motivated faculty members and employees to organise and promote solid union activism.

The students employed different means in managing their struggle. They produced several infographics showing the extent of the fees increase in recent years. They successfully managed a media campaign clarifying the students' position and responding to each statement of the university administration. For instance, on 29 August 2016, the student council and the student movement issued a statement titled 'why the strike' stating that the Birzeit student movement which represents an extension and producer of national activism aimed to first put an end to the university policy in recent years which targets the pocket of poor students as the easiest way to solve its financial problem. Second, it aimed to pressure the university to find other ways to solve its financial problem such as demanding that the PA, the main reason for the problem, allocate more money to higher education. Third, they demanded the revision of academic, financial, administrative and social policies adopted by the university which negatively affected students.

The student movement statement diagnosed the structural political and economic reasons behind the fee increase. Thus, it challenged the economic policy of the university directed by the privatisation logic and simultaneously challenged the Palestinian political system, which allocates a much greater portion of its budget to the security sector than to education. Additionally, the student movement called for structural changes at the university level concerning administrative, financial and academic dimensions. The leftist student bloc, Al-Qotb al-Tollabi, took the demand for institutional changes further by defining its vision for a popular university, democratic education and liberation. During the strike, leftist activists organised multiple activities to discuss radical student struggles, forms of popular education and ways to revive the voluntary collective culture that characterised the first Intifada.

On 4 September 2016, the 11th day of the strike, the student movement called for a protest titled 'Sunday of Anger' in front of the Council of Ministers to demand support for the university and the transfer of allocations earmarked for higher education. That is, students carried their demands outside the walls of the university directing them to the formal political system, a task that should be done by university administrations. During that protest, Palestinian security forces arrested a student council member.

Throughout the strike, student activists proved their readiness to sacrifice for their cause, taking student activism many steps forward. They spent Eid al-Adha (one of the most important feasts) within the walls of the university apart from their families, and on the 26th day of the strike, four students began an open hunger strike until the cancellation of the fees decision. Throughout the strike, the student movement received supporting delegations and letters of solidarity from public figures, including a statement of support from Muhammad Alqiq, a former Palestinian political prisoner acknowledged by Palestinians for his long period of hunger strike. Alqiq, formerly a head of Birzeit's student council, stated that the students at Birzeit had always been at the forefront of defending the Palestinian cause, Palestinian prisoners and the families of martyrs, calling for support of their struggle for the right of education for all, and encouraging joining their rejection of the inhuman economic policies.

On 23 September, the student movement reached an agreement with the administration. The university administration agreed that it would not raise fees for four years and that any future increase would be conditional on consultation between all university constituents. On 25 September, the student movement announced its victory and the end of the strike, stating that the victory was a result of the unity and persistence of the students.

The strike and its success constitutes a turning point in the student movement's struggle. Student activists from all factions were unified despite the deep division that characterises current Palestinian society. This unity had been carved around a class issue which de-emphasised ideological divisions and highlighted the material conditions and their deterioration because of the economic policies adopted by the PA and higher education institutions. Throughout the long period of the strike, the other issue was that of Palestinian political prisoners. This points to the fact that national liberation and class issues are two dimensions with the ability to unify students.

Students also adopted new tactics for achieving their goals. Shutting down the university gates and occupying the university continuously until their goals were achieved constituted a new tactic that proved to be successful and strengthened the students' confidence in their collective power. Moreover, the strike's time span provided students with the space and time to perceive and discuss important issues related to the structure and content of higher education. That is, they gained theoretical consciousness through praxis and gained confidence in their agency. Also, during the strike, female student activists, especially members of leftist blocs challenged the objection of conservative male students to their involvement in some types of actions and activities, especially staying on campus at night.

Finally, the student struggle went beyond the university's walls and opened a societal debate around the form of education and the form of society that the masses need and envision, restoring the student movement's vanguard role.

UNION STRUGGLES: OPENING A NEW POLITICAL HORIZON

The struggle waged by the student movement at Birzeit University was not the only union struggle that year. The summer of 2016 also witnessed the union struggle of the Palestinian schoolteachers who collected 15,000 signatures to form a new union after their abandonment by their weak formal union. On 22 October 2016, the teachers announced a strike protesting the oppressive practices of the ministry of education toward the teacher activists and also against security forces' policies in harassing and arresting teachers engaged in activism. Recently, various unions such as that of 'Ambulance and emergency services in the Red Crescent' and the newly formed union at Dar Al Shifa (Pharmacare), a private company, are fighting to improve their members' work conditions.

These union struggles represent the response of the masses to the material conditions caused by the PA's neoliberal economic policies and supported by its security apparatus. These in turn are both consequences of the post-Oslo conditions and the submissiveness of the PA to the Zionist colonial dictates supported by the US empire. Union struggles have recently been spreading in all Palestinian sectors, endowing their participants with organisational skills. Strong union organisation and activism open a new horizon of possibility that link union-class struggles with liberation struggles – a path that entails the potential to transcend the post-Oslo impasse.

NOTES

1   The earlier history of Palestinian student activism goes back to the period of British colonialism (mandate) in Palestine in which students in different educational institutions began to form associations calling for forming a student union to confront the colonial plans. In 1929, following the events of the Al-Buraq revolution, a student conference was held in Akka, calling for confronting British colonialism and its support for Zionist immigration to Palestine. In 1936, the student committees' conference in Jaffa was

attended by representatives from various Palestinian schools and the elected student union called for supporting the six-month long strike to confront British colonialism and its collusion with the Zionist settler colonial project in Palestine (Ghaiathah, 2000; Encyclopedia Palestina, 2013; Salem, 2000).

2   The Palestinian Liberation Organisation (PLO) was established in 1964 as the embodiment of the Palestinian National Liberation Movement. It has been a broad front comprised of various Palestinian political parties, independent figures, and the popular organisations which were part of the resistance movement during the time of its establishment.

3   Historical leaders of the Palestinian revolutionary movement such as Yasser Arafat and George Habash began their political engagements during the 1950s as student activists in Cairo University and the American University of Beirut.

4   It is worth noting that student activism inside the borders of colonised Palestine had begun earlier when the Palestinian students at Hebrew University established the Arab Students Committee in 1959. The emergence and development of the Palestinian student movement within the parts of Palestine occupied in 1948 is outside the scope of the current chapter. On the student movement in the 1948 occupied parts of Palestine see Ibrahim Makkawi (2004).

5   In 1972, Birzeit College transformed into a university, to become the first Palestinian institution to award a bachelor's degree. In 1973, Bethlehem University was established, followed by An Najah National College which transformed into a university in 1977, and the Islamic University of Gaza in 1978.

6   For instance, the student movement and the union of employees at Birzeit engaged in activities to confront the occupation practices in cooperation with the administration, such as the battle against the military decision of the occupation military chief which provided the occupation the right to interfere in higher education institutions.

7   In recent years, Birzeit student activism regarding the universities' cafeterias had been focused on boycotting Israeli products.

8   For detailed documentation of the history of Birzeit closures by the occupation forces see: www.birzeit.edu/en/about/history/education-under-occupation/closures-history.

9   Birzeit University had been closed for 1571 days from 1 October 1988 to 29 April 1992.

10   Before the PA was established, the PLO funded the greater portion of higher education institutions, as the contributing portion from student fees did not exceed 10 per cent of the real student cost (Muhammad & Batta, 2019).

REFERENCES

Abu Duhou, R. (2009). Between Nationalism and Feminism: Maha Mustaklem Nassar. *Women Studies Review*. Birzeit: Institute of Women's Studies. (Arabic).

Encyclopedia Palestina (2013). *The General Union of Palestine's Students.* Retrieved from www.palestinapedia.net/topic/the General Union of Palestine's Students (Arabic) (Accessed 20 May 2019).

Ghaiathah, I. (2000). *Palestinian Student Movement: The practice and agency.* Palestine: Muwatin, the Palestinian Institute for the Study of Democracy. (Arabic).

Kuttab, E. (2000). The Palestinian Student Movement and Its Social and Feminist Dimensions. In M. Al-Malki (ed.), *The Palestinian Student Movement and the Tasks of the Current Period* (pp. 131–149). Palestine: Muwatin, the Palestinian Institute for the Study of Democracy. (Arabic).

Makkawi, I. (2004). National Identity Development among Student Activists in the Israeli Universities. *International Journal of Educational Policy, Research, & Practice,* 5(2), 19–59.

MIFTAH. (2014). *Political Participation Perceptions of Students in Palestinian Universities and Colleges: Analytical report.* Retrieved from www.miftah.org/Publications/Books/Political_Participation_Perceptions_of_Students.pdf (Accessed 20 May 2019).

Muhammad, G. (2000). The Student Movement: A unionist and democratic yeast. In M. Al-Malki (ed.), *The Palestinian Student Movement and the Tasks of the Current Period* (pp. 39–55). Palestine: Muwatin, the Palestinian Institute for the Study of Democracy. (Arabic).

Muhammad, G. (2012). Palestinian Student Movement: Decline in the national struggle and confusion in the struggle for students' demands. *Modern Discussion,* vol. 3619. Retrieved from www.ahewar.org/debat/show.art.asp?aid=292884 (Arabic) (Accessed 20 May 2019).

Muhammad, G. & Batta, H. (2019). *Palestinian Higher Education between Right and the Market Chaos.* Ramallah: Bisan Center for Research and Development. (Arabic).

The Palestinian Revolution. (n.d.) *Dreaming Revolution: Clandestine networks and public associations 1951–1967.* Retrieved from http://learnpalestine.politics.ox.ac.uk/teach/week/4 (Accessed 20 May 2019).

Rafidi, W. (2016). The Student Movement and The Political Party: The experience of Al-taqadom Bulletin. *Women Studies Review.* Birzeit: Institute of Women's Studies. (Arabic).

Ramadan, S. (2016). *The Role of the Palestinian Student Movement in National Liberation: Chances and obstacles.* Beirut: Alzaituna Center for Studies and Consultations.

Salameh, A. B. (2013). The Palestinian Student Movement between Reality and Possibility. *Modern Discussion,* vol. 4221. Retrieved from www.ahewar.org/debat/show.art.asp?aid=378866&r=0. (Accessed 20 May 2019).

Salem, W. (2000). The Student Movement between the Tasks of Completing National Liberation and the Tasks of Democratic Building. In M. Al-Malki (ed.), *The Palestinian Student Movement and the Tasks of the Current Period* (pp. 17–37). Palestine: Muwatin, the Palestinian Institute for the Study of Democracy. (Arabic).

Tamari, S. (1991). The Palestinian Movement in Transition: Historical reversals and the uprising. *Journal of Palestine Studies, 20*(2), 57–70.

Taraki, L. (1989). Mass Organizations in the West Bank. In N. H. Aruri (ed.), *Occupation: Israel Over Palestine* (pp. 431–463). Belmont, MA: Association of Arab-American University Graduates, Inc.

Tartir, A. (2017). The Palestinian Authority Security Forces: Whose security? *Al Shabaka: The Palestinian policy network.* Retrieved from https://al-shabaka. org/briefs/palestinian-authority-security-forces-whose-security/. (Accessed 20 May 2019).

Twam, R. (2010). The Palestinian Student Movement: The crisis of charisma and the loss of institutionalization. *Dirasat, 13–14,* 82–104. (Arabic).

Youssef, T. A. (2011). The Political and Demands-focused Approaches within the Palestinian Student Movement's Thought in Palestinian Universities: A critical evaluation of praxis. *Al-Quds Open University Journal for Studies and Research, 23*(1), 339–372. (Arabic).

9

The new student movements in Mexico in the twenty-first century

#YoSoy132, Ayotzinapa and
#TodosSomosPolitécnico

Alma Maldonado-Maldonado and
Vania Bañuelos Astorga

Mexico has a very long tradition of student revolts. Years before the movement of 1968 – a period of heightened politicisation in Mexico City and alliances between students, workers and the urban poor – there were many popular movements throughout Mexico. These included miners, railroad and other workers, *normalistas* (student teachers) and teachers demanding better working conditions, better social security and an end to exploitation. Yet the most important event in the Mexican student movement's history happened in 1968. Ten days before Mexico City hosted the 1968 Olympics, on 2 October 1968, the military opened fire on a rally of 10,000 university and high school students in Mexico City's Tlatelolco area. The students were protesting the hosting of the Olympics and the Mexican state's repressive actions during what was called Mexico's 'Dirty War'. The exact number of students and other civilians murdered and missing as a consequence of the Tlatelolco massacre is unknown, but many estimates of the death toll range from 300 to 400.

The 1968 Mexican student revolt can be explained by the economic, political and social crises the country was then facing, but was also connected to other youth movements in countries like France (Paris,

May 1968), Czechoslovakia (Prague, January 1968), and the United States (with the anti-Vietnam War movement in several states from 1965 to 1970). These movements culturally influenced the Mexican movement, which was not restricted to the participation of students but also included other actors such as workers and unions. The Mexican government did not pay attention to these social demands, but repressed the students. Besides the Tlatelolco massacre, there were many cases of illegal detention, torture and extrajudicial executions.

After the student revolt of 1968, several conflicts arose in the country involving students. These include the 'halconazo' also known as the Corpus Christi massacre (of student demonstrators) that took place on 10 June 1971, and later movements as a protest of the paramilitary repression suffered by students. During the 1970s, there were many social movements that included teachers. There were other revolts at universities such as Sinaloa, Oaxaca, Nuevo Leon and Puebla. Then during the 1980s, an important 21-day student strike took place at the Autonomous National University of Mexico (UNAM) in 1986, resulting in a University Congress that happened in 1990. The 1990 UNAM University Congress was a unique experience because students and faculty were elected to participate in a space to define the future of the institution; nothing similar has happened before or since. There were student revolts at some other institutions like Guerrero, Chapingo, Puebla and Sonora but these were isolated movements. In 1994, with the uprising of the Ejército Zapatista de Liberación Nacional (Zapatistas) in the southern state of Chiapas, most universities participated in the subsequent peace movements from the Universities of Chiapas, Michoacana to UNAM. In 1999 there were other small isolated student protests at the Universities of Zacatecas, Coahuila, Chapingo until the largest student strike that took place at UNAM which lasted almost ten months and ended with army intervention. Finally, the student teachers (*normalistas*) of 'El Mexe', a rural teacher training college in Hidalgo, went on strike in January 2000 and ended after police intervention (Pérez Durán & Magaña Vargas, 2001).

This chapter will analyse the three latest Mexican student and youth movements in the last decade that mostly emerged as a result of the country's social, political and insecurity crisis. The first of these is #YoSoy132 ('I am 132') a youth movement against a presidential candidate and a fight to open the mass media to more democratic content. The second, #TodosSomosPolitécnico (We are all Polytechnic), was a series of mass demonstrations and a 79-day strike at the National Polytechnic Institute (Instituto Politécnico Nacional – IPN). This movement protested against administrative and academic reforms which were almost imposed on 17 September 2014. Finally, the Ayotzinapa protests are discussed, organised after the disappearance of 43 rural teacher education students in Guerrero who have been missing since the night of 26 September 2014. The 43 students were preparing to journey to Tlatelolco to commemorate the 1968 massacre.

#YoSoy132, Ayotzinapa and #TodosSomosPolitécnico

As the literature on student movements and social movements highlights (Berrío, 2006), there are two main explanations for these types of movements: situations within higher education institutions, reforms, or changes that students disagree with and factors outside the institutions that help protests or revolts to emerge. The three Mexican student movements discussed here respond to each of these characteristics, including a third type which perhaps falls in the middle of both and will be discussed later.

Some research on collective action (Melucci, 1999; Tarrow, 1989; Tilly, 1977) uses 'events' as analytical units. This methodological device results in a very effective research strategy and contributes to the renewal of this field, offering great empirical evidence for the study of collective action and social movements (Melucci, 1999, p. 36). This chapter follows the idea of selecting events as a way to explain the movements while discussing their characteristics.

As Lipset and Schaflander (1971) note, generally speaking it is very difficult to predict the development of a student movement. In the case of the three movements here, perhaps the #YoSoy132 and the #TodosSomosPolitécnico movements were the hardest to anticipate. On the other hand, the issues that sparked the Ayotzinapa movement were predictably going to catalyse important national protests. The #YoSoy132 movement was not motivated by problems within the universities or colleges, but from the broad social and political concerns of the country. It took place in 2012 as a protest against Enrique Peña Nieto, the official presidential candidate of the *Partido Revolucionario Institucional* (PRI)[1], whose electoral victory was only a matter of time. The movement began at Ibero-American University, a prestigious private university in Mexico City, with the students protesting previous human rights violations during Nieto's time as governor of the State of Mexico.[2] However, the mass media accused the protesters of not being real Ibero-American students. The students were then forced to make a video where they introduced themselves and proved that they were enrolled there. One of their main demands was the democratisation of mass media, asking them to be objective and to open spaces to all voices and opinions. In responding to this situation, students produced their own Internet media messages. Later, the movement spread widely across the metropolitan area of Mexico City and other states.

The second movement is a clear example of a collective university student action. It was a 79-day strike at the National Polytechnic Institute (IPN). The IPN is a federal higher education institution that was established in 1936 with the purpose of integrating the system of technical education. The IPN has an enrolment of about 177,983 students and about 16,556 academics. Of the students, 35 per cent are enrolled at the high school level, 61 per cent are higher education students and 4 per cent are graduate students (IPN-SGE, 2017; SGE, 2017). The IPN offers about 293 educational programmes, 68 technical programmes, 77 bachelor's degrees and 148 graduate programmes (28 specialisations, 61 Master's programmes and 42 Ph.D. programmes). At high school level, the IPN has two types of programmes – general education to offer the basis for the next level (higher education) and the opportunity to obtain a technical career diploma. When students learned that at the higher education level they would be given another technical diploma if they were unable to finish their higher education programme, they felt the IPN was going to transform into a purely technical school. Consequently, for most students, this was a sign that the institution wanted to orient itself more towards technical training than professional or more academic education and lower the institution's educational level. The IPN's director at that time also questioned the student participation in the movement, claiming that they were outsiders, offending the activists with such a suggestion. Another administrative change took place at the federal government when there was an attempt to modify the IPN's legal status. The IPN did not want to become part of the Tecnológico de México and preferred to interact directly with the Ministry of Education and to remain a more comprehensive educational institution and not a technical one. The outcome of the IPN student movement is still pending: a compromise was made to organise a congress in 2019 to discuss the IPN's academic and administrative problems, but as of writing this has yet to happen.

The third movement is not a student revolt but rather a collective action in response to a tragedy that affected the whole country after 43 students from a rural teaching school went missing on the night of 26 September 2014. These students disappeared with the complicity of the police and military in Iguala, Guerrero. According to the Interdisciplinary Group of Independent Experts (GIEI, 2015), around 180 people, 100 of them students, were direct victims of various human rights violations during the events of 26 September 2014. The students from the Ayotzinapa Rural Teachers College were travelling in three buses to the nearby town of Iguala when they went missing. These students wanted to fundraise in order to attend a march in Mexico City in remembrance of the 1968 Tlatelolco student massacre. Once the news spread, Mexican society started to protest this outrageous incident. College students were a key part of protests along with other sectors of society such as groups of teachers, farmers, students and citizens in general who were demanding justice and insisted that the 43 students should be found alive. This movement's inspiration came from a request for justice to punish those responsible for the murder and disappearance of the 43 missing students (allegedly with the involvement of the local and federal authorities). The fact that the missing students were enrolled at a higher education institution (rural teaching school) and that they belonged to the less privileged social classes (farmers and Indigenous people) was also significant. Part of the history of rural teaching schools is that they preserve an agenda of social justice and educational aspirations that include demanding a space for poor people to study higher education (Elortegui, 2017). Ayotzinapa is the only rural teaching school in the state of Guerrero (Fernández-Poncela, 2015). Established in 1926, its students belong to one of the oldest student organisations in the country, the Student Federation of Socialist Farmers of Mexico [Federación de Estudiantes Campesinos Socialistas de México (FECSM)], founded in 1935. This organisation has consistently demanded that the authorities maintain the minimum academic conditions and the necessary infrastructure to offer their educational programmes (Hernández-Navarro, 2015). Since the beginning of the protests by the Ayotzinapa movement, the FECSM showed its organisational capacity and discipline to train the students of the teaching schools (Hernández-Navarro, 2015). The Rural Teaching School 'Professor Raúl Isidro Burgos' had 522 male students and 52 teachers in 2014. It offered the following programmes: Primary School Teacher, Intercultural Bilingual Primary School Teacher and Physical Education (Ayotzinapa, 2019; Candelas, 2016).

For the most part, the most recent youth and student movements in Mexico are more collective actions than previous university movements. Perhaps the main explanation is the country context. In two cases, the revolts are responses to broader public outrage concerning the 43 missing students, the murder of six people, the injuries of 27 people in Iguala (Concha-Malo, 2015; Fernández-Poncela, 2015) and the lack of democratisation and plurality of the mainstream mass media (#YoSoy132). This is explained in the following sections.

STRATEGIES, TACTICS AND DEMANDS

These three movements are the first Mexican youth/student movements that have really used social media. The #YoSoy132 movement began with a home video that introduced the 131 Ibero-American University students who protested against the campus visit of the PRI presidential candidate. The video was produced when they were questioned whether they were real students at that university. In this video, 131 students gave their names and enrolment numbers, presenting their official IDs in order to prove their identities. Very soon, people in Mexico were saying that these college students were not alone, that all Mexican dissidents were 'the student number 132'. Then, more home videos were produced of people referring to themselves as 'number 132'. Shortly after, students and other members of society continued to identify as 'number 132'. Social media was essential to spread this movement. The most important event of the #YoSoy132 movement was displayed on Facebook, Twitter and YouTube with the campaign, 'Do you want to change the history of Mexico?' Additionally, the use of the hashtag #YoSoy132 was very popular and effective (Cerrillo & Lay, 2014; Torres, 2015). The #YoSoy132 movement organised several demonstrations, mostly in Mexico City but also in other cities. They also organised several assemblies in public and private universities.

Table 9.1 Tactics, media and legal approaches

| | Traditional tactics | | | | Media | | Legal approaches | |
	Demonstrations	Strikes	Assemblies	Occupations	Mass media	Social media networks	International	National
Yo Soy 132	x		x		x	x		
Ayotzinapa	x	x	x	x		x	x	
IPN	x	x	x	x	x	x		x

Table 9.1 explains the type of tactics used by each movement in order to compare different strategies. There are interesting differences between them in terms of the scope and location but there is no question these are the three more important recent youth and student movements with national impact. They all use demonstrations and assemblies. Two of them held strikes that can be considered more of a traditional tactic. The use of social media networks was similar across the three movements but perhaps the Ayotzinapa protests did not have the mass media impact that they should have had. Although the Ayotzinapa activists pursued the legal fight at the national and international courts, since it was mostly a justice issue. In the Ayotzinapa protests, social media networks were used to inform people about the tragedy, to ask for a response from the Mexican government regarding the investigations, and report the human rights violations involved in this case. In order to understand the type of participation in this movement, it is important to talk about civic engagement. According to Adler and Goggin (2005), civic engagement can be 'the ways in which citizens participate in the life of a community in order to improve conditions for others or to help shape the community's future.' Robert Putnam (quoted in Hopf, 2011) defines civic engagement in terms of social capital, as 'features of social life—networks, norms, and trust—that enable participants to act together more effectively to pursue shared objectives.' In this particular case, the role of social media networks like Facebook, Twitter and others were very relevant forms of civic engagement (Hopf, 2011). The social networks served mainly as mechanisms of organisation among the university community, but also as an effective way to inform the wider population about their demands. The use of the hashtags #YoSoy132, #TodosSomosPolitécnico and #Ayotzinapa were a symbol of collective action.

The IPN movement is a traditional student movement. 'Students have almost invariably been more responsive to political trends, to changes in mood, to opportunities for social change, than any other group in the population, except possibly intellectuals', as Lipset and Schaflander (1971, p. 14) suggest. The movement used traditional strategies: demonstrations, strikes and assemblies, which are drawn from two major social movements of the twentieth century, farmers and trade unions. It held two large demonstrations (over 70,000 people) and other smaller demonstrations (3000 and 20,000 people). Additionally, multiple assemblies took place in each IPN school located in Mexico City, several general assemblies were also organised and finally, the student strike took place over a 70-day period. There were nine dialogues between authorities and students before signing eight agreements. Another result was that 25 IPN directors were fired, together with its lawyer, general secretary, and general director (Celestino & Iglesias, 2014; Rojas, 2014). Also, since the IPN movement is more of a traditional student movement, it had a shorter lifespan. As Altbach (1989) points out, student movements have a short life because of students' limited stay in college. On 10 February 2015, IPN general director, Fernández Fassnacht, stated that until that date, 36 out of the 73 agreements signed were in the process of implementation. Recently, on 23 March 2019, the IPN director communicated that most of the specific agreements have been fulfilled, in particular the integration of the organisational commission of the congress (Rodríguez, 2015). However, since the organisation of the congress is at a standstill, it is difficult to guess if it will happen in the near future or not. Table 9.2 presents the three movements classified depending on the type of movements and demands made.

Table 9.2 Classification of the three Mexican movements according to the type of movements and demands

| | Type of movements (Tarrow, 1989) | | |
	Protest organisation	Movement	Protest acts
Type of demands (Tilly & Wood, 2010)			
Identity	Yo Soy 132		
Programmatic		IPN	
Positional			Ayotzinapa

#YoSoy132 had more to do with creating an identity of subversion and was more a protest organisation with a specific agenda to democratise the mass media and oppose the top presidential candidate. The IPN student revolt must be classified as a movement with a programmatic setting of demands for administrative and academic changes. The Ayotzinapa protests could be defined more as protest acts since the demands related to the clarification of the crimes and disappearance of the 43 students. Table 9.2 illustrates the different scales of the movements and suggests a way to identify each of them. The Ayotzinapa protest tactics were concentrated in the mass media and in social networks. Their principal demands focused on pressuring the government to open an independent investigation coordinated by some human rights international organisations, resulting in considerable national and international attention. In the Ayotzinapa case, the impact was also international since Mexican communities living abroad also organised protests. In the case of the #YoSoy132 and #TodosSomosPolitécnico, international TV networks disseminated news about these movements.

One of the main characteristics of these movements is that they created coalitions with students from other universities and sectors. In Mexico, there tends to be an ideological separation between public and private universities. Since the 1968 student movement, the country did not witness a movement that combined both sectors and shared agendas. The Ayotzinapa protests went beyond public and private higher education institutions, spreading throughout Mexican society but also internationally. Furthermore, the #YoSoy132 movement took place in both public and private education sectors. Its tactics in particular were based on social media, first filming a video and secondly generating many messages that were reproduced on a massive scale.

Information about #YoSoy132 emerged and spread quickly. Its specific demands were:

1. Ask mass media (radio, TV, press) to take an interest in social concerns.
2. Let communication schools create public media productions.
3. Provide Internet access as a constitutional right.
4. Open spaces to have debates between young people.
5. Offer safety to all the participants in the movement, especially the protection of journalists who had been threatened with violence.

Other demands of #YoSoy132 concerned the organisation of a third independent presidential debate and rejection of the candidacy of Enrique Peña Nieto. Perhaps one of the movement's main immediate victories was the organisation of the third debate. On 19 June 2012, the third debate took place, organised by the #YoSoy132 movement with the participation of three of the four presidential candidates: Josefina

Vázquez Mota, Gabriel Quadri and Andrés Manuel López Obrador. Enrique Peña Nieto declined the invitation. The debate was transmitted by Hangout in Google+ and by some radio stations. The cultural channels such as Once TV and Channel 22 televised the debate.

Another important political event organised by the #YoSoy132 before the first university assembly that took place at UNAM was held on 31 May 2012. The meeting was very successful. Over 50 educational institutions participated, mostly higher education institutions. That day, many roundtable discussions were held on different social, economic, cultural and political issues. Instead of explaining the movement's dynamic and debates, the mass media basically reported that the assembly had an anti-Enrique Peña Nieto tendency, instead of reporting the broader positions discussed.

The IPN movement is the only one primarily related to the problems within educational institutions that is included in this chapter. The ten demands of this movement were: 1) Cancelling the Internal Regulation approved by the Consulting General Council on 23 September. 2) Abolition of the programme that decided to establish a technical exit to the higher education programmes, as well as the high school programmes that belong to the high school national reform. 3) Discharge of Yoloxóchitl Bustamante as the general director of the IPN. 4) Removal of the banking and industrial police of the IPN. 5) Eliminating the life pension of former directors. 7) No academic or legal repression against the participants of the movement. 8) Increase spending on higher education, science and technology to at least 2 per cent of the GDP. 9) Make privatisation measures in the institution more transparent. 10) Dismantle the shock groups[3] at the institution.

A second series of demands asked the Polytechnic National Congress to do away with the plan to create the National Technological Institute of Mexico (a public university system which had been created in July 2014). A third package of demands included the opening of public discussions between representatives of the movement and the official authorities. After 67 days of a student strike, classes resumed but the important changes that were expected at the institution did not occur (Rodríguez, 2015).

As in earlier periods in Mexico, recent student movements have been able to stop reforms or changes in institutions but are unable to take their energy to make profound transformations in their institutions. In the case of the IPN, most of their demands were solved during the negotiations. The ones that were not resolved were sent to be discussed at the general congress that has not taken place. Therefore the process of IPN transformation has not been completely solved.

CITIZENSHIP BUILDING AS A COLLECTIVE POSSIBILITY

In the Mexican context, the fight for democracy and respect for human rights can be considered part of citizenship construction, particularly for the youth. According to Tarrow (1997), research has shown that people join movements based on a broad spectrum of reasons that range from wishing to receive personal advantages, to solidarity with others, and from the engagement of principles to the desire of being a part of something collective. This heterogeneity makes it more complicated to understand participants' motivations. Secondly, social movements do not need to be defined by a minimum number of participants. Thirdly, they do not need a formal structure.

The Ayotzinapa story revealed some of the deepest concerns for a group of students who were presumably murdered with the complicity of the local police and military forces (Gómez, 2015). At the same time, the Ayotzinapa movement made many college students aware of the problems of the rural teaching school. Many of these university students did not know about the existence of this student population and showed empathy for them and wondered: who are these students and why does the government want them to disappear? Many people wonder that if these were college students instead of students from a rural teaching school, would they have been treated differently. Equally, the movement was also important for the students of the teaching school, because it helped them to build a sense of identity. This came as a result of the 2013 educational reform, which questioned the training quality of the *normalistas*. In some ways, the Ayotzinapa movement helped to reinforce a sense of dignity and self-esteem for the *normalistas* who are constantly viewed as students rejected by other universities for their poor academic quality.

There are two other characteristics that help to understand the development of youth and student movements: the desire to become part of something collective and the necessity of creating an identity. Age plays a very important role in explaining these movements. As Lipset and Schaflander (1971, p. 17) point out, 'student activism in particular, is among other things an expression of the need for a distinct youth culture'. The #TodosSomosPolitécnicos is a clear example of this. The IPN movement created a collective identity around a higher education institution. It reinforced the students' pride and identity for their institution: 'We are all Polytechnic'. In contrast to the Chilean movements that were promoted by highly structured organisations (student federations, student centres, student coordinations) (Fernández, 2013; Guzmán-Concha, 2012; also see Chapter 6 in this collection); the IPN movement started with small coordinated groups who had a specific conflict with their authorities.

After learning about some of the dynamics of the Brazilian student movements (Arroyo, 2016) and the Chilean movements (Maldonado-Maldonado & Acosta, 2018) where some of these protests were led by women, the contrast with the Mexican case is apparent. Although Mexico has some of the highest rates of murdered and missing women (García, 2018), the number of protests in response to these issues at schools and colleges do not correspond to the seriousness of the problem. Another example of gender disparity is the fact that student enrolment in higher education is almost 50 per cent women and 50 per cent men, but the movement leaders, especially the speakers, are mostly men. Men were the main leaders of the #TodosSomosPolitécnicos but in the dialogues (between authorities and students) the best speeches and arguments came from women (Olivos, 2014).

Tilly and Wood (2010) say that a social movement, as an invented/imaginary institution, 'can disappear or get transformed in a very different political way' (p. 42). This idea applies perfectly to the movements #YoSoy132, #TodosSomosPolitécnicos and the Ayotzinapa protests. But this also happens to the participants themselves. Some of the participants of #YoSoy132, who are now 28–30 years old, have decided to start building new forms of political organisations. Some participants took part in self-governance collective projects within the universities. Others completed their studies and began work as digital rights and human rights lawyers, activists in the defence of digital rights (Colectivo Horizontal y R3D), in organisations that defend the land and Indigenous communities, feminists (such as FEMEN), publicity agents who support NGOs and civil society movements, or worked on alternative media and documentaries (for instance: Colectivo Más de 131). Other former #YoSoy132 activists have sought to influence politics working in an independent platform to publish corruption reports (MexicoLeaks); others decided to work with a network of independent candidates called Wikipolitica ('sons of the 132', as they like to be called). Another group of the former #YoSoy132 are part of the current political party in power (MORENA). Many of them still participate in TV or radio programmes.

Despite the differences in terms of how many of the leaders and participants sought personal advantage, importantly, the movements analysed in this chapter helped most participants build their character and their agency. These movements became spaces of conscience, reflection and activism; they created a historical memory and a way to develop critical thinking. #YoSoy132 was the base for developing a new generation ready to creatively transform the idea of citizenship. Ayotzinapa put Mexico's insecurity problem in the middle of the debate and has reminded the country about the situation of the most excluded populations: Indigenous, poor people and small farmers to name a few. The IPN movement woke the students up, got them together, and was a reminder that student revolts can happen at any time.

CONCLUSION

In weak democracies, traditional political participation does not take young people and youth demands into consideration and indeed, they are largely excluded from political participation. The situation is extreme in weak societies (with deep inequalities) where there is no space for social movements but for more radical movements like guerrillas. In more democratic societies there are more spaces for participating and demanding social change. Mexico cannot be broadly considered to be a very democratic country. It has elections, but corruption runs through all its structures, including the purchase and sale of votes in every election. The other problem is that in developing societies there is always a lack of resources in general, and social movements including youth movements require resources (human, networks, time, media) that are not necessarily available in societies that are struggling.

For the students and youth who participate in these movements, there are always lessons and informal apprenticeships in areas such as public speaking, debating, writing and communications, amongst others, enforcing the agency of the activists. Some movements are vital in marking or redefining future generations, such as movements for minority rights or women's rights.

The 2 October 1968 massacre was a major setback to social movements in general and especially for student movements. Later movements in Mexico took inspiration from this to continue the tradition of rebellion. In 2012, when the #YoSoy132 movement was getting stronger, a source of inspiration was the uprising in Tunisia and the start of what was called the 'Arab Spring'. The Mexican students saw in that movement the possibility to fight totalitarian regimes and to fight for democracy. Since 1968, youth and students in Mexico have learned that rights are not to be taken for granted, but need to be defended, as they are constantly contested.

Finally, student and youth movements are not only the results of a failed state, as in the case of the activism related to Ayotzinapa, but can also represent a possibility to transform societies, which can be seen from #YoSoy132. Mexico is facing a regime change (with the new, supposedly left-wing government of Andrés Manuel López Obrador) which is transforming the political map of the country, ostensibly placing the youth and students in a stronger position, the majority of whom voted for this particular government. The government though has ominously started to cut spending on universities, science and the arts. These changing contexts are compelling reasons for the student movement to be vigilant and strengthened by learning lessons from past struggles.

NOTES

[Date last accessed for all links: 20 June 2019]

1   The political party that ruled Mexico continually for 71 years, from 1929 to 2000.

2   In May 2006, police forces used excessive violence against farmers in the town of Atenco, Texcoco because they protested against Mexico City's airport construction in 2001. The farmers were organised as the Frente de Pueblos en Defensa de la Tierra (FPDT). Six people were murdered, 27 injured and eleven women sexually abused during these events.

3   *porros* – semi-fascist shock groups which attacked student protesters.

REFERENCES

Adler, R. & Goggin, J. (2005). What Do We Mean By 'Civic Engagement'? *Journal of Transformative Education, 3*(3), 236–253.

Altbach, P. G. (1989). Perspectives on Student Political Activism. *Comparative Education, 25*(1), 97–110.

Arroyo, A. (2016). Los recientes movimientos estudiantiles de ocupación en Brasil: Lute como um estudante. *Blog de educación Distacia por tiempos*. Retrieved from https://educacion.nexos.com.mx/?p=375.

Ayotzinapa. (2019). Oferta educativa de la Escuela Normal Rural 'Raúl Isidro Burgos'. *Página oficial*. Retrieved from www.ayotzinapa.26omb.com/oferta.html.

Berrío, A. (2006). La perspectiva de los nuevos movimientos sociales en las obras de Sydney, Tarrow, Alain Touraine y Alberto Melucci. *Estudios Políticos*, (29), 219–236.

Candelas, R. (2016). *La política educativa y su impacto en las Escuelas Normales*. Centro de Estudios Sociales y de Opinión Pública (CESOP). Cámara de Diputados. Documento de trabajo núm. 233. Retrieved from www5.diputados.gob.mx/index.php/esl/content/download/61225/309090/file/CESOP-IL-14DT233EscuelasNormales-28102016.pdf.

Celestino, E. & Iglesias, C. (2014). IPN: segundo round, en A Contracorriente. *Rompeviento Tv*. Retrieved from www.youtube.com/watch?v=j5VqbWfaDeA.

Cerrillo, O. & Lay, I. (2014). #Yosoy132: redes digitales como comunicación e identidad en la acción colectiva. *Enfoques, 13*(1), 294–317. Retrieved from www.researchgate.net/publication/286624512_yosoy132_redes_digitales_como_comunicacion_e_identidad_en_la_accion_colectiva.

Concha-Malo, M. (2015). Ayotzinapa: preocupaciones abiertas. *El Cotidiano*, (189), 45–49.

Elortegui, M. (2017). Un recorrido histórico de las Escuelas Normales Rurales de México: el acto subversivo de hacer memoria desde los acontecimientos contra los estudiantes de Ayotzinapa. *Estudios Latinoamericanos, Nueva Época*, (40), 157–178. Retrieved from www.revistas.unam.mx/index.php/rel/article/view/61600.

FEMOSPP. (2008). *Informe Histórico presentado a la sociedad mexicana: Fiscalía especial FEMOSPP. Serie: México: Genocidio y delitos de lesa humanidad. Documentos fundamentales 1968–2008*. Tomo IX. Mexico: Comité 68. Retrieved from https://nsarchive2.gwu.edu/NSAEBB/NSAEBB180/index2.htm.

Fernández, J. (2013). Movimiento estudiantil en Chile (2011): repertorios de acción marcos de acción colectiva, impactos y desafíos para la política pública. *Circunstancia, 11*(31), 1–10.

Fernández-Poncela, A. M. (2015). Ayotzinapa, protestas, solidaridades y movimientos juveniles en México. *Boletín Científico Sapiens Research, 5*(2), 61–65.

García, A. (2018, 20 November). 14 de los 25 países con más feminicidios se ubican en América Latina. *El Economista*. Retrieved from www.eleconomista. com.mx/politica/Violencia-de-genero-14-de-los-25-paises-del-mundo-con-mas-feminicidios-se-ubican-en-America-Latina--20181120-0048.html.

Gómez, M. (2015). Ayotzinapa: de la crisis humanitaria a la crisis de Estado. *El Cotidiano*, (189), 50–59.

Grupo Interdisciplinario de Expertos Independientes (GIEI). (2015). *Informe Ayotzinapa. Investigación y primeras conclusiones de las desapariciones y homicidios de los normalistas de Ayotzinapa*, Ciudad de México.

Guzmán-Concha, C. (2012). The Students' Rebellion in Chile: Occupy protests or classic social movement? *Journal Social Movement Studies*, *11*(3–4), 408–415.

Hernández-Navarro, L. (2015). Ayotzinapa: el dolor y la esperanza. *El Cotidiano*, (189), 7–17.

Hopf, A. C. (2011). *Social Media's Impact on Civic Engagement in Mexico*. (Master's thesis). Texas: A&M University.

IPN-SGE. (2017). *Estadística básica. Fin de ciclo escolar 2016-2017 e Inicio de ciclo escolar 2017–2018*. Retrieved from www.gestionestrategica.ipn.mx/Evaluacion/ Documents/Estadistica/EBASICA_2017-2_V1.pdf.

Lipset, S. M. & Schaflander, G. M. (1971). *Passion and Politics: Student activism in America*. Boston, MA: Little Brown and Co.

Maldonado-Maldonado, A. & Acosta, F. (2018). An Agenda in Motion: Women's issues in Latin American higher education. *International Higher Education*, (94) Summer, 2–4. Retrieved from www.die.cinvestav.mx/Portals/ die/SiteDocs/Investigadores/AMaldonado/Articulos/IHE_ingles.pdf.

Melucci, A. (1999). Capítulo 1. Teoría de la acción colectiva. En A. Melucci (ed.), *Acción colectiva, vida cotidiana y democracia* (pp. 25–54). Mexico City: COLMEX.

Pérez Durán, J. & Magaña Vargas, H. (2001). *Los movimientos estudiantiles en México*. Retrieved from: www.cuestiones.ws/revista/n2/feb01-jp-hm1.htm.

Olivos, T. (2014). Mensaje final de la última mesa de diálogo. *Canal de YouTube*. Retrieved from www.youtube.com/watch?v=Cbk1nih9K90&t=28s/scielo. php?script=sci_arttext&pid=S0187-57952014000200004.

Rodríguez, R. (2015). El conflicto politécnico: Desarrollo, presente y horizonte. *Campus Milenio* no. 604. Retrieved from http://campusmilenio.mx/index. php?option=com_k2&view=item&id=2845:el-conflicto-politecnico-desarrollo-presente-y-horizonte&Itemid=140.

Rojas, H. (2014). Movimiento politécnico, cronología. *Educación Futura*. Retrieved from www.educacionfutura.org/movimiento-politecnico-cronologia/.

Secretaria de Gestión Estratégica (SGE). (2017). *Anuario Estadístico 2017 del IPN*. Retrieved from www.gestionestrategica.ipn.mx/Evaluacion/Documents/ Anuarios/ANUARIO_2017_V1.pdf.

Tarrow, S. (1989). Struggle, Politics and Reform: Collective action, social movement, and cycles of protest. Ithaca, NY: Cornell University Press.

—— (1997). *El poder en movimiento. Los movimientos sociales, la acción colectiva y la política*. Madrid: Alianza Editorial.

Tilly, C. (1977). *From Mobilization to Revolution.* Michigan: University of Michigan.
—— & Wood, L. (2010). *Los movimientos sociales, 1768–2008. Desde sus orígenes a Facebook.* Barcelona: Editorial Crítica.
Torres, L. (2015). ¿Quién programa las redes sociales en internet? El caso de Twitter en el movimiento #YoSoy132 en México. *Revista Internacional de Sociología, 73*(2). doi: http://dx.doi.org/10.3989/2013.05.29. Retrieved from http://revintsociologia.revistas.csic.es/index.php/revintsociologia/article/view/622/669.

Table 9.3 Appendix: List of IPN-related events

Dates	Events (2014)
17 September	Strike at the Architecture and Engineering School (Escuela Superior de Arquitectura e Ingeniería) (ESIA).
25 September	First student demonstration at the General Management of the Institute.
26 September	Most IPN schools go on strike.
28 September	The General Polytechnic Assembly is founded.
30 September	Second student demonstration at the Interior Affairs Ministry. Students deliver first set of demands to the Secretary Osorio Chong.
10 October	Third demonstration to deliver a response to their demands to the Ministry of Education and the Interior Affairs Ministry.
20 October	Students delivered their third set of demands to the Ministry of Education, Interior Affairs Ministry, the Internal Revenue and Public Credit Ministry, the Deputies' Camera and the Presidency.
28 October	IPN students symbolically took to TV Channel 11 (the IPN's open channel) as a way to show support for the Ayotzinapa movement.
4 November	First roundtable of dialogue at the IPN with the Ministry of Education authorities.
9 November	Authorities named a new director (Enrique Fernández Fassnacht).
5 December	Government authorities and students signed the eight agreements and the engagement letter with the director.

10

How did they fight? French student movements in the late 2000s and their contentious repertoire

Julie Le Mazier

From 2006 to 2010, four national-level student mobilisations happened in France. In the winter and spring of 2006, university students, joined by high school students and workers, opposed the French government's project of creating a precarious labour contract specific to young people, the *Contrat première embauche* (CPE), which was abolished in April that year. In the summer of 2007, they fought an overhaul of higher education, through the *loi relative aux Libertés et Responsabilités des universités* (LRU). This reform made universities manage their material and human resources, without giving them enough public money. Students contested it in the autumn and winter of 2007, and once again in the winter and spring of 2009, as higher education employees went on strike against some decrees enforcing the law. Finally, students joined an interprofessional movement against pension reform in the autumn of 2010. These last three mobilisations were unsuccessful.

During these four mobilisations, students mostly used strikes, mass demonstrations, occupation of campuses and general assemblies as their main decision-making tools, the latter being a direct democracy procedure in which any student can participate, speak and vote. The fact that activists often adopt the same modes of action over time is well documented by sociologists of social movements. Referring to this, Tilly (1977) called contentious repertoire 'the whole set of means [any particular group] has for making claims of different kinds on different individuals or groups' (Tilly, 1986, p. 4). Like musicians or actors, activists protest by adapting parts of a repertoire they already know. Tilly argued that history may explain types of collective action available to social movements. Macro-structural changes, such as industrialisation, urbanisation, the development of mass-media and migrations, and the construction of the nation-state in Europe at the beginning of the nineteenth century gave birth to the set of practices we still know: strikes, demonstrations, meetings and campaigns. But several unresolved questions (Fillieule, 2010) are partly addressed in Tilly's last work (Tilly, 2008), such as the identification of the brokers and communication channels through which means of action were diffused. We might also pay attention to the symbolic dimension actors confer on some modes of action, which may foster their use (Steinberg, 1995; Traugott, 1995). Most of all, social movements are not homogeneous, and the different groups involved may have different preferences within the pieces which compose a repertoire, depending on the meaning they give to tactics, their ideology or their competition for leadership in the mobilisation (Ennis, 1987).

How did French students come to adopt their modes of collective action in the late 2000s? History certainly matters, since this repertoire has been used by French student movements since at least the 1960s, and by the French labour movement before. But how do protesters appropriate some means of action from an already known repertoire? This is to pose a question about the conditions of the reproduction, recurrence and regularity of contentious repertoires. The point here is that the use of a mode of collective action stems from both practical and symbolic grounds. First, strikes, demonstrations, occupations and general assemblies fit with the constraints French students were facing. They allowed them to gather as many people as possible despite academic obligations on the one hand, and the long-standing existence of student unions combined with a low rate of unionisation among this population, on the other hand. But means of collective action are also used because they become markers of identity for activist groups who work towards promoting them and succeed in implementing them. In other words, we argue that contentious repertoires are also symbolic goods. Forms of action are not only tools, with tangible effects, which make the mobilisation possible and visible. They have a symbolic value, which changes depending on power relations between movement entrepreneurs who promote them and their adversaries who try to diminish their legitimacy.

This study is based on an ethnographic investigation, through long-time immersion among student activists, about these mobilisations in three higher education establishments, and the social history of French student movements (Le Mazier, 2015). Ethnography helped capture internal competition between groups of activists within the movements, their contentious practices as well as the way they justified them. The three establishments were chosen for the variety of student unions and political youth organisations present. I conducted in-depth interviews with 60 participants, and collected information through informal talks, mailing lists, websites, leaflets and public or internal texts produced by organisations. In order to have access to diverse spaces and to control the possible biases of my observer position in each field, I practiced non-participant observation in one establishment (in 2009 and 2010) and participant observation in another (in 2010). I continued to mix with student activists outside periods of mobilisation, as a member of a student union from 2006 to 2012. For the social history of French student movements, this chapter relies on secondary literature, edited primary sources about the 1968 student strike (Perrot, Perrot, Rebérioux & Maitron, 1968; Schnapp & Vidal-Naquet, 1969), and archives of the 1960s student movements. It ends with insights into the way students slightly changed their tactical tools during the last mobilisation, in 2018, when they fought for free access to university for all high school graduates.

HISTORY MADE THE STUDENT CONTENTIOUS REPERTOIRE AVAILABLE

The French student contentious repertoire changed during the 1960s, becoming closer to the labour movement's one. One particularity of higher education activism in France is the long-standing existence of student unions, the oldest and most powerful one being the *Union nationale des étudiants de France* (UNEF). In 1946, just after World War II, UNEF adopted a manifesto (reproduced and analysed in Morder, 2006), including a founding text of the French student movement called the *Charte de Grenoble*, and a detailed list of means of action, which gives insights into their repertoire before the 1960s. It mixed practices borrowed from the labour movement repertoire: petitions, demonstrations, strikes (when students refuse to attend classes), and old student modes of action, such as *monôme*, a procession of lined-up students holding each other's shoulders. It also mentioned occupation, used during the 1936 French general strike (Penissat, 2005b), although we do not find any occupations during student mobilisations before the 1960s.

A first turn in French student movements happened during the Algerian war of independence, from 1954 to 1962, which deeply divided French society. This period is known as the first step of the mass politicisation of youth (Bantigny, 2007b). Indeed, military conscription meant that young people were directly involved. Hence youth organisations, UNEF in particular, engaged more clearly against the war than other left-wing organisations, becoming the vanguard of the mobilisation (Monchablon, 1983; Sabot, 1995). In wartime, access to information was difficult, some activities happened underground, and clashes with the far right were frequent. Consequently, students, including members of non-student organisations, began to organise outside formal organisations. They gathered every day at noon in the Sorbonne courtyard to exchange the latest news. They created a grassroots network, the *Front universitaire antifasciste*, to fight the far right (Bantigny, 2007a).

The end of the Algerian war marked UNEF's highest point: one in two students was a member. Paradoxically, it began a long decline just after the end of the war. It failed to build another federative project throughout the 1960s. Meanwhile, the student population deeply changed quantitatively and qualitatively with the rise of mass education. As a result, only one in ten students belonged to the organisation in 1968. In order to stay attractive to students and to mobilise them, some UNEF activists, from the organisation's left wing, who had been part of the *Front universitaire antifasciste*, tried to rely on this experience to set up organisational forms open to non-members and new means of action. They planned to occupy the Sorbonne in 1963 but gave up the day before. They tested bottom-up decisions of going on strike, class by class, instead of top-down ones inside the union. They created grassroots groups in colleges, course union delegates who were supposed to be elected by every student and not only UNEF members, and organised many meetings and debates. During the 1960s, leftist groups, mainly Trotskyist and Maoist ones, also set up grassroots organisations, in particular to fight against the Vietnam War (Pas, 2000). Breaking with the Communist Party, they tried thus to contest the party leadership within social movements.[1]

Despite this constant political turmoil during the 1960s, the huge May and June 1968 student strike started while no one had prepared or anticipated it. What was first at stake was freedom of speech on campuses and the fight against repression (Gruel, 2004). Student meetings were prohibited, attacked by the police or the far right, in Nanterre (a Paris suburb), Toulouse and Sorbonne universities. Student protest was a reply to this repression, even if contention rapidly spread to other claims, other sectors, becoming a general worker strike.[2] It gave birth to a renewal of the student contentious repertoire. Demonstrations often turned into clashes with the police. Students occupied campuses. They debated all day long inside the occupied universities, and the most important meeting became the daily general assembly, gathering all interested people participating and voting on an individual basis, whether or not they were members of organisations. Innovation relied on the experimentations of the 1960s, but the crisis and the rapid massification of the movement precipitated their setting up and diffusion. The initial strike goals, the fight for freedom of speech, fashioned this repertoire: occupying the universities and debating were a sort of direct action, getting and putting into practice what was demanded. The organisational form of the general assembly, used in the French labour movement since the first strikes at the beginning of the 19th century (Aguet, 1954; Sirot, 2002), was then very suitable.

In the following decades, the 1968 student contentious repertoire was transmitted, primarily within student movements themselves. Indeed, student mobilisations are frequent in France (Legois, Monchablon & Morder, 2007). Therefore, despite the constant renewal of this population, a student strike almost never happens without actors who have already participated in the previous one, becoming brokers who diffuse tactics and means of action. Secondly, the continuity of the student repertoire may be explained by the work of what Verta Taylor (1989) called 'abeyance organizations' (p. 761). 'In nonreceptive political environments', such organisations 'provide continuity from one stage of mobilization to another' (p. 761), making networks, goals, tactics and collective identity survive. In France, political organisations, youth organisations and unions kept alive the memory of student means of actions and their justification.

They mostly belonged to the far left and justified tactics such as occupation and general assembly by using watchwords from 1968 (Hatzfeld, 2011) like 'autogestion' or 'direct democracy'. That is the case of the *Ligue communiste révolutionnaire*, a Trotskyist political organisation, and the *Jeunesses communistes révolutionnaires*, its youth movement, which both founded the *Nouveau Parti anticapitaliste* in 2009. Anarchist networks also mattered, in particular the *Organisation révolutionnaire anarchiste* and the *Union des travailleurs communistes libertaires* which became *Alternative libertaire* in 1991 (Rival, 2013). The ideal of autogestion was principally diffused in the union field by the *Confédération française démocratique du travail*, notably to promote occupation (Penissat, 2005a) and general assembly. When this reference became less and less central in its principles during the 1980s, some activists continued to promote them and eventually created new unions with the label SUD (*Solidaires, Unitaires et Démocratiques*) at the end of the decade (Denis, 2001). At the end of the 2000s, student activists, members of these organisations, had become acquainted with these repertoires and watchwords, through internal literature and by interpersonal relationships with older activists. Then, the diffusion of the student repertoire happened through brokers from the far left, who made it part of their activist identity by associating them with a symbolic set of justifications. To what extent do the symbolic dimension of means of action also favour their appropriation?

THE PRACTICAL AND SYMBOLIC CONDITIONS OF REPERTOIRE APPROPRIATION

History alone does not account for the 2000s student contentious repertoire. Indeed, it does not explain why social movement actors resort to a particular mode of action among all the ones they know. Other groups in France, within the labour movement, also have recourse to strike, occupation, demonstration and general assembly when they protest. The difference here is that occupation and general assembly are recurrent in student contention, whereas they are not in other mobilisations. The practical resources students had and the constraints they were facing help understand this particularity but are not sufficient. Conversely, symbolic reasons do matter, but should not be considered in isolation, lest we give an excessively idealistic vision of protesters' behaviour. We need both, as we try to show through the cases of occupation and general assembly.

In the second half of the 2000s, students called the occupation of campuses '*blocage*'. Indeed, they not only occupied, but also prevented classes from happening through barricades in front of the doors, picket lines and walkouts which practically blocked access to classrooms. This mode of action was used to enforce student strikes. French law does not recognise the student right to strike and considers student unions only as associations. Moreover, academic rules regarding attendance became more and more severe, so that it was increasingly more difficult for students to go on strike. Therefore, *blocage* was a way to stop classes for everyone without penalising only the strikers. The succession of the means of action during student movements is revealing. Most of the time, general assemblies happened first, secondly, they voted for strike action, and after several days or weeks, strikers began to complain about the costs of this action: they missed important classes, they risked failure due to attendance rules. Then general assemblies voted for *blocage*. But there was not a full consensus about this means of action. It was contested by some teachers and students. That is why strikers strived to make it legitimate by votes in general assemblies open to anyone.

This linear narrative is not sufficient. Indeed, *blocage* is also used, conversely, to enhance participation in strikes and general assemblies. It is a coercion technique to enrol everybody, de facto, in the strike and a selective incentive (Olson, 1965) to make students come to general assemblies: only those who attended the latter could be part of the decision. Therefore, *blocage* usually increased the number of participants, up to hundreds or even thousands of people, making assemblies more and more legitimate in return. Spectators included some opposed to *blocage*, a captive audience who had to listen to the strikers' arguments and, for some of them, changed their mind to join the mobilisation. This mechanism is unveiled by this striker's speech in a general assembly, using a recurrent justification of *blocage*:

> You don't want us to block. But I have a question. Would you be here debating with us without *blocage*? ['No', 'no' from the audience] Yeah! Yeah! I'm glad you are here, now we gonna talk about politics, it matters

too, and that's what a general assembly is, and that wouldn't have happened without *blocage*.

(Field notes, general assembly, Pierre Mendès France Centre,
Université Paris 1 Panthéon-Sorbonne, 26 October 2010)

Here the coercion dimension is explicit, as is its legitimacy, for the sake of the value of political debate. Thus we see that tactics, practical concerns and power relations were constantly combined among strikers in a process of legitimation of what they did. Another incentive to *blocage* was, meaningfully, that it came to be used to measure and demonstrate the conflict's intensity, by students who enumerated the occupied campuses in assemblies, by organisations in their communication, by media and even by the government. It was then put forward as a sign of the force of the mobilisation. So was the number of participants in general assemblies.

It seems obvious that the general assembly was used for democratic reasons, as it is a direct democracy procedure where attendees are considered to be legitimate to make decisions by the sole virtue of their gathering, without relying on representatives. Literature about democracy in social movements often infer ideological, cultural or identity motives from the use of participatory organisational forms (Curtis & Zurcher, 1974; Downey, 1986; Della Porta, 2005). But in her research about democracy in US social movements (2002), Polletta also discovered strategic benefits that activists attributed to such modes of organisation. They also disagreed about what was or was not democratic and changed their minds over time. Similarly, my research found that there was a democratic dimension in the use of general assemblies in French student movements, but that strategic concerns should not be neglected either: students did many things during assemblies besides deliberating and making decisions, and not all participants considered them to be democratic.

The observation of general assemblies showed that they were given a whole set of roles, which sometimes had nothing to do with democracy. They gathered most of the people who were more or less interested in the movement. Therefore, the assemblies were used to mobilise the audience. Actions were announced or people were reminded of them there: meetings, demonstrations and conferences. In the assemblies, strikers also explained how they organised to potential newcomers.

They tried to convince more people and to give information through speeches about the contested reforms, the social and political situation, or the mobilisation in other universities, as they would have done in a public rally. Assemblies were also where students practically organised the fight, for instance by inviting those present to support a strike fund or to join a mailing list. They gave mandates to individuals or groups to carry out tasks and later they listened to their reports.

They also debated and voted by a show of hands about claims and means of action. In this activity, it was not only democracy which was at stake. Gathering hundreds or thousands of people in the same place, and making them raise their hand, applaud and scream in favour of claims is a mode of collective action as such, since it gives force and publicity to them by making visible a mass who supports them. Making students vote for means of action was supposed to incite the voters, committed to the decision, to participate in them, as when the president of a general assembly reminded the audience, after a vote for strike action: 'That means everybody here should participate in this strike' (Field notes, general assembly, Censier Centre, Université Paris 3 Sorbonne nouvelle, 3 February 2009). Eventually, the general assembly was both a place where enough people gathered to produce a mass effect, and where the co-presence of debating participants gave the performance of democracy – if not its reality. The plasticity of this organisational form, a big fair hosting a heterogeneous set of actions, incited many students with divergent interests to get involved in it, including paradoxically their own members. Indeed, even if student unions have a long tradition in France, in 2009 only 1 per cent of students declared that they belonged to one (Institut français d'opinion publique, 2009). Therefore, general assemblies were valued by activists because they gave the feeling that they influenced a mass of students while the organisations that they belonged to were not capable of mobilising in such large numbers on their own. Among the audience, opponents of *blocage* denied the legitimacy of general assemblies, but participated only to vote against this mode of action. On the contrary, members of the majority faction of UNEF, the main student union at that time, were partisans of general assemblies, but did not consider them to be democratic. They viewed assemblies as a forum, like a public rally, in order to convince a large audience, which could potentially be mobilised to support their positions. That is why they made speeches, but barely made propositions for votes. As one of them said: 'in the movement, our compass is the mass of students' (Interview, May 5, 2009), that is, including those who did not come to assemblies but whom UNEF claimed to represent as the majority union in the student elections and in terms of the number of adherents. Eventually, a lot of students viewed general assemblies as democratic, but very few did so after the alternative conceptions implied by the watchwords of 'autogestion', 'auto-organisation' or 'direct democracy'. The latter, far-left activists, nevertheless were well positioned to raise the symbolic value of this organisational form.

REPERTOIRES AS SYMBOLIC GOODS

The various political and union currents involved in student movements in the 2000s disagreed about the means of action and tactics. For instance, they were all partisans of general assemblies, but opposed each other about their role, the democracy they provided and the right time to organise them. Initiators of these mobilisations, mostly youth organisations and unions, usually began with public rallies, to inform and test the popularity of the cause. Then, general assemblies replaced rallies, meaning that a movement was growing and organising. They faced a dilemma though: when should they start using general assemblies? The answer depended on their political position, with regular disputes, such as the one analysed below, in the Pierre Mendès France Centre of the Université Paris 1 Panthéon-Sorbonne, while organisations of this university prepared for the 2010 fight against pension reform.

A week before classes began, several organisations met in order to plan actions for the first weeks and initiate a mobilisation. Thousands of leaflets had already been disseminated during the university enrolment days. Three options emerged. SUD-Étudiant suggested a general assembly during the first week of classes in order to immediately set up a contentious atmosphere. The *Nouveau Parti anticapitaliste*, a student union called *Fédération syndicale étudiante* and the left-wing minority faction of UNEF supported a general assembly during the second week, on a demonstration day, in order to have time to prepare them. UNEF's majority faction wanted to organise a public rally first. The organisations' representatives gave examples from other universities in favour of the options they promoted. UNEF's representative said: 'A UNEF conference call has just been held. It seems that general assemblies don't work much. But public rallies gather a lot of people. Students need information about the reform.' A member of the *Nouveau Parti anticapitaliste* and the left-wing minority faction of UNEF replied: 'I'm not surprised by the UNEF majority faction analysis, because it supports public rallies everywhere. I have different feedback. In some universities, general assemblies gathered people, like in Clermont-Ferrand.' Eventually, after long discussions, a compromise was found: an informative general assembly, a kind of mix between general assembly and public rally, would be organised during the first week (Field notes, organisations' meeting, Pierre Mendès France Centre, Université Paris 1 Panthéon-Sorbonne, 27 September 2010).

Research on mobilisations distinguishes 'issue entrepreneurs' from social movement organisation activists who strive to prepare and build protest (McCarthy & Zald, 1977). Here we see them at work. But this work does not only deal with gathering resources and defining strategies to foster the mobilisation, but also with internal competition among them: they select information and arguments which give symbolic credit to the tactic they promote. The positions they take are not situational: I found the same structure of oppositions between those who want general assemblies sooner, or later, at other times and places. They are coherent with their conceptions of democracy, which also fit with their interests. The UNEF majority faction values representation, not general assemblies. To them, the main union is seen as legitimate to give guidelines to students, like in public rallies, or general assemblies they use as if they were rallies. Indeed, its hegemony in the student world is much clearer after the barometer of student elections and the number of adherents than after their weight in general assemblies. In the latter, far-left minority currents, like the *Nouveau Parti anticapitaliste*, UNEF's left-wing faction or student unions such as the *Fédération syndicale étudiante* and SUD-Étudiant feel more at ease. Their members have learnt to promote alternative organisational forms, to legitimate them through the watchwords of 'autogestion', 'auto-organisation' and 'direct democracy' and to practice them in the internal functioning of their organisations. For these activists who support a rupture with the existing institutions, general assemblies during mobilisations are prefigurative (Breines, 1980) of the kind of society they seek to create. A member of SUD-Étudiant and *Alternative libertaire* related his practice of general assemblies during the 2006 movement to a 'project of society' (Interview, March 27, 2007). In his view, they allowed participants 'to realize that, yes indeed, direct democracy does work'. As outsiders, these activists are also disposed to contest current modes of representation and to challenge UNEF's usual leadership in general assemblies where they hope to reshuffle the cards of power relations between organisations.

Depending on their position in the internal competition among social movement organisations, activists use means of action as markers of identity. They work towards promoting them, because, if they succeed, it will show that they took the lead within the mobilisation. As there are issue entrepreneurs and owners of problems (Gusfield, 1981), there are in social movements owners and entrepreneurs of modes of action. Then the use and appropriation of a contentious repertoire also depends on successful enterprises of promotion and symbolic justification conducted by owners of means of action. Thus, we may develop a conception of repertoires as symbolic goods, based on a free interpretation of Bourdieu (see for instance Bourdieu, 1984). They are not only used for their practical effects, but also for their symbolic value, which is not given and stable but changes according to the concerned actors fighting for raising – or depreciating – it. That does not mean that the use of repertoires is only a matter of culture and ideas, since the legitimacy ascribed to a means of action, reinforcing that of those who use it, veils the power relations it stems from. We will try now to support this statement through insights into the slight transformations of the student contentious repertoire during the 2018 strike.

In 1968, students, based on the revolutionary demands against capitalism and political representation expressed by the movement, did not gain substantially. At least they gained the right, guaranteed by law, for every high school graduate to attend university. In 2018, the French government changed the law and implemented university selection, resulting in the most important student movement since 2010. Students still organised in general assemblies and occupied campuses. But since the end of the 2000s, university administrations have developed a tactic around closing the campuses as soon as they are occupied, preventing strikers from meeting and enrolling other students. As a response, students switched from daytime to permanent occupation: then administrations could only rely on police eviction – which eventually happened, for most of them. Permanent occupation was also the result of the new leadership in the student mobilisation of the autonomous political current, which values this means of action. Meanwhile, keeping hold of the campuses by night and day cost a lot of time and energy. The high level of police repression of demonstrations in France since the beginning of the state of emergency in 2015, and secondly, the radicalisation strategy of the autonomous movement among the demonstrators reduced the number of those participating.

During the movement, as usual, protesters were involved in a fight with their targets, the government and the university administrations, for the (de)legitimation of the mobilisation, notably by raising or lowering the value of their means of action. Practicing occupation made reference to May 1968, during its 50th anniversary year, but also to other historic events, to make it appealing. In the Pierre Mendès France Centre of the Université Paris 1 Panthéon-Sorbonne, the occupation was called 'Commune libre de Tolbiac' and the Université Paris 3 Sorbonne nouvelle's one, 'Commune de Censier' (Tolbiac and Censier being the name of the streets where the sites are located), in memory of the 1871 Paris Commune. Conversely, the president of the Université Paris 1 Panthéon-Sorbonne declared in the press: 'I am afraid that Tolbiac might become a university ZAD' (Brigaudeau, 2018). ZAD (originally meaning 'zone d'aménagement différé'/'deferred development zone') is an acronym used by the French administration to refer to a place where a development project was scheduled, for instance the Notre-Dame-des-Landes airport project. There, opponents of the airport have occupied the sector for years and diverted the acronym in order to mean 'zone à défendre' ('zone to defend'). By mentioning the ZAD, the president relied on the connotation of chaos and illegality this giant squat has for some sections of the public. As a response, the students who occupied the Tolbiac site reclaimed the name, on a huge banner wrapped around its facade. Thus, they intended to benefit from the reputation of this emblematic movement which had just won the fight against the airport project.

Ethnography allows us to capture how protesters appropriate an existing contentious repertoire, then to extend and amend current theories of the sociology of social movements. Means of action are both practical resources and symbolic goods, unequally valued by the different groups of activists, their targets and their public. The symbolic value acknowledged about a mode of action or organisation fosters its use, but also reinforces the legitimacy of the mobilisation and the leadership of its promoters. It invites us to analyse the power relations embedded in the adoption of a form of action, and the way activists strive to impose it.

During these strikes, students learnt how to use a repertoire, then reproduced it in subsequent student mobilisations, with some variations. But students do not stay students forever. Some former student activists later engaged in other social movements, in particular at their workplace. They sometimes imported parts of the student contentious repertoire, notably their assembly practices. The 2018 and 2019 *Gilets jaunes* protests are revealing in this matter, even if research on them has just begun. Initial studies have noted their assembly practices although these were neither systematic nor homogeneous (Devaux, Lang, Lévêque, Parnet & Thomas, 2019). There is some evidence though that where they existed, they may have been influenced by current or former student activists.

NOTES

1   The organisational repertoire (Clemens, 1993) of student movements during these years is identified through a systematic analysis of archives from several mobilisations and organisations (press, leaflets, public or internal texts) kept in Bibliothèque de documentation internationale contemporaine de Nanterre, Fonds Comités Vietnam de base, F delta 2089.

2   The chronology of the 1968 student mobilisation, as well as its claims and repertoire, are determined by combining different sources, i.e. Perrot et al., 1968, Viénet, 1998 [1968], Schnapp & Vidal-Naquet, 1969, Dreyfus-Armand & Gervereau, 1988, Duteuil, 1988, Gobille, 2008, Bibliothèque de documentation internationale contemporaine de Nanterre, Fonds Maupeou-Abboud, Nicole de, Mai 68 en régions, Mai 68 à Toulouse, F delta 1061 (8) / 2.

REFERENCES

Aguet J.-P. (1954). *Contribution à l'histoire du mouvement ouvrier français. Les grèves sous la Monarchie de Juillet (1830–1847)*. Genève: E. Droz.

Bantigny, L. (2007a). Jeunesse et engagement pendant la guerre d'Algérie. *Parlement[s]*, 8(2), 39–53.

—— (2007b). *Le Plus Bel Âge? Jeunes et jeunesse en France de l'aube des 'Trente Glorieuses' à la guerre d'Algérie*. Paris: Libraire Arthème Fayard.

Bourdieu, P. (1984). La délégation et le fétichisme politique. *Actes de la recherche en sciences sociales*, 52–53, 49–55.

Breines, W. (1980). Community and Organization: The new left and Michels' 'Iron Law'. *Social Problems, 27*(4), 419–429.

Brigaudeau, C. (2018), Fronde dans les facs: 'J'ai peur que Tolbiac se transforme en ZAD universitaire', interview with Georges Haddad. *Le Parisien,* 6 April. Retrieved from www.leparisien.fr/societe/fronde-dans-les-facs-j-ai-peur-que-tolbiac-se-transforme-en-zad-universitaire-06-04-2018-7649121.php (Accessed 27 September 2019).

Clemens, E. (1993). Organizational Repertoires and Institutional Change: Women's groups and the transformation of U.S. politics, 1890–1920. *The American Journal of Sociology, 98*(4), 755–798.

Curtis Jr, R. L. & Zurcher Jr, L. A. (1974). Social movements: An analytical exploration of organizational forms. *Social Problems, 21*(3), 356–370.

Della Porta, D. (2005). Deliberation in Movement: Why and how to study deliberative democracy and social movements. *Acta Politica, 40,* 336–350.

Denis J.-M. (2001) *Le Groupe des Dix, un modèle syndical alternatif?* Paris: La Documentation française.

Devaux, J.-B., Lang, M., Lévêque, A., Parnet, C. & Thomas, V. (2019, 30 April). La banlieue jaune. Enquête sur les recompositions d'un mouvement. *La Vie des idées.* Retrieved from https://laviedesidees.fr/La-banlieue-jaune.html (Accessed 25 May 2019).

Downey, G. (1986). Ideology and the Clamshell Identity: Organizational dilemmas in the anti-nuclear power movement. *Social Problems, 33*(5), 357–373.

Dreyfus-Armand, G. & Gervereau, L. (eds). (1988), *Mai 68. Les mouvements étudiants en France et dans le monde.* Nanterre: Bibliothèque de documentation internationale contemporaine.

Duteuil J.-P. (1988). *Nanterre. 1965–66–67–68. Vers le mouvement du 22 mars.* Mauléon: Acratie.

Ennis, J. (1987). Fields of Action: Structure in movements' tactical repertoires. *Sociological Forum, 2*(3), 520–533.

Field notes, general assembly, Censier Centre, Université Paris 3 Sorbonne nouvelle, 3 February 2009.

Field notes, organisations' meeting, Pierre Mendès France Centre, Université Paris 1 Panthéon-Sorbonne, 27 September 2010.

Field notes, general assembly, Pierre Mendès France Centre, Université Paris 1 Panthéon-Sorbonne, 26 October 2010.

Fillieule, O. (2010). Tombeau pour Charles Tilly. Répertoires, performances et strategies d'action. In É. Agrikoliansky, O. Fillieule & I. Sommier (eds), *Penser les mouvements sociaux. Conflits sociaux et contestations dans les sociétés contemporaines* (pp. 77–99). Paris: La Découverte.

Gobille, B. (2008). *Mai 68.* Paris: La Découverte.

Gruel, L. (2004). *La Rébellion de 68. Une relecture sociologique.* Rennes: Presses universitaires de Rennes.

Gusfield, J. (1981). *The Culture of Public Problems: Drinking-driving and the symbolic order.* Chicago, IL: University of Chicago Press.

Hatzfeld, H. (2011). De l'autogestion à la démocratie participative: des contributions pour renouveler la démocratie. In M.-H. Bacqué & Y. Sintomer (eds), *La Démocratie participative. Histoire et généalogie* (pp. 51–64). Paris: La Découverte.

Institut français d'opinion publique (2009). *Le Baromètre étudiant.*

Le Mazier, J. (2015). *'Pas de mouvement sans AG': les conditions d'appropriation de l'assemblée générale dans les mobilisations étudiantes en France (2006–2010). Contribution à l'étude des répertoires contestataires* (Doctoral dissertation). Paris: Université Paris 1 Panthéon-Sorbonne. Retrieved from https://tel. archives-ouvertes.fr/tel-01610685 (Accessed 25 May 2019).

Legois, J.-P., Monchablon, A. & Morder, R. (eds). (2007). *Cent ans de mouvements étudiants.* Paris: Éditions Syllepse.

McCarthy, J. D. & Zald, M. N. (1977). Resource mobilization and social movements: A partial theory. *American Journal of Sociology, 82*(6), 1212–1241.

Monchablon, A. (1983). *Histoire de l'UNEF de 1956 à 1968.* Paris: Presses universitaires de France.

Morder, R. (ed.). (2006). *Naissance d'un syndicalisme étudiant. 1946: la Charte de Grenoble.* Paris: Syllepse.

Olson, M. (1965). *The Logic of Collective Action: Public goods and the theory of groups.* Cambridge, MA: Harvard University Press.

Pas, N. (2000). 'Six heures pour le Vietnam'. Histoire des Comités Vietnam français 1965–1968. *Revue historique, 312*(613), 157–185.

Penissat, É. (2005a). Les occupations de locaux dans les années 1960–1970: processus sociohistoriques de 'réinvention' d'un mode d'action. *Genèses, 59*(2), 71–93.

—— (2005b). 'Occuper les lieux de travail' en 1936. Usages et enjeux sociaux et politiques. *Mots. Les langages du politique, 79,* 131–142.

Perrot, J.-C., Perrot, M., Rebérioux, M. & Maitron, J. (1968). La Sorbonne par elle-même: Mai–Juin 1968. *Le Mouvement social, 64.*

Polletta, F. (2002). *Freedom Is an Endless Meeting: Democracy in American social movements.* Chicago, IL: University of Chicago Press.

Rival, T. (2013). *Syndicalistes et libertaires. Une histoire de l'Union des travailleurs communistes libertaires (1974–1991).* Paris: Éditions d'Alternative libertaire.

Sabot, J.-Y. (1995). *Le Syndicalisme étudiant et la guerre d'Algérie. L'entrée d'une génération en politique et la formation d'une élite.* Paris: L'Harmattan.

Salles, J.-P. (2005). *La Ligue communiste révolutionnaire (1968–1981). Instrument du Grand Soir ou lieu d'apprentissage?* Rennes: Presses universitaires de Rennes.

Schnapp, A. & Vidal-Naquet, P. (1969). *Journal de la commune étudiante. Textes et documents. Novembre 1967–juin 1968.* Paris: Seuil.

Sirot, S. (2002). *La Grève en France: une histoire sociale (XIXe–XXe siècle).* Paris: Éditions Odile Jacob.

Steinberg, M. (1995). The Roar of the Crowd: Repertoires of discourse and collective action among the Spitalfields silk weavers in nineteenth-century

London. In M. Traugott (ed.), *Repertoires and Cycles of Collective Action* (pp. 57–87). Durham, NC and London: Duke University Press.

Taylor, V. (1989). Social Movement Continuity: The Women's movement in abeyance. *American Sociological Review,* 54(5), 761–775.

Tilly, C. (1977). Getting It Together in Burgundy, 1675–1975. *Theory and Society,* 4, 479–504.

—— (1986). *The Contentious French.* Cambridge: Belknap Press.

—— (2008). *Contentious Performances.* New York: Cambridge University Press.

Traugott, M. (1995). Barricades as Repertoire: Continuities and discontinuities in the history of French contention. In M. Traugott (ed.), *Repertoires and Cycles of Collective Action* (pp. 43–56). Durham, NC and London: Duke University Press.

Viénet, R. (1998) [1968]. *Enragés et Situationnistes dans le mouvement des occupations.* Paris: Éditions Gallimard.

Archives

Bibliothèque de documentation internationale contemporaine de Nanterre: Fonds Comités Vietnam de base, F delta 2089.

Fonds Maupeou-Abboud, Nicole de, Mai 68 en régions, Mai 68 à Toulouse, F delta 1061 (8) / 2.

11

The mustfall mo(ve)ments
and *Publica[c]tion*
Reflections on collective knowledge production in South Africa
Asher Gamedze and Leigh-Ann Naidoo

FALLIST MOVEMENTS AND THE EMERGENCE
OF *PUBLICA(C)TION*

The year 2015 was an intense one for campus revolt at South African universities. The movements for decolonisation at universities (#rhodesmustfall (#rmf) at the University of Cape Town (UCT), #blackstudentmovement (#bsm) at the University Currently Known As Rhodes (UCKAR[1]), etc.)[2] prefigured, laid the groundwork for and made possible the later eruptions around mobilisation and demands for free education and an in-sourced workforce (#feesmustfall (#fmf), #outsourcingmustfall (#omf)). The mustfall hashtags signal and symbolise a particular historical moment in student organising and modes of information-sharing in an era of Facebook, Twitter, Instagram and other social media sites. Great as they are at sharing images and hashtags far, wide and fast, what these modes often miss out on are the more complex stories of actual organising efforts of students and staff that made the eruptions possible. Also largely missing in the era of the hashtag and the image are the perspectives and deep analyses, the processes of producing knowledge that the protagonists were engaged in through struggle and in reflection on struggle.

In the relative calm of December 2015 after the mayhem of the first iteration of #fmf, we (Leigh-Ann and Asher) had a conversation about initiating a collective, Black student publication project that could function as a site of communing to share, think and ask questions together. We had both been involved in various Black student movement formations and projects prior to the massive student protests of 2015. These experiences included the radical education experiments which formed the inception of #rhodesmustfall at the student occupation of Azania House at UCT as well as the RhodesMustFall (RMF) writing and education subcommittees.[3] The writing subcommittee was one space in which we had experimented with a collective writing and publishing project.[4] We found these spaces for collective work exciting and generative. The deep grappling with political questions related to the oppressive structures of society, and the university in particular, provided a different way into education processes than what students were offered and accustomed to at school and in university. These occupations were critical, urgent and politicised spaces which, not uncomplicatedly, also held a generousness and a generative atmosphere for learning and sharing.

These types of spaces were largely criminalised and shut down by university managements across the country. The later wave of popular energy following #October6 – a Johannesburg-based decolonial student and worker collective with members from the University of the Witwatersrand (Wits) and the University of Johannesburg (UJ) – that ignited in late 2015 in #fmf and #omf, led to many campus occupations. However, in these moments of intense resistance and repression, in a similar way to Leigh-Ann's reflections on SASO (South African Students Association) in the 1970s (Naidoo, 2015), the political project moved away from the critical consciousness work of the earlier 'decolonial mo(ve)ments' and became centred on very intensive, almost-continuous, daily direct action. These mass revolts were demobilised by police repression, university disciplinary actions and punishment, and partisan forces with directives from their leadership structures.

At the end of the year, following the mayhem of the #fmf moment, Leigh-Ann, along with others, had been involved in coordinating some regional and national meetings. These gatherings brought student activists together from across the country and were an attempt to coordinate struggles on a scale broader than individual institutions. They were generative in that they created a space for students to meet and learn about each other's experiences in a highly differentiated South African tertiary education landscape. The national meeting concluded with some agreement around five principles that comrades would organise around in their respective contexts (Naidoo, 2016, pp. 180–191). These gatherings were also problematic in a number of ways. The homophobia and misogyny displayed by some and, relatedly, disagreements between the various conflicting political tendencies collapsed especially the national meeting at numerous points, which undermined many possibilities for collaborating.

This reflected a moment in the movement.

The mass and urgent nature of the #fmf uprisings, as well as the repression and shutting down of autonomous Black student spaces on campus – like Azania House at UCT and Solomon House at Wits – largely alienated the movement from its earlier basis in occupations where students had the time, space and desire for collective discussion and critical education, where it was possible to have more productive engagements around issues. The intense focus on planning and coordinating action with the absence of space for real study – emblematic of the #fmf and #omf moments – magnified a number of contradictions internal to the movement and fragmented it along those fractures.

In addition to the disillusionment with the landscape at the end of that year – the fragmented movement and the decreasing amount of space for deep engagement with the political issues – many students had been critiquing the ways in which the student movement was being written *about*. There were two major issues at play here. First, the majority of work being produced about students was not written by students but by people who were far away – either organisationally, politically or both – from students. This included news reporters, so-called public intellectuals and academics (with the increasingly more frequent token inclusion of students as 'co-writers'). The second issue was the unequal coverage of institutions. (Historically) white universities like UCT, Wits, UCKAR (University Currently Known As Rhodes) and Stellenbosch tended to feature prominently in the media while Black campuses like UniVen (University of Venda), NWU-Mahikeng (North West University, Mahikeng campus), Fort Hare and TUT – Shoshanguve (Tshwane University of Technology) – many of which had protests almost annually over fees and other issues for the previous ten years – hardly attracted a mention.

It was out of this morass – the crises of the moment, the movement and the writing about it – that the project of *Publica[c]tion* emerged: An attempt to make space for students to write and publish our own stories and perspectives on our own terms. An attempt to connect Black students across different institutions in a more generative pedagogical space that didn't have to make urgent direct action decisions. An insistence on the importance of the reflective, intellectual and emotional lives of a movement. An insistence on the importance of some of the questions student activists had been asking and the critiques and analyses we had been making – of society, the economy, of racism, the country, of the curriculum, pedagogy and heteropatriarchy.

PUBLISHING BLACK STUDENT PUBLICS

When I think about the way we use the term 'study', I think we are committed to the idea that study is what you do with other people.

(Harney & Moten, 2013, p. 110)

Following our initial conversations around wanting to do a publication project, we put together a proposal and managed to secure some funding from an academic at UCT who agreed to fund the project on our terms. We started meeting as the coordinating collective – Leigh-Ann, Asher and Thato – in February/March 2016.[5] Parts of these meetings were catching up on current developments in student politics internationally. There had been student uprisings in many parts of the world including Brazil, USA, India and England. Internal to South Africa, the #rureferencelist, where women had organised protests against a culture of sexual harassment at UCKAR, another national meeting at Wits that went horribly awry – collapsed by violent masculinities and a culture of silence around the organising, #shackville[6] at UCT, etc., all of these events influenced how we were thinking about and planning the process – what would be important to include, how to make particular interventions that would be politically useful to the movement.

Those meetings were made of long discussions about how decolonisation, the political project that we were committed to, should inform our approach to publication. One of the central questions that the project continued to ask us was around pedagogy. Without being a textbook, how does a publication do pedagogical work? We really wanted it to be a resource that could be used to deeply study and engage with the student movement. As we wanted to encourage collective learning, particularly in activist groupings, we wanted to conceptualise and design something that could, through *Publica[c]tion*'s form itself, facilitate that kind of engagement. We imagined a *pedagogical device*, conceived as a separate, supplementary document to the main publication. In the form of possible workshop plans, this *device* would attempt to facilitate a deeper engagement with some of the trajectories and the political questions that the movement had raised.

Another set of questions concerned our approach to the norms of the publishing racket. The first thing we committed to was that the eventual published product would be free – for obvious reasons. Beyond this, in response to mainstream publishing which is fixated on the product, we chose instead to focus on the process and make it as collective and collaborative as possible.

We planned, and then went on an intense and exhausting five-day trip where we rented a kombi[7] and drove over 3000km. In total, we held six workshops in six provinces at different institutions, all of which brought together Black students from at least three or four different universities. At the workshops, we did three things. First everyone introduced themselves, gave the rest of the group a sense of the context at our respective institutions, how we were involved and what the current situation was. The second aspect of the workshop was the longest and probably the most generative. We did some collective reading and thinking together about the practices and importance of reading, writing and publishing. We discussed radical Freirean (1983) ideas of reading the word and reading the world,[8] spoke about the importance of writing in moments of chaos and despair (Morrison, 2015),[9] and thought about autonomous and collective publishing (Muller & Jordan, 1995)[10] as an alternative to capitalist presses.

Although we did the workshop six times, altering the process only slightly based on post-workshop reflections, each time we did it, it was completely different. These were spaces of radical critique of university teaching and learning as well as sites of generative creativity. During the discussions on publishing we came to a critique of the standard and boring format of book launches, suggesting that launches should be fun and exciting and they should most fundamentally be about sharing what was produced in the process. And, further, that the sharing itself might take on different forms – a party, a poetry performance, a ritual, a discussion, etc. – depending on the context. During the third section of the session, students got into their university groups and brainstormed potential pieces that they might want to contribute together.

After the workshop, most of the work was periodic checking in and reminding the contributors of the deadline. The deadline eventually got pushed back a few months because of the intensity of #fmf 2016 which escalated an already-packed year of student resistance and repression. Once we had all the pieces in, we went into a collective design workshop process with a designer and an illustrator. The five of us sat together three or four times over about two months, getting everything laid out in a way that was interesting and felt somewhat aesthetically representative of the process. By July 2017, the copies were printed and in August and September we entered the launch phase of the project.

The launch phase in some way mirrored, or perhaps replicated the initial workshop phase. We did six launches: at the Workers' Museum in Johannesburg, Community House in Cape Town, Durban University of Technology in Durban, Walter Sisulu University in Umtata, University of Fort Hare in East London and Nelson Mandela University in Port Elizabeth.[11] Again, they were radically different in each place. Where possible, at most of the launches, we collaborated with local students, cultural activists and progressive organisations and people to collectively organise and shape the events. As an attempt to not centre *Publica[c] tion* and present it in conversation with other forms of 'text in struggle', the launches featured performances of avant-garde jazz, hip-hop, radical theatre as well as poetry recitals. In addition to these elements, we had sections where we introduced people to the A3 publication via its unwieldy, A1 foldout map/contents page. People were also invited, in groups, to read and discuss one piece and then share some reflections. Our favourite section was when all the contributors who were present spoke about their pieces – either the story of writing them, what they were about or why they thought it was important.

THE ENTAILED EDITOR, ENTANGLEMENT AS METHOD

Central to the mode of *Publica[c]tion*'s production – which included discussions internal to the coordinating collective, workshops with contributors, communication with contributors and launch/sharing events – was a methodology of, and a commitment to dialogue. The process's ontological basis was collective. The collective's basis was a shared political project – dynamic, multiple, divergent, contradictory and even incoherent as it was at particular moments. The foundation of getting together was an involvement in Black student politics. This co-involvement profoundly shaped the nature and character of the process. This entailment, this 'openness to being affected by others, dispossessed and possessed by others' (Harney & Moten, 2013, p. 116), this entanglement with one another, all this raised serious questions about hierarchies, roles, divisions of labour, power and responsibility within publishing. Many of these questions seemed to be directed towards the position of the editor wherein power is centralised: What are the hierarchies embedded in the position of the editor in mainstream and academic publishing? What should the editor's role be in an entailed political process? Is it sufficient to merely mimic and replicate the academic editor or does their entanglement require of them something else? If entailment is the ontological positioning of the collective process, what are the social relations that this entailment implies, inscribes and insists on, and what are the relations that it by necessity rejects and refuses?

Publishing divisions of labour: Power, responsibility and editing

Our response, ongoing reflections and praxis of 'editing' emerged from the contradictions at the intersection, coalescence and divergence of two strands of thought and practice. Coming from largely consensus-based, horizontally structured Black student spaces, and working on a project emerging from those politics, the first strand was one critical of the academy and how the hierarchies internal to it replicated those of society. These critiques we extended to the position of the editor, refusing to mimic the types of power relations we were accustomed to challenging. The second strand was the very real situation we were in. We had proposed and initiated a project and were the ones responsible for carrying it out. We felt the project was important for the moment and once we had started it, and spoke about it, we were accountable to our comrades, the other contributors. There was a whole range of work that needed to be done – coordinating, organising, communicating, negotiating, planning, ordering and facilitating – and we couldn't refuse that.

The first thing that confronted us as we engaged the question of the editor was the process of getting contributors and submissions. The contributors were going to be Black student/worker/academic activists and, as our commitment was to create a space for all the universities in the country, we decided on two pieces per institution with some wiggle room.[12] Beyond trying to get pieces from all the universities, around 24 at the time, there were some other provisos for contributions. We thought it important that instances of political organising around particular issues were highlighted, such as the #rureferencelist,[13] Pathways to Free Education, the Trans Collective and UCT for Disability Justice. Similarly, with regards to knowledge and analyses around some specific questions such as securitisation, discourses of violence and intersectionality. We wanted to make space for women and LGBTQIA+[14] activists to contribute as the archive of Black activist history remains dominated by cis-het[15] men. These and other considerations framed who we approached to potentially contribute.

We had to use our own networks of comrades to find potential contributors, people who had been active and might be interested in participating in the project. As Leigh-Ann had been involved in some of the regional/national-level organising, many of the contacts were people she had met at those gatherings, while others were referred by comrades we knew from other organising spaces. It is important to acknowledge that these are some of the first points of 'selection' or 'curation', that sit within the editor's power – deciding what the important questions are, and who gets to contribute. There are certain logistical realities here that cannot be avoided. But there are aspects that can be reconfigured by different practices and processes.

Something that felt very important to us was to spend time with contributors. We decided not to merely email people asking for a submission on a topic we chose as that would feel deeply impersonal, individualised and antithetical to some of the most generative moments of the student movement which came out of people sitting together, thinking together, singing together, eating together and studying together. The commitment to meeting people allowed us to shape different kinds of relations with contributors versus what is possible in an email or over the phone. In the workshops, we were able to think together and *listen* for the important questions and stories rather than imposing ours on comrades.

In the last part of the workshops we asked contributors 'what do you think are the most important and interesting stories to tell and questions to be raised from your context? You can contribute in any form you choose – cartoon, essay, poem, history piece, anything – and you can write in any language you choose. There is a guideline of two pieces of up to 1500 words each per university, you can divide that up how you want, write together, write individually, etc.' That was the basics of the brief, which formed the basis of an ensuing discussion. We also committed to publishing everything that we received – i.e. we wouldn't decide on whether pieces were 'good enough' or not. And we decided that we wouldn't 'edit' anything. We committed to continuing a conversation with contributors after submission if there were particular questions or suggestions for their piece, and correct typos or make grammatical suggestions only in instances where we felt that what was written was too difficult to understand. Beyond that, we would publish what came in as it came.

Publica[c]tion received and, in the final instance, is constituted by a range of pieces so multiple and even divergent in form, style, content and ideological orientation, that, as editors we wondered how they might sit together. Through our process of grappling, we came to this non-introductory introduction, entitled 'This here collection is incoherent' Publica[c]tion Collective (2017, p. 3):

> there is something about a decolonial moment that requires incoherence
> or just perhaps is incoherent
>
> conversely there is something about an intellectual tendency
>
> or perhaps just an academic one that seeks to impose order: coherence
>
> by most measures this here collection is incoherent
>
> if we think decolonially, we might see this as a strength
>
> if we think academically, we might fail to grasp this moment and the thoughts of those writing it
>
> if you ask people to write on whatever they choose to, whatever they think is important, they might write about the revolutionary core at ufs [University of the Free State], they might write about the serial killer at univen, they might write about how feesmustfall relates to the struggle of poor black families in ct [Cape Town], they might write a letter to the academy, they

might write a history of fort hare, or the genesis of #openstellenbosch …
that's what we did, and that's what we've got, and it would be in some
way dishonest to attempt to frame the unframeable, to impose order on
disorder, to cohere the incoherent. but in the interests of unveiling the
thing, de-fetishising the commodity, we thought as an introduction, we
would not try to frame the unframeable but rather speak about our process
so you might come to appreciate it for what it is

we set out to reimagine publication, we collectively fumbled through
critiques and may have stumbled upon an alternative, welcome to
publica[c]tion.

This introduction reflects our grappling with the work of the editor. As
the ones who receive all of the pieces, unless one takes the fairly obscure
decision to arrange everything at random, there is the responsibility of
ordering and organising the work somehow. In our workshops with
contributors in Durban, one comrade, Shabashni, had critiqued or, at
least raised questions about our concept of the *pedagogic device*. She
said that what it seemed like, or could be perceived as, was a kind of
ghettoisation of knowledge – in the main publication the 'raw data
and experience', and in the *pedagogic device*, the deeper analysis and
overviews. While that was never quite how we imagined and planned to
separate the two documents – contributors were providing perspectives,
reflections, critiques, theories and a whole range of other things beside
'experience' – the critique was important in that it highlighted the skewed
power relations of academic publishing: Who gets the responsibility and
role of abstraction, overview and analysis? What are the power relations
vested in that work? And what does that type of work do to the relations
between 'editors' and 'contributors'?

These were some of the questions at play in our minds. Understanding
and being critical of the problematic nature of these divisions of labour,
we still wanted to do our best to facilitate some sort of engagement with
what is a very dense, varied and complex collection of work. We grappled
for so long about whether or not we should write an introduction or
just leave the collection to speak for itself. While we refused to write a
piece that attempted to tie everything together or provided the master
narrative or the overview – work that would have felt dishonest and
would be destined to fail in some way – it felt somewhat irresponsible
to leave the reader entirely to their own devices. Our introductory frame
of chaos, disorder, incoherence and unframeability was one way we

responded to this contradiction. Apart from the introduction, we made a number of other, what we think of as pedagogical interventions, or editing decisions about how to help people find a way into *Publica[c] tion*. One of these was a foldout with a map of South Africa doubling as a contents page on the one side, and a history of student activism on the African continent on the reverse side.

Knowledge production under conditions of entailment

Asher's notebook contains the following notes from the first set of meetings of the editorial collective:

> <<What are we trying to do?>>
> – Students writing themselves
> – Going and <u>listening</u> for the unasked questions
> – Diff[erent] forms of reflection
> – Not present authoritative text
> – Chronology & historical process up to Oct 2015

In reflection on the processes and relations of *Publica[c]tion*, the critical practice of listening (underlined in original notes) was indeed one of the central pillars of our method. This method, emerging from a certain kind of entailed sociality, was rooted in and fixated on dialogue as well as engagements, through dialogue, with the practices of reading, writing and sharing/publishing. In engaging these practices, we were grappling with what it might mean to do these things both collectively and generously. Upon reflection, we realise that our process itself was to a significant extent not only shaped, but also constituted by this grappling. And this experimenting with what mode of knowledge production might emerge from, resonate with and respond to the particular political and historical moment and community we found ourselves in. Part of this was practising critique of academic modes of knowledge production which many of us found alienating, limited and restricting. The other part of the process was being together in various ways and settings.

In *The Undercommons*, Fred Moten raps about the potentialities and spaces inside texts and their outsides and their invitations (Harney & Moten, 2013, p. 108):

Fanon's text is still open and it still opens. Now you have to go inside it. When you're inside, now, you have to go outside of it. Actually you're being blown out of it – this happens within the context of a single authored piece ... Recognising that text is intertext is one thing. Seeing that space as a social space is another. It's a deeper way of looking at it. To say that it's a social space is to say that stuff is going on: people, things, are meeting there and interacting, rubbing off one another, brushing against one another – and you enter into that social space, to try be part of it ... There are things to do, places to go, and people to see in reading and writing – and it's about maybe even trying to figure out some kind of ethically responsible way to be in that world with other things.

Friend, Stefano Harney listens and responds, reflecting Fred whilst simultaneously stretching out (Ibid., Italics added):

The one thing that I was thinking about as you were talking about the text being a social space is it's exciting for me when we get to that point where *the text is open enough that instead of being studied, it actually becomes the occasion for study. So, we enter into the social world of study* ... That seems to me to be not about saying there's no longer somebody who might have insisted or persisted in getting us into that time-space of study, but rather that the text is one way for that kind of insistence on study to be an open insistence, to be one that doesn't have to be about authority or ongoing leadership or anything like that, but a kind of invitation for other people to pick stuff up.

What *The Undercommons* is asking or raising here we understand somewhat in conversation with David Scott's notion of attunement (2018). It asks what being attuned might mean for our relation to text and the multiple ways we move into, through, out of it and back in. Fred Moten raises the politics of an 'ethically responsible' way to be in a text. How do we read in a way that is 'ethically responsible': what might that look like? How do we get open to entering the text, into the writer's world and being there with them? How do we get attuned to what's going on there – which is the writer's world? For us, these questions were somewhat answered by our ability to travel to visit writers' contexts all over the country and study with them. This physical travel preceded and facilitated the metaphysical entering into their texts and the openness to see some of what was going on inside it because we had a sense of the texts' many outsides.

But beyond the question of travel, the mode of getting together and be-ing together that was the basis of *Publica[c]tion* entailed a practice of dialogue and generous listening that prefigured our practice of reading. In the collective reading exercises in the workshops with contributors, we were able to have such interesting, generative, and exciting conversations which went to such a variety of places that were implied either by the text and the texts' worlds, or introduced by our own experiences, imaginations and worlds – the context in which the texts were read. What we remember most about these conversations was the willingness to step out and think out loud with not yet fully formed thoughts. There was an openness to people sharing personal stories that related them to the texts, improvisations and theory-making, critique of the way we are expected to read at University, and many tangential and creative detours. This sensibility, this thinking out loud and these speculative sojourns, were matched by a willingness to listen and hear as well as an openness to build something together through conversation, an openness to step out and go with someone as they take the discussion to a place you couldn't have imagined it going. Dialogue became a site, not only of clarification, learning and questioning, but also one of collaboration and creation.

By the time we received submissions, this practice of dialogue influenced and shaped the ways we were able to read them. It might well have also shaped the way contributors wrote, in the sense that the submitted texts became the continuation or elaboration of both a conversation began with each other and a feeling of being together. In this there is a form of transposition from the oral, the aural and the dialogic to the textual. In dialogue there is a very fluid move between what someone says to its context – brought in the form of comments, questions, thoughts and reflections from another person. From its insides to its outsides. These moves are continually happening such that dialogue, or conversation, itself is constituted and animated by this dialectical movement. In true dialogue, there is the understanding that there are at least two people present and participating. What happens to this relationship as dialogue is transposed through text in the context of the University? Can the writer still assume an engaged reader, a participant reader, a generous listener?

Generosity brings the creative and critical conversational mode of sociality to the act of reading. It opens the possibility of entering the text as a social space and seeing all the things going on and adding to them. Generosity takes seriously the collaborative creative act between the listener/reader and the speaker/writer. Whereas the University's mode of criticality is so often mobilised to poke gaps, identify holes and limitations, and tends to 'diss' or attack presented work (captured in the normalised practice of 'defending' a dissertation or a paper), generosity opens reading and listening to be-ing potentially generative, rather than merely absorptive of critical practices. Something new is produced or generated in the dialectical encounter between reading and writing and the context in which the encounter takes place.

PUBLICATION AS PROCESS, EDITOR AS LISTENER AND ORGANISER

What we have been interested in here is thinking about how the editor can play that role in a collective process of production. By way of moving forward rather than concluding, which always seems to close what remains open and declare a stasis or finality of that which is in flux, we thought we would reflect on our improvised attempts to be editors as well as comrades, to simultaneously be with others in struggle and hold the responsibility of the publishing process. We have found it generative to consider the editor-in-struggle's role as that of an organiser. And when we reflect on our process, we realise that a lot of what we were doing was organising: communicating with multiple groups and individuals, coordinating timelines, booking venues, organising travel and meetings, running workshops, and so on, a significant part of all these activities and responsibilities are based on building: relationships, consciousness and community.

All of these questions and practices – around editing, organising and publishing – grew very organically out of our own involvement in student politics in 2015 onwards. In addition to urgent material questions of fees and outsourcing, an important aspect of the work that Black students did was to raise critical questions about the politics of knowledge production. As a site of knowledge production, *Publica[c] tion* attempted to archive the moment, spaces and processes out of which the questions and reflections emerged by making space for us to write about ourselves, our theories and our perspectives, and experiment with responses to questions posed by the project of decolonisation in the context of a publication.

Fixating on process as central to a collective and truly collaborative publishing project, which emerged out of a critique of capital's fetishisation of the product, opened *Publica[c]tion* to the necessity of meeting each other, reflecting and asking questions together. Getting people together in any circumstances requires and is a form of organising, as is planning what you do together and coordinating that process. Being with people in pedagogical processes where there is the space to think creatively and openly, where, as an editor, one doesn't assume that they know the best or most important story, opens one up to the humbling intellectual practice of listening. Being in a space with comrades where there is an understood political urgency to the pedagogical process, one's orientation to each other, because we need each other, is potentially one of generosity rather than the fierceness and cold of academic critique. Which is not to say that there is no criticality: a form of criticality is built into dialogue, as is creativity. It is rather to say that, as comrades, we are or should be more interested in building something together – whether in dialogue or in material struggle – rather than merely poking holes or gaps in people's positions and thoughts. The mode of sociality that any productive process is based in will imply both a theory and practice of 'the public' and certain forms of action based on who and how that public is constituted. Publication is a mode of public action.

NOTES

1 The term students used for Rhodes University signifying their rejection of their institution being named after the imperialist Cecil John Rhodes.
2 For an overview and archive of the Black-led student formations at [historically] white universities that emerged before #fmf, see *Publica[c]tion* pp. 29–32 downloadable at https://gorahtah.files.wordpress.com/2017/11/publicaction_pdf-for-web_pages1.pdf.
3 RMF was also engaged in various forms of action outside of the education spaces.
4 To download the full volume of writing, go to http://jwtc.org.za/resources/docs/salon-volume-9/FINAL_FINAL_Vol9_Book.pdf.
5 Thato Magano is a writer and was a literature student at Wits who had been involved in organising Wits #fmf as well as some independent publishing

with a Black feminist online platform called *Vanguard Magazine*, (http://vanguardmagazine.co.za). They completed the team, helping to shape it in particular ways and bringing lots of difficult questions and generative conversations to the project. Thato was preparing to pursue a PhD programme at a university in the USA, and because of that and some other personal reasons, decided to pull back from the project around August 2017.

6 Shacks built by students on the UCT campus during the protests signifying both the poverty in the country as well as the lack of accommodation for students. The shacks were later destroyed by UCT's private security.

7 A kombi is a minibus. Ours was rented but, as a public transport form, it is a ubiquitous feature of South African life.

8 Expanding 'reading' to include reading the world and not merely texts allowed for most participants to bring experiences and ideas from wide personal archives into the conversation.

9 Encouraging and reminding activists and artists that when things get lit/intense/fired-up, writing is imperative.

10 This encourages autonomous and collective publishing rather than waiting for commercial publishers to get material out – if we believe that our work is important, we can't leave its fate in the hands of capitalists.

11 *Publica[c]tion* has also been distributed in many different parts of the world. Copies have been taken to, and shared at a pan-African socialist gathering in Dar es Salaam, a fringe art festival in Rygge, a graduate student conference in Nairobi, an independent publishing festival in Paris and more.

12 Although the final publication only has contributions from South Africa, India and Puerto Rico, the intention was to have much broader coverage. There were meant to be contributions from Chile, Angola, Ethiopia, Brazil and a few other places, but activists were experiencing severe repression, and writing at that particular moment was not possible for all of them.

13 Activist campaign against rape culture at UCKAR.

14 Lesbian, gay, bisexual, transgender, queer or questioning, intersex, and asexual or allied.

15 Cis-het describes someone who is cis-gendered and heterosexual. Cis-gender/Cis describes people whose gender identity aligns with that of their biological sex.

REFERENCES

[Date last accessed for all links: 20 June 2019]

Freire, P. (1983). The Importance of the Act of Reading. *Journal of Education*, 165(1), 5–11.

Gamedze, A., Magano, T. & Naidoo, L.-A. (eds). (2017). *Publica[c]tion*. Publica[c]tion Collective: Johannesburg.

Harney, S. & Moten, F. (2013). *The Undercommons: Fugitive planning and black study*. Wivenhoe / New York / Port Watson: Minor Compositions.

Morrison, T. (2015, 23 Marc). No Place for Self-Pity, No Room for Fear: In times of dread, artists must never choose to remain silent. *The Nation*. Retrieved from www.thenation.com/article/no-place-self-pity-no-room-fear.

Muller, L. & Jordan, J. (1995). *June Jordan's Poetry for the People: A revolutionary blueprint*. New York: Routledge.

Naidoo, L.-A. (2015). The Role of Radical Pedagogy in the South African Student Organisation and the Black Consciousness Movement in South Africa, 1968–1972. *Education as Change, 19*(2), 112–132.

—— (2016). The Rise of the Black-Led Student Movements of #RhodesMustFall and #FeesMustFall in 2015. In A. Heffernan & N. Nieftagodien (eds), *Students Must Rise: Youth struggle in South Africa before and beyond Soweto '76* (pp. 180–191). Johannesburg: Wits University Press.

RhodesMustFall Writing SubCom (eds). (2015). *The Johannesburg Salon, 9*.

Scott, D. (2018, 24 November). 'Marxisms, radical traditions and the South: Reflections on Stuart Hall's voice', Panel discussion at Community House, Cape Town.

12

Revolutionary vanguard no more?

The student movement and the struggle for education and social justice in Nigeria

Rhoda Nanre Nafziger and Krystal Strong

The student movement in Nigeria has been central to the fight against imperialism, militarism and neocolonialism in the struggle for human rights and equitable, accessible public education. It has been a crucial training ground for democratic practice and struggles for social justice, from the founding of higher education in Nigeria to the present (Adejumobi, 2000; Beckman & Ya'u, 2005). Nigerian students have assumed a critical role in shaping and transforming institutions of higher education and society as a whole, forming part of a rich tradition of resistance, which includes movements representing labour, youth, women and civil society more broadly. Organised bodies representing these interests have resisted the Nigerian state, controlled by economic and political elites in its military and civilian formations.

Despite this legacy, some scholars have noted a marked decline in radical student politics in concert with a wider systemic retreat of the radical left in Nigeria (Beckman, 2006; Odion-Akhaine, 2009). Others reframe this narrative of decline and focus on emerging political patterns and structural distinctions between today's student movement and those of previous eras (Strong, 2015). This chapter considers both perspectives, and how analysis of the student radical tradition as a historical revolutionary formation lends itself to understanding the conditions, contingencies and possibilities of student radicalism in the present. Historical analysis, coupled with analysis of current political movements, offers insight into the conditions that once enabled vibrant student activism and their relationship with broader developments within the Nigerian state. To this end, this chapter advances three interrelated arguments: (1) the history of the Nigerian student movement articulates a revolutionary vision and praxis of decolonial education and socially just societal transformation that remains instructive for contemporary conditions; (2) the apparent decline of revolutionary student politics must be interpreted within a broader context of neoliberal state formation, elite consolidation and the suppression of radical politics; and (3) contemporary resurgences of student political protest may indicate emerging possibilities in the struggle for education and social justice.

We begin with a discussion of the relationship between the Nigerian state and higher education and the theoretical framework informing our analysis. Then, we present the chapter's three arguments related to the past, present and future horizons of the Nigerian student movement and conclude with an assessment of broader conditions for student-led social movements.

THE STATE AND THE PLIGHT OF HIGHER EDUCATION

The Nigerian state is characterised by political and economic crisis related to 'deepening regional cleavages, pervasive political discontent, profound economic disparities, and ... a culture of political racketeering' (Joseph, 2014). Quadri (2008, 2018) argues that this poverty exists despite various development plans and poverty reduction strategies implemented within the context of neoliberal ideologies and strategies for development.

The conditions of higher education are deeply entwined with formations of the Nigerian state, and struggles around it. At its inception under British rule, higher learning in Nigeria was foundational to the colonial project of re/producing a native proto-elite class, ensuring that university access was a sure trajectory to power and privilege (Ayandele, 1974; Van den Berghe, 1973). After underwriting ambitious national development plans for education with the newly established oil economy during the 1970s and early 1980s, Nigeria's education sector shifted from an elite to a mass education model, drastically expanding the nation's educational infrastructure. However, the prioritisation of education within the state agenda changed dramatically in the 1980s after Nigeria adopted structural adjustment programmes (SAP) and defunded and deskilled higher education. The latter development created both conditions for radical student struggles for public education and the turn towards the privatisation of education. Decades later, many institutions are still recovering from this era of austerity policies.

Nigeria's crowded higher educational landscape comprises over 500 post-secondary institutions, including dozens of federal and state universities, colleges of education and polytechnics, and an increasing number of private universities. Students today seek educational credentials, but they do not necessarily lead to socio-economic mobility. Furthermore, similar to other African nations, higher education in Nigeria can be described as a 'neglected institution, a crumbling edifice' (Zeilig, 2007, pp. 60–64) with neither the economic structures nor political will to keep pace with public demands for accessible public education.

STUDENTS: A CONTESTED ELITE

Nigerian students occupy a unique position in society today which must be understood within the historical context of social, economic and political events that shaped public education in the country. Western education in Nigeria has its foundations in colonial institutions set up by European missionaries and later the British government. Colonial schools in Nigeria focused on training Nigerians to occupy positions within churches, missionary establishments and the British colonial administration. Over time, Nigerians demanded their own forms of education, and advocacy for Nigerian universities led to the establishment of the first higher institution, the Yaba High College in 1932 (Fafunwa, 1971).

Fanon (1967) contends that colonial education entrenched class struggle and gave rise to a new class of educated elite. This educated elite, trained in the best Nigerian schools and abroad, had tremendous privilege and power, which placed it at the negotiating table with the

British government for Nigeria's independence (Ayandele, 1974). However, despite their status, many members of the elite fought for the expansion of higher education in Nigeria, helping to establish what were recognised as some of the best institutions in Africa by the 1960s. This included the prestigious University of Ibadan, Nigeria's first university, Ahmadu Bello University, Obafemi Awolowo University and the University of Nigeria at Nsukka (Fagbulu, 1983, p. 143).

While a significant body of scholarship describes how the Nigerian educated classes have contributed to the nation's degradation for their own self-aggrandisement (Ayandele, 1974; Ayling, 2016; Mann, 1985), we contend that the struggle of student activists within higher education compels a more nuanced understanding of the power of the educated 'elite'. A Gramscian analysis allows us to understand that education is a contested terrain in which the elite have to give certain concessions in order to maintain their hold, as we describe in the following discussion.

Nigeria's student movement has always contested Nigerian political and economic elite classes, which have governed the country through military rule and into the current democratic dispensation. Over the past six decades, Nigeria's elite classes have grown richer while poverty continues to rise. The student movement has historically pushed back against the policies of elites, at times against their own interests as a proto-elite group, working to counter destructive state policies that affect schooling as well as broader social issues. By understanding the student movement's history, we become more keenly aware of the possibilities for radical student activism in the future. We turn now to the student struggle led by the National Association of Nigerian Students (NANS) and how it historically responded to social, political and economic conditions.

THE STUDENT MOVEMENT AS REVOLUTIONARY VANGUARD

Though student resistance has existed throughout the history of higher education in Nigeria, the student movement assumed a revolutionary character beginning in the 1980s with resistance against neoliberal economic policies imposed by the military regime and elite ruling classes in collaboration with international financial institutions

(IFIs) such as the International Monetary Fund (IMF) and the World Bank. The student movement resisted austerity measures in Nigeria in coalition with the labour movement and civil society. As a result, they were targeted with state violence, expulsion, detention and even death. The broader student movement was strategically undermined, with the suppression of campus student unions and the creation of pro-government counter-organisations to undermine the role of radical student and popular activism (Beckman, 2006). Radical aspects of student unionism largely declined by the 2000s, while similar economic policies continued under a civilian government, using the revisionist neoliberal language of participation, transparency and government reforms (Adejumobi, 2000).

Nkinyangi (1991) notes that the general decline in social and economic conditions was the most important factor contributing to student protests in African countries since the early 1980s. Indeed, the Nigerian student movement aligned with radical civil society, trade and labour unions to push back against military rule and state efforts to impose neoliberal economic reforms in tertiary education that would defund and limit state responsibility for public education. Students protested the general decline in education standards, including the 'book famine, crowded classrooms, lack of consistent electricity, water supply and learning equipment, lecturers not showing up to teach, unpaid scholarships, and lack of general concern of the government to the deteriorating conditions of the universities' (Nkinyangi, 1991, p. 3). Campus conditions were exacerbated by the entrenchment of military rule and worsening social economic conditions, including the rising cost of living and increasing poverty levels.

Nigeria's national student unions have their roots in radical activism. The National Union of Nigerian Students (NUNS), formed out of the West African Student Union (WASU) in 1956, advocated for decreases in fees, students' rights and improved conditions on campus as well as broader social issues. In 1978, NUNS staged nationwide protests against university fees where over 20 students were killed and scores wounded. NUNS was subsequently banned and the National Association of Nigerian Students (NANS) was founded in 1980 to replace it. By 1986, NANS had followed in the historical tradition of its predecessor with national protests, where more students were killed leading to nationwide riots after which NANS was also banned.

NANS has consistently been an anti-imperialist organisation and, thus, a threat to the ruling class (Odion-Akhaine, 2009). Students were at the forefront of the anti-SAP protests against the removal of petrol subsidies, which led to an increase in the cost of living (Beckman, 2006). NANS also alerted the public to federal government and IMF plans to make significant changes to universities, including the introduction of fees, phasing out certain university departments and the commercialisation of student accommodation (Amidu & Okweocha, 1989).

NANS opposed plans for rationalisation in education and at the end of its 20th Senate meeting in November 1988 gave the federal government a ten-point demand accompanied by a six-month ultimatum to meet the demands. Among the demands were the abolition of the SAP, an end to the rationalisation of education which included fees, course changes and decreased funding, an end to the invasion and closures of universities by security forces as well as free health care and free education for all. When the ultimatum lapsed on 6 April 1989, NANS directed mass mobilisation of its members at a press conference which condemned the SAP and IMF/World Bank inspired policies, which included 'privatisation, devaluation, retrenchment, mass unemployment, high military expenditure, trade liberalisation, under-funding of the universities, rising cost of education, arrests and detention of student leaders and activists, among other things' (Adejumobi, 2000). These demands indicate a broad revolutionary vision of both educational and societal transformation grounded in free public education and an end to state policies that deepened social inequalities.

NANS joined labour, the Academic Staff Union of Universities (ASUU) and radical civil society organisations to respond to the government's increasing austerity measures. Peaceful actions engulfed the nation as citizens, including schoolchildren, poured out into the streets chanting 'SAP must go, we are dying of hunger in the name of SAP' (Shettima, 1993, p. 87). The military government met peaceful protests with violence, tear gas and live bullets, issuing curfews and shoot-on-sight orders. The situation deteriorated into large scale riots in cities across Nigeria. The police and security services arrested movement leaders along with the NANS leadership and put them on trial. Despite this repression, the riots continued. The federal government closed 31 tertiary institutions, banned student leaders and sponsored conservative groups to attack students. NANS continued to meet and work with other members of civil society to resist the SAP, so the government began to sponsor alternative movements such as the Association of Nigerian Students, to provide a pro-government alternative to NANS (Shettima, 1993).

The anti-SAP riots pressured the federal military government to make a number of concessions in order to quell the rising tide of resistance. Having undermined the government effort to reschedule $23 million in debt with the World Bank (Nkinyangi, 1991), in early 1989 the Federal Government of Nigeria signed a memorandum of understanding with trade unions (NANS was still proscribed). This guaranteed nine years of free schooling, books at affordable prices, student unionism as a right and the removal of the ban on NANS. In July 1989, selective schools were opened and the federal government introduced relief measures. It allocated 9.4 million naira to the education sector for teachers and federal institutions, and jobs were created. Trade tariffs were removed and the federal government directed states to pay a bursary to all of their students. Britain, Japan and the European Community issued over US $380 million in bilateral SAP-relief loans. In 1990, a $20 million grant was given to each university and Nigeria took out a $140 million World Bank loan for higher education (Shettima, 1993).

Although these concessions were made, the student movement was significantly undermined in its capacity to effectively organise students and contest the state. The federal government issued the promulgation of Student Union Activities (Control and Regulation) Decree of 1989, which made student unions voluntary and delegitimised national student unions. Local student unions could also be proscribed if they were 'not in the interest of national security, public safety, public morality or public health' (Shettima, 1993, p. 88). The Military Head of State and the Minister of Education were both authorised to expel individual students and ban individual student unions, bypassing university procedures.

Despite this response to student leadership in the anti-SAP protests, the student movement continued to align itself with other progressive movements in the 1980s and 1990s around the broader struggle for democracy and economic justice. NANS' struggle against neoliberal policies and military rule was integral to the fall of Ibrahim Badamasi Babangida's military regime. Following the annulment of the June 1993 elections and the failed transition to democratic rule, the pro-democracy movement grew stronger and led to increased instability. In 1993, a largely unpopular Babangida was forced to step down, handing over to an even more brutal military dictator, General Sani Abacha. The latter continued the Babangida government's neoliberal economic policies and instituted a reign of terror against student activists, until his death in 1998, when Nigeria transitioned to democracy.

IS STUDENT RADICALISM DEAD? INTERPRETING PRESENT CONDITIONS FOR STUDENT MOVEMENTS

Scholarly literature is united in its assessment that, by the early 2000s, the student-led movement that birthed resistance to the neoliberalisation of the Nigerian state, the entrenchment of military governance, and radical visions for decolonial education and social transformation had largely lost its revolutionary character (Beckman, 2006; Odion-Akhaine, 2016). This section considers five primary factors, which ultimately led to the movement's demobilisation, and continue to shape the conditions of possibility for student radicalism in the present. They are: (1) violent state suppression of student leaders and unions; (2) the deliberate funding of counter-revolutionary student organisations by state agents and their university collaborators; (3) the delinking of the Nigerian left from the ideologies and praxes of radical internationalism after the end of the Cold War; (4) the transition to constitutional democracy, which shifted student politics from state opposition to incorporation into the political establishment and (5) the systemic deterioration of higher education and the social and economic fabric of the nation.

Repression of student unionism, through government and university policies, and targeted violence against student leaders and protesters, was the most heavy-handed state tactic used to dismantle the student movement. Military rulers in the 1990s were notoriously ruthless towards student organisations, and civil society generally. The government issued decrees specifically banning student unions and penalised their leaders (Odion-Akhaine, 2009). For instance, Decree No. 47 of 1989, promulgated after the anti-SAP riots, stipulated draconian penalties for student radicalism, effectively extending the reach of military dictatorship to campuses through persistent harassment, rustication (temporary expulsion) and detention of students suspected of being involved in political activism. Initially, this decree failed to curtail student activism or demobilise NANS: in 1991, students demanded academic reform through national protests. In 1992, anti-SAP student protests continued, and after the 1993 annulment of the 12 June elections, students formed the nucleus of the pro-democracy movement alongside national organisations such as the Campaign for Democracy (CD), the Civil Liberties Organisation (CLO) and the Committee for the Defence of Human Rights, which also maintained chapters on major campuses (Olamosu, 2000).

Still, the military government was relentless. Fear became widespread as the military disregarded human rights and targeted activists with brute force, even on campuses, which became heavily militarised and lost what little autonomy they had (Olamosu, 2000; Beckman, 2006; Odion-Akhaine, 2009). In 1995, the Ogoni Nine were publicly executed for their role in agitating for the disenfranchised Ogoni people and the destruction of Ogoniland by major oil corporations like Shell and Chevron. In 1996, Kudirat Abiola, the wife of imprisoned presidential aspirant of the 12 June elections, M. K. O. Abiola, was killed in prison in Lagos. Student leaders alongside other civil society leaders were imprisoned and tried for treason. Amnesty International named many Nigerian leaders as prisoners of conscience and decried the Nigerian government's human rights abuses, as well as the complicity of multinational corporations (Amnesty International, 1999). When Abacha died in 1998, many student and civil society leaders were still imprisoned. By the time civilian rule began in 1999, civil society had already 'lost steam' (Aiyede, 2009, p. 2), the student movement had 'lost its ideological direction' (Odion-Akhaine, 2009, p. 247), and 'political fatigue' had set in partially as a result of the fierce and bitter battles against the Abacha regime (p. 430).

State sponsorship of counter-revolutionary campus organisations represents another tactic to weaken radical student organisations and dramatically shift the balance of power on campuses across the country (Olamosu, 2000). The rise of violent 'cultism' on Nigerian campuses compromised the security of educational institutions, making campus communities fearful, and discrediting student unions (Beckman, 2012; Odion-Akhaine, 2009; Olamosu, 2000). Cults such as the Pyrate Confraternity and Black Axe, while originally formed as anti-imperialist secret societies, became notorious for rape, harassment and violence against student leaders, and even murders on campuses across the country (Rotimi, 2005). As Olamosu notes:

> The rise of cultism became visible with the gradual crippling of student unions, progressive, radical, political, social and cultural organization that were banned by the authorities ... Since life abhors a vacuum, the repression against the radical movement in the campuses eventually caused the diversion of youthful energy underground leading to the emergence of various anarchist cult groups.
>
> (2000, p. 57)

With government support, cult groups disrupted student unions and organisations with the intention to infiltrate and co-opt them, a process which typically led to the banning of democratic political organisations on campus, further entrenching the strength of underground associations. These groups operated with impunity, brutalising student leaders, often in gruesome fashion (Beckman, 2006). While violent cultism has significantly declined, the stain of association with cult activity continues to mire the credibility of student unions today.

In addition, the end of the Cold War weakened the hold of radical internationalism, which adversely affected the Nigerian left and its capacity to support radical student activism (Beckman, 2006). The Soviet Union's collapse adversely impacted Nigerian social movements which had strongly aligned with Marxist-Leninist ideology (Odion-Akhaine, 2009). This included the student movement, which had operated with strong ideological commitments to strategic alliances with other leftist organisations in Nigeria and international solidarity with organisations in Cuba and South Africa. Thus, with the decline of the global leftist international and leftist organisations in Nigeria, NANS and the student movement lost their ideological footing (Beckman, 2006).

Where the Nigerian left's decline shifted the student movement ideologically, the transition to civilian rule changed the political nature of student organisations. With no clear enemy in the form of a repressive military government, campus politics, among students, faculty and staff, turned inward and became more focused on internal campus political contests (Beckman & Adeoti, 2006). The student movement transformed from being ideologically aligned to the mass resistance movements in the 1980s and early 1990s during the pro-democracy struggles to become aligned with the politics of the civilian rule post-1999. Beckman (2012) and Aiyede (2009) both attribute this to the contentious class position of students themselves.

The changed political space has impacted on how students see their role in society. Many student union leaders today see themselves as either part of the political establishment or politicians-in-training (Strong, 2015). Student unions are often closely tied to the political establishment, and candidates for student political offices are frequently sponsored by politicians and political parties, which undermines students' autonomy and the inclination to critique the political establishment.

Nigeria's deteriorating economic situation further compromised the student movement's ideological clarity, giving way to corruption and other survival strategies. In essence, the struggle for democracy and economic justice became secondary to the struggle for survival. Mohan and Stokke (2000) note that popular struggles are often determined by economic necessities, while Beckman (2006) adequately recognises the plight of Nigerian students:

> Students became the immiserated victims of a collapsing university system. How could they organize and fight for university reforms? How could these starving, overcrowded and deprived students defend themselves against a repressive state and reactionary university autocrats?
>
> (p. 114)

Impoverished student activists became increasingly reliant on external sources of income, such as externally funded human rights organisations (Beckman, 2006), while unions were vulnerable to being 'hijacked' by political 'godfathers', who enticed students with resources in exchange for political allegiance (Odion-Akhaine, 2009). Students were impoverished, while inflation and skyrocketing costs of living also meant that the unions of faculty and non-academic staff shifted their political focus to the welfare of members. This in turn has led to frequent strike actions to increase pay increments leading to disruptions in academic activities and student degree progress, unintentionally sowing division between students and faculty, who once formed strong alliances.

Nigerian universities and institutions of higher learning continue to suffer from poor funding, cramped classrooms, inadequate infrastructure, rampant closures, corruption and misappropriation of funds, delayed staff salaries, lack of research grants to universities and collapsed library systems without books. The university system continues to be plagued by a regional imbalance of education opportunities between the north and the south[1] (Davis & Kalu-Nwiwu, 2001), a ratio system based on ethnicity[2] which exacerbates ethnic divisions (Adeyemi, 2001), as well as the lack of autonomy and leadership in university administration.

The current condition of the university system reflects the broader state abandonment of public education at all levels (Atteh, 1996; Ekundayo & Ajayi, 2009; Enu & Esu, 2011). While Nigerian educational institutions were once recognised as among the best in Africa, many universities have become unaccredited, and the overall decay in the system has led to a mass exodus of faculty and students abroad. Nigerian elites have turned to private and foreign education for their own children, leaving those with less economic power with few options for quality education through public schools. Although many Nigerian leaders were trained in public schools, today members of the economic and political elite, and civil servants, rarely educate their children at public schools (Udey et al., 2009). Factors that include state suppression and co-optation of student radicalism, the decline of public education and the left in Nigeria and internationally, produced the conditions for the collapse of the student movement. These dynamics also continue to impede the movement's revitalisation.

EMERGING FORMATIONS OF STUDENT RADICALISM

Today, many student unions struggle to exist. In the past decade, university authorities have banned or suspended historically strong student unions for extended periods of time at the University of Ibadan, University of Ilorin, University of Lagos, Polytechnic Ibadan, Obafemi Awolowo University, Lagos State University, among dozens of other documented cases of student union suppression by university management (Etadon, 2013). Similarly, universities continue to punish leaders of student protest activities with suspension and expulsion, even for non-violent actions and offences as petty as critiquing university authorities, as in the case of a University of Ibadan student, Kunle Adebajo, who was suspended for writing an opinion piece in 2016 about the poor condition of student dormitories (Sahara Reporters, 2018).

Students are collectively punished as university authorities use the state policy that permits schools to be closed indefinitely after extended protests, a tactic that produces anxieties around academic instability and weakens political solidarities among students. Furthermore, where student unions are still permitted to exist, they often find themselves without genuine autonomy, since their leaders are under constant threat of discipline and lack an independent economic base now that compulsory student union dues, once mandatory for all students, are forbidden by law. These factors make students unduly beholden to university management and politicians in order to function. At Nigeria's growing number of religious and secular private institutions, student unionism is typically banned and student political activities are often limited to voluntary associations, which do not represent student interests as a whole, and are frequently organised around regional, ethnic and religious divisions. Thus, students lack the organisational conditions for meaningful political representation and radical activism across public and private institutions.

However, despite tremendous impediments, the structural conditions of higher education, and the socio-economic and political realities facing most Nigerians regularly catalyse significant student protest activities. At the time of writing, since 2009, at least 168 unique student protest events have been documented in over 70 different locations throughout the nation, encompassing a range of political action. This includes non-violent demonstrations, class boycotts, property vandalism, social media-based organising and even riots. Incidents of campus unrest today are rarely tied to a specific political movement, but instead form in response to perennial grievances, such as unsafe infrastructural conditions (i.e. lack of running water, electricity and health care access); administrative policies like tuition fee hikes; and the targeting of student leaders and unionism.

Some recent student protest activities have aligned with larger political mobilisations and popular struggles around unfavourable state policies and continued attacks on public education. For the post-military generation of Nigerian students, Occupy Nigeria is the closest representative of what the anti-SAP and pro-democracy movements signified for the Nigerian student movement of the 1980s and 1990s. Occupy Nigeria formed in January 2012, after former Nigerian president, Goodluck Jonathan, removed the 20-year standing government subsidy on petroleum products, which kept Nigeria's fuel prices among the lowest in Africa. The drastic policy shift was met with popular disdain and catalysed nearly two weeks of mass protests and acts of disruption in 17 cities, reportedly the largest in the nation's history. Though the labour strike led by older labour officials provided legitimacy to what began as a loose constellation of uprisings, the movement was first incited and sustained by tens of thousands of nameless young people, including university students, who provided leadership to several nodes of the Occupy Nigeria movement.

Though the movement was ultimately ended by the collusion of labour leaders with the federal government, since then, the rhetoric and praxis of 'occupation' has enlivened student activism, as the Occupy University of Ibadan movement of April 2012 signalled. The formation of Occupy Nigeria, the first broad-based political movement of the democratic era, and the frequency of student protest activities should not be interpreted as a harbinger of the revitalisation of the Nigerian student movement. However, its existence, despite the current condition of political mobilisation in the nation, should signal the enduring salience and possibilities of revolutionary student activism even after its separation from organised movement building.

REIMAGINING THE NIGERIAN STUDENT MOVEMENT: CONDITIONS AND POSSIBILITIES

Student activism has both failed and succeeded. The failure is evidenced in the banning or suspension of student unions across the country, the continued closure of universities as well as the continued decline in the quality of education at public tertiary institutions nationwide. But the war is far from being lost. Nigerian universities remain the last bastion of hope for aspiring radical activists. Student activism, though repressed and embattled, has taken on different forms and may yet still live to see another day. While the elites may view the movement as comatose, there continue to be stirrings within the universities, and the fight against imperialist subjugation and capitalistic hegemony is far from over.

Beyond critique and analysis, it is imperative to use the rich history and traditions, as well as insights into the challenges and pitfalls of the student movement to reimagine radicalism in the student movement of the future. Nigeria's objective conditions have experienced little change from the early days of NUNS and NANS. Nigeria is still experiencing high rates of poverty and inequality. While university fees remain low, public institutions are in poor condition and public education is in crisis. The Nigerian elite has continued to corner the country's material resources while most Nigerians wallow in literal darkness without electricity, potable water, affordable food of high quality or access to basic sanitation. If these objective conditions that facilitated radicalism in the first four decades of Nigeria's independence continue to exist, what prevents student activism from sustaining itself? We argue that the subjective conditions which gave strength to its antecedents may still be fanned to give life back to the fire of radicalism that may appear to be smouldering.

Some suggestions on the way forward include:

1 *Rebuilding the ideological base and historical consciousness of the student movement* would include reviving reading and study groups which were a strong feature of organisations such as the Patriotic Youth Movement of Nigeria (PYMN).

2 *Democratising the internal structure of student unions and getting rid of money politics* is central for the student movement to undergo its own cleansing mechanism and provide it with the necessary strength to pursue a wider social agenda.

3 *Collectivisation and rebuilding solidarity;* the student movement must re-establish strategic coalitions with labour and working people's associations which include women's organisations and farmers' associations. Within the campuses, student unions must rebuild relationships with academic and non-academic staff unions at every level. At the international level, strategic alliances can be formed or reactivated.

4 *Rebuilding an economic base for student struggles;* the struggle for political and social rights cannot be separated from the struggle for economic rights. Advocating for financial assistance for poor students as well as state and national bursaries is critical for student well-being. Addressing rising fee structures and skyrocketing prices of both on-campus and off-campus accommodation is essential, as is the need to support jobs for students on campus. In addition to addressing the welfare of individual students, there is a need to

address the welfare needs of student organisations. A modest student fee, payable to the student union and managed by it, will help them to reduce their dependence on external funds to run their most basic functions and programmes.

To revive radical student activism, it is critical to place the focus on the existing conditions and structures, rather than to be nostalgic about the student movement's history. The student movement can never return to its past to fully reclaim it; it can only reflect and learn from it. In order for Nigerian students to reclaim their position as a revolutionary vanguard, their struggle must extend again beyond issues relating directly to their own welfare and into broader goals for social justice and human dignity for all Nigerians. In rallying for the greater good, students may find once again their own fate well supported by the people they seek to defend.

NOTES

1   Western education in Nigeria was first established by missionaries in the former Southern Protectorate of Nigeria. Due in part to strong agitation from Muslim leaders in the Northern Protectorate resisting missionary education, the Northern part of Nigeria became educationally disadvantaged, and this trend continued despite the dominance of Northern leadership in the country through the first 30 years of independence.

2   The development of higher education in Nigeria was also seen to advantage some areas, particularly the Yoruba south-west region of the country. Further agitation for equal access to education led to the formation of the Joint Admission Matriculation Board (JAMB) which was created to promote equity and fairness in university admission. This gave room for universities to admit students based on four criteria; merit, educational disadvantage, university discretion and catchment area. A quota system thus enforced admission to sometimes underqualified candidates into universities in the South region, where students of greater merit often exceeded the quotas outside their states and are subsequently denied admission. This has led to further tension concerning ethnic based admission policies.

REFERENCES

Adejumobi, S. (2000). Structural Adjustment, Students' Movement and Popular Struggles in Nigeria, 1986–1996. In A. Jega (ed.), *Identity transformation and identity politics under structural adjustment in Nigeria* (pp. 204–233). Uppsala: Nordic Africa Institute.

Adeyemi, K. (2001). Equality of Access and Catchment Area Factor in University Admissions in Nigeria. *Higher Education*, 42(3), 307–332.

Aiyede, E. R. (2009). The Political Economy of Fiscal Federalism and the Dilemma of Constructing a Developmental State in Nigeria. *International Political Science Review*, 30(3), 249–269.

Amidu, A. & Okweocha, O. (1989). Communique issued at the 8th annual convention of NANS, University of Illorin, 22–23 July.

Amnesty International (1999, 1 January). Amnesty International Report 1999 – Nigeria available at: www.refworld.org/docid/3ae6aa0824.html (Accessed 1 October 2019).

Atteh, S. O. (1996). The Crisis in Higher Education in Africa. *Issue: A Journal of Opinion*, 24(1), 36–42.

Ayandele, E. A. (1974). *The Educated Elite in the Nigerian Society*. Ibadan: Ibadan University Press.

Ayling, P. (2016). 'Eliteness' and Elite Schooling in Contemporary Nigeria. In C. Maxwell & P. Aggleton (eds), *Elite Education: International perspectives* (pp. 148–161). New York: Routledge.

Beckman, B. (2012). Trade Unions and the Politics of Crisis. In P. Utting, S. Razavi, R. V. Buchholz & R. Varghese Buchholz (eds), *The Global Crisis and Transformative Social Change* (pp. 237–256). London: Palgrave Macmillan.

Beckman, B. (2006). Student Radicalism and the National Project: The Nigerian student movement. In B. Beckman & G. Adeoti (eds), *Intellectuals and African Development: Pretension and Resistance in African Politics* (pp. 98–123). Dakar: CODESRIA.

Beckman, B. & Adeoti, G. (2006). Predicament and Response: An introduction. *Intellectual and African Development: Pretension and Resistance in African Politics*, 5–8.

Beckman, B. & Ya'u, Y. Z. (2005). *Great Nigerian Students: Movement politics and radical nationalism*. Kano: Centre for Research and Documentation.

Davis, T. J. & Kalu-Nwiwu, A. (2001). Education, Ethnicity and National Integration in the History of Nigeria: Continuing problems of Africa's colonial legacy. *The Journal of Negro History*, 86(1), 1–11. https://doi.org/10.2307/1350175.

Ekundayo, H. T. & Ajayi, I. A. (2009). Towards Effective Management of University Education in Nigeria. *International NGO Journal*, 4(8), 342–347.

Enu, D. B. & Esu, A. E. O. (2011). Re-Engineering Values Education in Nigerian Schools as Catalyst for National Development. *International Education Studies*, 4(1), 147–153.

Etadon, F. I. (2013). Campus Conflicts Involving Students' and University Management in Nigeria: The case of the University of Ibadan. *International Journal of Educational Sciences*, 5(3), 333–343.

Fafunwa, A. B. (1971). *A History of Nigerian Higher Education*. Yaba, Lagos: Macmillan and Co. (Nigeria) Ltd.

Fagbulu, A. M. (1983). Trends in Education and Employment in Nigeria. In S. Adesina (ed.), *The Development of Modern Education in Nigeria*. Nigeria: Heinemann Educational Books.

Falola, T. (2009). *Colonialism and Violence in Nigeria*. Bloomington, IN: Indiana University Press.

Fanon, F. (1967). *Towards the African Revolution (Political Essays)*. New York: Grove Press.

Fanon, F. (1961). *The Wretched of the Earth*. New York: Grove Press.

Isichei, E. A. (1983). *A History of Nigeria*. Lagos, Nigeria: Indiana University Press.

Joseph, R. (2014). Boko Haram and the Nigerian State Crisis. *Brookings* (blog). Retrieved from www.brookings.edu/blog/africa-in-focus/2014/05/19/boko-haram-and-the-nigerian-state-crisis/ (Accessed 19 May 2014).

Mann, K. (1985). *Marrying Well: Marriage, status, and social change among the educated elite in colonial Lagos*. Chicago, IL: Cambridge University Press.

Mohan, G. & Stokke, K. (2000). Participatory Development and Empowerment: The dangers of localism. *Third World Quarterly*, 21(2) 247–268.

Nkinyangi, J. A. (1991). Student Protests in Sub-Saharan Africa. *Higher Education*, 22(2), 157–173.

Odion-Akhaine, S. (2009). The Student Movement in Nigeria: Antinomies and transformation. *Review of African Political Economy*, 36(121), 427–433.

Olamosu, B. (2000). *Crisis of Education in Nigeria*. Ibadan: Book Farm Publisher.

Quadri, M. O. (2008). Their Programs, Our Programs: Poverty reduction strategy in Africa. In I. M. Zulu & A. Aderemi (eds), *Global Peace Leadership Summit 2007: Africa and the Diaspora* (pp. 147–166). Los Angeles, CA: African Diaspora Foundation.

Quadri, M. O. (2018). Neoliberalism and the Paradox of Poverty Reduction: A Synthesis of the Poverty Reduction Strategy Paper Experience in Benin and Nigeria. *Journal of Pan African Studies*, 11(6).

Rotimi, A. (2005). Violence in the Citadel: The menace of secret cults in the Nigerian universities. *Nordic Journal of African Studies*, 14(1), 79–98.

Sahara Reporters New York (2018, 16 June). The Article that got 'Kunle Adebajo Rusticated by The University of Ibadan. *Sahara Reporters*. Retrieved from http://saharareporters.com/2018/06/16/article-got-%E2%80%98kunle-adebajo-rusticated-university-ibadan (Accessed 15 November 2018).

Shettima, K. A. (1993). Structural Adjustment and the Student Movement in Nigeria. *Review of African Political Economy*, 56, Challenging Gender Inequalities in Africa (March 1993), pp. 83–91. Retrieved from www.jstor.org/stable/4006127 (Accessed 15 November 2018).

Strong, K. S. (2015). *Political Training Grounds: Students and the future of post-military Nigeria* (Doctoral dissertation, University of California, Berkeley).

Udey, F. U., Ebuara, V. O., Ekpoh, U. I. & Edet, A. O. (2009, August). Management and Administration of Nigerian Education System: Problems, challenges, and the way forward. In *11th International Conference of Educational Management Association of South Africa (EMASA)* (pp. 7–9).

Van den Berghe, P. (1973). *Power and Privilege at an African University.* Piscataway, NJ: Transaction Publishers.

Zachernuck, P. S. (2000). *Colonial Subjects: An African intelligentsia and Atlantic ideas.* Charlottesville, SC: University Press of Virginia.

Zeilig, L. (2007). *Revolt and Protest: Student politics and activism in Sub-Saharan Africa.* (Revised edition). London: I. B. Tauris.

13

Postcolonial and transformative education in the University of the Philippines

Sarah Raymundo and Karlo Mikhail I. Mongaya

During the 2018 championship of the University Athletic Association of the Philippines (UAAP), the University of the Philippines Fighting Maroons (UPFM) men's basketball team enthralled the University of the Philippines (UP) community as it fought its way to the top after years of being at the losing end of the competition. Ultimately UPFM lost to the well-oiled Ateneo de Manila University's Blue Eagles. But this did not dampen the celebratory mood in the campus, since the last time UPFM won the championships had been in 1986.

This fighting spirit is best captured by the passionate chants by UP Fighting Maroons fans which goes: 'Unibersidad ng Pilipinas! Matatapang! Matatalino! Walang takot! Kahit kanino!' (University of the Philippines! Courageous! Intelligent! Not afraid of anyone!). Such cheers have parallels with the chants of student activist groups, for which UP has become known in recent decades. They include slogans that describe their activist organisations as 'tunay, palaban, makabayan!' (genuine, militant, patriotic!) and 'lumalakas, lumalawak, lumalaban!' (building strength, ever-expanding, daring to struggle!).

This relation between sports and activism is not new, as we can see from the insights of Angel Baking: 'If a simple basketball game, as it sometimes happens even among our college teams, erupts into violence, how much more a revolution which seeks to resolve more complex difficulties' (Baking, 2008, pp. 106–107)? Baking posed the question of revolution as a career for the young activists who were part of the revolutionary upsurges of the 1960s.

In November 2018, UP Regent Angelo 'Jijil' Jimenez extolled the UP Fighting Maroons as an inspiration for the Filipino people: 'Basketball is life after all. But I like the deeper significance, not just to my fellow Iskos and Iskas [UP students]. Let our boys [sic] fight and be an inspiration to the country.' For Jimenez, belief in the UP men's basketball team functions as a nodal point that articulates the UP community and wider society's hopes for national renewal. 'Let us believe, for our country, for all,' he concludes (Jimenez, 2018).

These statements, which both refer to basketball, are separated by only 48 years. Yet they seem to be worlds apart in terms of the relation they make between education, struggle and society. Baking simply compares the scale of violence involved in basketball and in revolutionary struggles. Meanwhile, Jimenez's statement makes the UP Fighting Maroons a synecdoche of the struggle against poverty and inequality. For him, it is by deriving inspiration from an institution of education that we may begin to change society. This runs opposite to the materialist approach to transformation in which a rupture in social relations of production is decisive in effecting changes in institutions such as education.

What follows is an attempt at tracing this shift from a materialist perspective to an idealist view of education which sits well with policies of neoliberalism. We argue that this shift is expressive of the struggle between postcolonial education and transformative education. 'Post' in this context does not refer to a moment in linear history, but to a transhistorical moment of crisis largely defined by global conditions of unequal development.

This chapter examines the struggles in Philippine public higher education within the context of its colonial function as a tool for imperialist control in the 'post-colonial era'. Nationalist historian Renato Constantino (1978) rightly refers to this colonial legacy as a 'continuing past'. By transformative education, we mean the continuing mass struggles and institutional projects of militant groups in the University in which local issues are raised and linked to national liberation as the articulation of class struggle in semi-colonial social formations.

POSTCOLONIAL EDUCATION AS SYMPTOM

Militant activists describe the Philippine educational system as colonial, commercial and repressive owing to continuing colonialism that has been naturalised through the institutionalisation of its new forms. Public education in the Philippines is a colonial legacy of American occupation. The Treaty of Paris in 1898 legitimised the transfer of the remaining countries under the Spanish Empire to the United States (US). The US paid Spain US $20 million for it to become the Philippines' new coloniser. However, there was a crucial lesson to be learned from the anti-colonial and armed revolutionary uprising of the Katipuneros[1] who defeated Spain in 1896: no coloniser can rule in the old way.

UP's founding in 1908 guaranteed the production of Filipino bureaucrats and technocrats who would govern the US-installed Philippine Republic. The process that took place in between the founding of the UP, a decade after the beginning of US colonialism (1898), and the contemporary period is a preparatory phase in the continuing colonisation of the Philippines by US imperialism.

UP's flagship campus is located in Quezon City, named after Commonwealth of the Philippines President Manuel L. Quezon. UP campuses were also established in the regions to cater to local ruling classes who wish to give their sons and daughters a 'UP education' in their own backyard, or as part of policy recommendations by multilateral institutions like the International Monetary Fund (IMF) and the World Bank (WB). UP Cebu was founded in 1918, UP Iloilo in 1947, UP Baguio in 1961, UP Tacloban in 1973 and UP Mindanao in Davao City in 1995. The dictator Ferdinand Marcos' Presidential Decree No. 1200, signed in 1977, provided for the establishment of UP Visayas as a centre of fisheries and marine sciences, a development made possible in 1980 by a World Bank educational loan. Marcos' 1972 Presidential Decree No. 58 founded the UP Los Baños campus in Laguna as a hub for agricultural research.

US colonialism's efforts to establish public higher education alongside its calculated and incremental granting of independence to the Philippines have had a foundational and continuing impact on UP and public higher education. Thus, rather than an exceptional phase in UP's history, the colonial period is a condition of possibility for UP's postcolonial becoming.

The 'postcolonial' is presumed to be a condition that constitutes the present as a rupture from the colonial past. In doing so, it can only treat current issues in public higher education as managerial problems devoid of history, and ignores the powerful influence of the global political economy on education.

The other symptom is the transformative one, which while laying latent for much of the early periods of direct American colonisation, occasionally surfaced through student and nationalist unrest. Student demonstrations during the term of UP President Guy Benton (1921–1923) slammed the infringing of academic freedom and due process with the dismissal of Professor Austin Craig.[2] UP president Rafael Palma's (1923–1933) term was a time of opposition to what the university's constituency saw as the 'despotic tendencies' of then Senate President Manuel Quezon (Ordoñez, 2008, pp. 6–7).

While the American colonisers were able to suppress the last pockets of Filipino armed resistance with the suppression of the Moros in Mindanao by 1913, peasant uprisings and workers' agitation would testify to growing disquiet under the new colonial regime. This reached its height with the establishment of the Partido Komunista Pilipinas (PKP) on 7 November 1930. Many promising young intellectuals were radicalised, with some writers forming the Philippine Writers League publishing socially conscious literature.

The PKP would be declared illegal and radical nationalist articulations deflected by reinforcing the campaign for the gradual handing over of independence in 1944. Japanese occupation intervened during World War II but 'American liberation' in 1945 and the granting of formal 'independence' in 1946 signified a return to business as usual. During the post-war years, the country was not just a conduit of anti-communism coming from the West but, as Colleen Woods (2012) argued, the Philippines served as one of the leading laboratories for the production of anti-communist discourse by diplomats, counter-insurgency experts, professors and administrators, missionaries, and social workers providing models for use across the world.

THE LONG '60S AND 'THE UNIVERSITY WITHIN THE UNIVERSITY'

By the late 1950s and early 1960s, the initial disparate protests in UP centred on particular grievances were later anchored in a wider critique of imperialist domination and unjust social structures, enabling the emergence of mass struggles and movements. This radicalisation found its strongest impetus in the global wave of Marxist-inspired national liberation struggles that reached an apex in the 1970s, that came to be called the 'long '60s' by some scholars (Ness & Cope, 2016).

The defeat of the Huk rebellion of the old PKP in the 1950s seemed to have precluded the fortunes of radical politics in the Philippines. The Anti-Subversion Law was crafted in 1957 to suppress Marxist ideology and the communist movement. But the heightened anti-communist campaign instead accomplished the opposite by becoming the very object of resistance for freedom-loving Filipinos. At UP, this spirit of dissent was particularly buoyed by the rift between liberalism and religious sectarianism, which politicised the students of that generation.

In 1959, students led by Jose Maria Sison established the Student Cultural Association of UP (SCAUP), the name of which is a play on the then dominant religious organisation, UP Student Catholic Action or UPSCA. SCAUP initiated a 5,000-strong protest on 14 March 1961 against a Committee on Anti-Filipino Activities (CAFA) hearing then conducting witch-hunts against UP faculty (Sison & De Lima, 2008). This was a foreshadowing of the changing times as SCAUP became an organised venue for the study of Marxism and Philippine social conditions. They thus:

> posed in strictly Marxist-Leninist terms the problem of the masses: How can a political force materialise among the toiling masses of workers and peasants of Philippine society? Indeed, for SCAUP members, the urgent question was how are we supposed to establish relations with this huge mass of exploited and oppressed people?
>
> (Raymundo, 2014)

These radical intellectual youths saw the necessity of engaging in ideological struggle against reactionary religious and anti-communist thinking, building what they called a 'progressive university within the reactionary university' (Sison & De Lima, 2008, pp. 46–47). But they harboured no illusion that this alone could transform the postcolonial character of UP without changing the dominant social order in broader society. The need for a movement on a national scale that could fulfil this mission was realised when the Kabataang Makabayan (KM or Patriotic Youth) was established on 30 November 1964. Since then, KM has been the comprehensive youth organisation not only for university-based students but also for the youth among the peasants, workers, professionals and women.

KM members would later form the core for the re-establishment of the Communist Party of the Philippines (CPP) on 26 December 1968. Repudiating what they called the 'revisionist treachery' of the old PKP, the CPP initiated a national democratic revolution to overthrow US imperialism, feudalism and bureaucratic capitalism. The new party's founding was made possible by the development of an uncompromisingly militant mass movement that struck roots among workers and peasants. This was decisive in allowing the CPP to effectively direct the defiant militant energies of the youth and toiling people in the following years.

The violent repression of a student rally in front of Congress during the state of the nation address of President Ferdinand Marcos on 26 January 1970 sparked what would become known as the First Quarter Storm. The first three months of 1970 saw an eruption of almost weekly militant protests of 50,000 people. In February 1971, the strike of jeepney drivers against successive oil price increases would spark a week of student barricades and pitched battles against besieging state security forces in the now celebrated Diliman Commune.[3]

The critical legacy of the 'long '60s' is crucial for the development of transformative education in UP. It moulded the 'radical' label that would come to be associated with UP. The revolutionary upsurge of this era spurred anti-imperialist institutional projects promoting the national language, local and popular histories and cultures, and social investigations into the conditions of marginalised sectors. Indeed, this was the backdrop to the founding of the UP Diliman Filipino Department in 1966 and the institutionalisation of various shades of Philippine Studies. These efforts persisted despite the Marcos dictatorship's suppression of radicalisation in academic sites which would dovetail with the intensification of the commercialised and labour-export orientation of Philippine education necessitated by the requirements of neoliberal globalisation (Mongaya, 2019).

NEOLIBERALISM AND RESISTANCE IN UP
AND BEYOND

Neoliberalism is first and foremost a class offensive (Harvey, 2018) of the global ruling elite against the global working poor, who prior to the late 1970s generated and sustained an anti-imperialist bloc from the formation of the League Against Imperialism in 1928, to the Bandung Conference in 1955, and finally, the Non-Aligned Movement in 1961. Prashad (2012) correctly claims that this series of anti-imperialist and internationalist advances is the Third World Project that mobilised for peace, bread and justice. It is the same project which neoliberalism or the Atlantic Project of the global ruling elite suppressed.

The moves by multilateral institutions like the IMF-WB to force neoliberal formulas of deregulation, privatisation, liberalisation and denationalisation on the 'underdeveloped' world through so-called Structural Adjustment Programmes (SAPs) have had a profound effect of accentuating the symptom of postcolonial education in the country. These 'reform packages' accelerated cutbacks on public spending for social services like education and intensified the role of the University as a resource for international labour markets.

The Marcos imposition of martial law on 21 September 1972 cleared the field for the imposition of such structural reforms by outlawing activist groups like KM, shutting down student councils and student publications, and repressing freedom of expression, the right to assembly and the right to organise. As many as 70,000 activists and suspected dissenters were detained, 35,000 tortured and 3257 murdered (McCoy, 2001). Many were compelled to go underground to join the armed resistance to the dictatorship led by the CPP, its armed wing, the New People's Army (NPA) and the National Democratic Front (NDF).

Gradually, activists were able to push the boundaries of legality to assert people's rights. Campaigns to revive student councils and student publications mobilised students, leading to the reopening of these institutions in the same decade they were closed. The militant student formation League of Filipino Students (LFS) was formed in 1977 and built chapters in major universities and colleges across the country, including UP. The Sandigan ng mga Mag-aaral para sa Sambayanan (SAMASA) party was founded in 1978 to contest UP campus elections.

Much of the 1980s would be marked by student militancy, exemplified by SAMASA's landslide electoral victories from 1981 to 1984.

Having revived the student councils, student leaders now set their eyes on reinstating student representation at the highest decision-making body in UP with a Student Regent in the UP Board of Regents. The Katipunan ng mga Sanggunian Mag-aaral sa UP (KASAMA sa UP), an alliance of UP student councils, was founded in 1981 for this purpose. The remaining years of the dictatorship in the 1980s were punctuated by dramatic protests in Diliman and other UP campuses.

By February 1986, economic crisis, the extreme political isolation of the Marcos ruling clique, massive unrest prepared for by over a decade of painstaking organising and armed resistance by the underground revolutionary movement climaxed with the overthrow of the Marcos dictatorship in the EDSA uprising.

One of the Marcos legacies with repercussions for decades to come is the Education Act of 1982 that gave schools the power to increase tuition and other fees. Comparison of data from a 1988 study (Riel, 1988) and 2016 tuition rates shows tuition costs in private schools increasing from an average PHP700–2,600 (US $13–49) per semester in 1982 to PHP40,000–80,000 (US $750–1,500) in 2015. Schools also collect other fees for medical services, laboratories, library and utilities, which should already be covered by tuition.

State universities like UP were also pushed to increase tuition to allow the deregulation of the entire education sector. A 'socialised' tuition scheme was first implemented in UP to purportedly only subsidise those in need. This only resulted in excluding students from less privileged classes as tuition soared from PHP40 ($0.75) per unit to PHP200 ($3.75) per unit in 1989 when the Socialized Tuition Financial Assistance Program (STFAP) was first implemented, and later to PHP1,000 ($18.85) per unit in 2007.

Ultimately, this shifting into high gear of the commercialisation of education coincided with the return of the oligarchic elites who ruled over the country before the Marcos family monopolised all political and economic power and thus represented continuity rather than a real rupture with the status quo.

The Philippines' entry into the World Trade Organization (WTO) in 1995 sparked the start of a campaign against the commercialisation of education. Youth activists countered neoliberal 'reforms' that reached full throttle under President Fidel Ramos. This campaign took place in the context of a split within the student movement between those who championed pluralist discourses but paradoxically excluded radical options, and those who reaffirmed the relevance of anti-imperialism. The student party SAMASA became a contested field between liberals who argued for the autonomy of alliance members to take different stands on issues, and student radicals who saw the need for forging one united stand for the alliance.

There have been two parallel struggles in the Philippines, differing in methods, but having the same goals of attaining genuine agrarian reform, national industrialisation and a socialist future. These are the underground armed revolution of the CPP-NPA-NDF and the urban mass movement composed of aboveground organisations. The latter has been the target of red-baiting and repression.

The split in the revolutionary movement in 1992 forced progressive formations to take stands across ideological lines. Underlying these debates was the shift in political claims-making with the fall of the Berlin Wall, the turn of China to capitalist markets, and the 'end of history' under capitalism, supposedly rendering struggles for economic redistribution obsolete and militancy inappropriate to pluralist 'empowerment'.

In 1996, militant student groups committed to the anti-imperialist line and the necessity of students linking their struggles with masses of workers and peasants would join the newly formed alliance, the Students for the Advancement of Democratic Rights in UP (STAND-UP). Disproving allegations of a monolithic activist youth milieu, there were different student formations catering to diverse fields that continue to organise up to the present: the research-oriented Center for Nationalist Studies, the artist collective Alay Sining, science advocates Agham Youth, the women's group Gabriela Youth and the Student Christian Movement of the Philippines.

In 1997, a group of progressive, anti-imperialist teachers formed the Congress of Teachers and Educators for Nationalism and Democracy (CONTEND) in the University. Throughout its existence, CONTEND has held exhibitions, fora and conferences, screened progressive films and published books on important milestones of the people's struggles. The group was central in establishing the All-UP Academic Employees Union and actively campaigned for the Alliance of Concerned Teachers

(ACT Teachers) when the teachers' union ran for the party-list elections starting in 2010. Entering Congress became a way of expanding modes of struggles and exposing the rottenness of the bureaucracy rather than falling into the trap of parliamentarism and careerism.

Responding to the realisation that in a semi-colony like the Philippines, the majority of the youth are out-of-school and unemployed, national student formations established Anakbayan (Children of the People) in 1998. Inspired by KM as an organisation for youth of all walks of life, Anakbayan would come to organise community youth, young workers, peasants and professionals alongside students. Militant youth groups would likewise form the core of Kabataan (Youth) Party-list which has become the broadest expression of organised youth in the country. It won its first seat in Congress in 2010, and would go on to win one seat each in the 2013 and 2016 national elections.

The militant movement in the UP community would have a vital role in the EDSA People Power 2 uprising on 17–20 January 2001 that cut short the term of President Joseph Estrada. His successor, Gloria Macapagal-Arroyo would intensify 'rationalisation' of public education budgets, hiking school fees and opening up to the private sector as recommended by the Philippine Commission on Education Reforms (PCER) formed under Estrada.

UP was opened to worsening commercialisation and marketisation under the 1997 Higher Education Modernisation Act (HEMA). This law pushed state schools to be run as 'self-sustaining' enterprises amidst chronic budget cuts. Boards of state universities were given power to set fees and enter into joint ventures with private business like the lease of University lands for the Ayala Techno-Hub and the UP Town Center Mall. In 2006, tuition hikes in UP were railroaded without student consultations and despite massive opposition.

The Arroyo years of intensifying neoliberalisation were characterised by increasing state terror and repression, including the abduction of UP students Karen Empeno and Sherlyn Cadapan by military men led by General Jovito Palparan. By the end of Arroyo's term, there would be over 1200 victims of extrajudicial killings. In 2008, a 'tenure for Sarah Raymundo' campaign was launched for one of this chapter's authors, who was then assistant professor at the UP Diliman Department of Sociology, and who had been denied tenure as a consequence of anti-communist witch-hunts.

President Benigno 'Noynoy' Aquino's term opened with massive walkouts against education budget cuts in 2011 followed by the tragic death of UP Manila student Kristel Tejada who committed suicide because of her inability to pay her tuition in 2013. The drastic restructuring of education with the adding of two years to the previous ten-year basic education curriculum under the K-12 programme and internationalisation of higher education under Aquino would intensify its postcolonial features.

Internationalisation meant changing UP's academic calendar to align with 'international standards'. The previous school calendar, starting in June and ending in March of the following year that was attuned to local climate and agricultural cycles shifted to an August-to-May calendar. It also meant the reduction of the UP General Education programme from the previous 45 units to a minimum of 21 units, thereby reducing history, language and literature, philosophy and social sciences subjects.

All these transformations of the University entailed the narrowing of its public character as students, parents, faculty and employees are deprived of a role in determining the direction of the institution. University administrators now decide school policies in boardrooms with 'industry leader' partners to align with 'business models' and 'international standards' without any accountability to the wider community. Nevertheless, decades of anti-commercialisation protests and campaigns have already borne fruit with students of UP and other state universities now enjoying free tuition.

Since taking power in 2016, President Rodrigo Duterte quickly revealed himself to be a fascist demagogue wedded to neoliberalism, whipping up anti-communist hysteria, and intensifying counter-insurgency campaigns. Duterte's throwing off liberal niceties in favour of militarist rule, however, resulted in the meeting of two historical milieus: the aging veterans of the anti-dictatorship movement against Ferdinand Marcos and the vocal young 'millennials' who are now at the forefront of actions against Duterte.

Young students quickly came together in large numbers in front of the UP Diliman Palma Hall, the historic venue of protest actions during the Marcos dictatorship, when news of Marcos getting a hero's burial at the Libingan ng mga Bayani was made public on 17 November 2016. Five thousand mostly UP students marched that afternoon from UP Diliman campus to the gates of the Jesuit-run Ateneo de Manila University and the American MaryKnoll Sisters-founded Miriam College in Katipunan Avenue where the protest programme continued into the night. Since then, UP students would become a mainstay in large and primarily youth-led anti-fascist mobilisations, including the 15,000-strong Day of Rage on 30 November 2016. Thousands of youth and students would mobilise for the 21 September martial law commemoration rallies in 2017 and 2018.

Militant youth not only took to the streets but also went to the picket lines of striking workers, campouts of protesting farmers, among others. They linked arms with workers of NutriAsia who were able to shut down the Filipino condiment company's factory in Bulacan province from May to July 2018. On 30 July, the picket line was violently dispersed by police and NutriAsia security, resulting in 20 hurt and 19 arrested. Starting on 8 March 2017, student activists integrated with homeless Filipino families who joined the Kadamay urban poor organisation-led occupation of 6,000 idle public housing units for police officers in Pandi, Bulacan. UP students also featured among the Lumad [Indigenous Peoples] who joined the people's march and caravan (Lakbayan) protests in 2015, 2016 and 2017 to the national capital as they sought refuge from brutal counterinsurgency operations in Mindanao. The Lumad made UP Diliman their temporary refuge for the duration of the 'Lakbayan'.

The Duterte regime responded with massive repression against student activists which dovetailed with a campaign of political killings against labour and peasant leaders and activists. In September 2018, UP was tagged by the military as one of a list of Manila-based schools implicated in a 'Red October' plot conspiracy to overthrow Duterte. In January 2019, teacher unionists of the ACT Teachers would expose police surveillance, profiling, harassment and detention of their members.

In the 2019 elections, Duterte was determined to stop progressive parties and candidates from winning any Congress seats through a campaign of vilification and repression. But progressive parties under the MAKABAYAN Coalition still won six seats.

CLASS STRUGGLE IN NATIONAL LIBERATION

Where do we go from here? What happens to the student and education worker who is unsettled by persistent attacks stemming from national oppression yet neither fully moved nor convinced by campaigns stemming from the politics of the national liberation struggle, socialism or even democracy? As advocates of national liberation and academic freedom, we cannot choose to ignore the destructive impact of four decades of neoliberalism on our academic and political organisations.

The fragmentation of political dissent remains a major challenge. New social movements still insist upon the primacy of identity politics, single-issue campaigning, the fragmentation of interlocking oppressions and the peculiar situation in the Philippines of the demonisation of the national democratic left alternative. Needless to say, the fragmentation of dissent is precisely the strategy of capital that largely shapes neoliberal policies. From the fragmentation of both knowledge and an approach to politics to the rise of the new right worldwide, it has become clear how neoliberalism has reduced democracy to what we are calling a populist-discourse-in-circulation. It is a discourse that merely highlights the conflict between 'the people' and a powerful bloc that is intent on marginalising them. Oppressive social relations can neither be denied nor resolved within the existing power structure.

The continued statements of the Philippine government, Armed Forces of the Philippines and the Philippine National Police about their 'war on the communists' must be understood as a reactionary hegemonic claim, standing alongside the Philippine government's participation in the WTO and other multilateral institutions like the IMF-WB. The IMF-WB-WTO's dispossession of the Global South will not be as successful without the constant rejection and dismissal of the struggles of its peoples. We contend that so-called postcolonial governments are no different from the colonial governments of Spain and the US. The Philippine government merely wants elite peace as it intensifies its war on the people through the maintenance of poverty and inequality.

In higher education, knowledge and skills are associated with its very own imaginary universalisms and the illusion of it being solely for the development of society in a neutral fashion. This results in the normalisation of ideology and naturalisation of class interest inherent in dominant paradigms and knowledge claims. Yet what is erased in this instance is the very context in which higher education materialises as a consumable commodity that is instrumentalised to serve the interest of finance and the exploitation of labour and resources in the Global South.

At the heart of this contradiction that takes place in one of monopoly capitalism's weakest links – the semi-colonial and semi-feudal Philippines – is the counter-hegemonic struggle of education workers and students aligned with the basic sectors of society (such as workers, small farmers, Indigenous Peoples and the urban poor). Their force constitutes a potentially broad anti-imperialist movement that is being weighed down yet also enabled by the contradictions that obtain from the simultaneity of structural stasis and destabilising changes. Both of which point to class struggle. Translating this counter-hegemonic potential into a massive force of anti-imperialist politics remains a challenge for militant organisations within the University.

While CONTEND's membership has grown significantly from when it was founded in 1997, its painstaking efforts at promoting an anti-imperialist politics can only subvert the fragmenting mechanisms of neoliberal policies in higher education through robust organisational programming. The democratic character of the politics of anti-imperialism is constrained by CONTEND's actual and current function as a campaign centre for local, national and international issues. While its function as a campaign centre is significant, its members agree on the necessity of running CONTEND as a mass organisation to concretise and give muscle to its calls and campaigns. It would thereby serve as an effective organised force that advances into the fray of the class struggle in a space like higher education dominated by pluralist discourses that result in depoliticisation.

CONTEND members share their assessment of this impasse in an interview. 'Foremost among the problems we face in terms of organising among faculty is the liberalism in the University combined with socially-engineered red scare and its real threats to professional security and opportunities', states a CONTEND member (2019). They add that 'there are varying degrees of careerism and continuing marketisation of the University alongside internal weaknesses in the organisation.'

For their part, members of Anakbayan share self-criticisms of belated efforts at seriously analysing the particularity of the neoliberal offensive in the University. This contributes to shortcomings in more concrete analysis of key issues like commercialised education as symptoms of imperialist class domination, thereby blunting the possibilities of more rapid organisational growth and wider mobilising capacity. This is compounded by neoliberalism's assault on public spaces within and outside academia from the restriction to outright removal of offices, halls, kiosks and bulletin boards up to the beefing up of campus security against activist organisers. This takes away physical spaces where the youth can convene to cultivate critical thinking and activism. These insights indicate tendencies even within militant organisations that are affected by the neoliberal consensus under global capitalism.

A well-known refutation of the class struggle is found in Jurgen Habermas' (1987) historicising of the so-called concrete conditions that eclipsed it. The pacification of class conflict, according to this view, can be traced to the development of welfare states since 1946 as a result of reforms which relied on Keynesian economics.

Domenico Losurdo (2016) contends that such analysis of the welfare state stems from a misconception of it being an essential and inherent tendency within capitalism. The welfare state was a materialisation of a set of demands pushed for by subaltern classes. While it did not take root in the US – as Roosevelt's New Deal was meant '[to contain socialism] and to reinforce the moribund capitalist mechanisms that were then shaken by the global crisis' (Raymundo, 2014, n.p.) – welfare states in Europe emerged at the peak of the trade union and labour movement. Does not this history demonstrate how the welfare state is primarily a result of class struggle rather than its pacification? (Losurdo, 2016, p. 3).

The reaffirmation of class struggle and its rejection of the postcolonial symptom in the academic field challenges the neoliberal claims of post-politics. It takes in the concrete struggles of national liberation movements. The particular form that this struggle assumes across militant organisations within UP is anti-imperialist. It unites generations of militants in the University from the 1960s, to the 1980s and 1990s, up to the current crop of activists. Yet this struggle is less a revolutionary solution than a problem to solve for the Philippine revolution.

In a 2018 Left Forum panel entitled 'The Imperial University', Raymundo argues that academic freedom is a claim on society, particularly, organising society in oppressive and exploitative ways. In this chapter, we trace the historical development of this mode of academic freedom alongside the history of the revolutionary movement whose seeds were scattered and which thrived in UP and beyond. While the University played a pivotal role in the organisation of political resistance, it cannot play a decisive role in clinching the relations of production in Philippine society. The common thread that ties the presence of militant organisations in the University to its past and future is their resolve to unite with a comprehensive programme for national liberation and socialism.

NOTES

1   Katipuneros were members of the Katipunan, a Philippine revolutionary society founded by Filipinos against Spanish colonialism in Manila in 1892.
2   The first chair of the UP Department of History, Craig was one of the first biographers of the Filipino national hero Jose Rizal.
3   The February 1971 uprising led by students, faculty members and residents of the University of the Philippines Diliman, and transport workers to protest the increase in oil prices during the second term of the Marcos administration.

REFERENCES

[Date last accessed for all links: 15 May 2019]
Baking, A. (2008). Revolution as a Career. In B. Lumbera, J. Taguiwalo, A. Alamon & R. Guillermo (eds), *Serve the People: Ang Kasaysayan Ng Radikal Na Kilusan Sa Unibersidad Ng Pilipinas* (pp. 106–108). Quezon City: IBON Foundation.
Constantino, R. & Constantino, L. (1978). *The Philippines: The continuing past.* Quezon City: Foundation for Nationalist Studies.
CONTEND Members. Interview by Karlo Mikhail Mongaya. Personal Interview. Quezon City, 18 March 2019.
Garcellano, E. (2001). Reading the Revolution, Reading the Masses. In E. Garcellano (ed.), *Knife's Edge: Selected Essays* (pp. 37–50). Quezon City: University of the Philippines Press.
Habermas, J. (1987). *Theory of Communicative Action, 2,* translated by Thomas McCarthy. Boston, MA: Beacon Press.
Harvey, D. (2018). *Seminar on Consciousness and Revolution 2017–2018.* Center for Place, Culture and Politics, The City University of New York Graduate Center.
Jimenez, J. (2018, 30 November). Inspiring Belief: Paul Desiderio and the UP Fighting Maroons. *ABS-CBN News.* Retrieved from https://news.abs-cbn.com/blogs/focus/11/30/18/inspiring-belief-paul-desiderio-and-the-up-fighting-maroons.
Losurdo, D. (2016). *Class Struggle: A Political and philosophical history.* New York: Palgrave Macmillan.
McCoy, A. (2001). Dark Legacy: Human rights under the Marcos regime. In *Memory, Truth-Telling, and the Pursuit of Justice: A Conference on the Legacies*

of the Marcos Dictatorship (pp. 129–144). Quezon City: Ateneo de Manila University Office of Research and Publications.

Mongaya, K. M. (2019, 18 February). 'Response to Immanuel Ness'. Message presented at Global Rupture, UP Center for International Studies World Experts Lecture Series, Diliman, Quezon City.

Ness, I. & Cope, Z. (2016). *The Palgrave Encyclopedia of Imperialism and Anti-Imperialism.* New York: Palgrave Macmillan.

Ordoñez, E. (2008). Dissent and Counterconsciousness in the Academe. In B. Lumbera, J. Taguiwalo, A. Alamon & R. Guillermo (eds), *Serve the People: Ang Kasaysayan Ng Radikal Na Kilusan Sa Unibersidad Ng Pilipinas,* (pp. 2–12). Quezon City: IBON Foundation.

Prashad, V. (2012). *The Poorer Nations: A possible history of the Global South.* New York: Verso.

Raymundo, S. (2014, 1 December). Towards a Sociology of KM*. *Bulatlat.* Retrieved from www.bulatlat.com/2014/12/01/towards-a-sociology-of-km.

—— (2018). 'Academic Freedom's Roots in Revolutionary Struggle' in *The Imperial University.* Left Forum 2018. John Jay College of Criminal Justice – City University of New York, NYC.

—— (2014, 5 May). Marx Lives. *Bulatlat.* Retrieved from www.bulatlat. com/2014/05/05/marx-lives/.

Riel, T. R. (1988). A Comparative Analysis of the Tuition Fees of Selected Tertiary Schools in Metro Manila from SY 1980–1988. (Undergraduate Thesis, Quezon City: University of the Philippines Diliman).

Sison, J. M. & De Lima, J. (2008). Foundation for Sustained Development of the National Democratic Movement in the University of the Philippines. In B. Lumbera, J. Taguiwalo, A. Alamon & R. Guillermo (eds), *Serve the People: Ang Kasaysayan Ng Radikal Na Kilusan Sa Unibersidad Ng Pilipinas* (pp. 43–62). Quezon City: IBON Foundation.

Woods, C. (2012). Bombs, Bureaucrats, and Rosary Beads: The United States, the Philippines, and the Making of Global Anti-Communism, 1945–1960. (Dissertation, University of Michigan).

Notes on contributors

Aziz Choudry is Associate Professor and Canada Research Chair in Social Movement Learning and Knowledge Production in the Department of Integrated Studies in Education, McGill University, and Visiting Professor at the Centre for Education Rights and Transformation, University of Johannesburg. He has been involved in a range of social, political and environmental justice movements and organisations since the 1980s. He is author of *Learning Activism: The intellectual life of contemporary social movements* (2015: University of Toronto Press), co-author of *Fight Back: Workplace justice for immigrants* (2009: Fernwood) and editor of *Activists and the Surveillance State: Learning from repression* (2018: Pluto/Between The Lines). His co-edited books include *Organize! Building from the local for global justice* (2012: PM Press/Between The Lines), *NGOization: Complicity, contradictions and prospects* (2013: Zed Books), *Unfree Labour: Struggles of migrant and immigrant workers in Canada* (2016: PM Press), and *Reflections on Knowledge, Learning and Social Movements: History's schools* (2018: Routledge).

Salim Vally is Professor and Director of the Centre for Education Rights and Transformation, Faculty of Education, University of Johannesburg, where he holds the DHET-NRF SARChI Chair in Community, Adult and Worker Education. He is also Visiting Professor at Nelson Mandela University (NMU), South Africa. He is the co-editor of *Education, Economy and Society* (2014: UNISA Press), and *Reflections on Knowledge, Learning and Social Movements: History's schools* (2018: Routledge). Vally worked as an education official in the trade union movement in South Africa for ten years before joining academia.

AUTHOR BIOGRAPHIES

Rabab Ibrahim Abdulhadi is Director and Senior Scholar, Arab and Muslim Ethnicities and Diasporas Studies programme, San Francisco State University.

Rula Abu Duhou is an instructor and researcher at the Institute of Women's Studies at Birzeit University, Palestine. She has an MA in Gender, Law and Development and a second MA in Democracy and Human Rights. She has published on Palestinian political prisoners, and contributed to the book *Small Places and Big Issues: Three Palestinian neighbourhoods under occupation*. A trade union activist, she volunteered for eight years at ADDAMEER Prisoner Support and Human Rights Association. She is currently writing a book on Palestinian women political prisoners based on her own experience as a political prisoner.

Vania Bañuelos Astorga was born in Mexico City. She studied pedagogy at UNAM. She started her experience as research assistant at the Department of Educational Research at CINVESTAV. She has participated as research assistant in several projects including *State of Art* published by the Mexican Association of Educational Researchers. Vania also participated in the evaluation of the international student mobility programme Sep-Bécalos-Santander Universidades 2014 and the IFP América Latina by the Ford Foundation and International Institute of Education (IIE). She is currently a Master's student at the Programme of Learning and Educational Policies in the CREFAL.

Javier Campos-Martínez is a Ph.D. candidate in Social Justice Education at the University of Massachusetts, Amherst. His research interests include the examination of teachers' identities from a social justice perspective as well as the effects of neoliberalism on schools and teachers' working conditions. Javier has worked as an instructor in several universities in Chile, including the University of Chile and the Pontifical Catholic University of Valparaiso. He is a founding member of the Chilean Collective for a New Education, which currently runs a national campaign to stop the harmful consequences of high-stakes testing. He is also a member of the working group 'Education Policy, Education Inequality, and the Right to Education in Latin America and the Caribbean' of the Latin-American Council of Social Sciences (CLACSO).

Asher Gamedze is a cultural worker working mainly in music, education and writing based in Cape Town, South Africa. He organises with a number of autonomous collectives.

rosalind hampton is an Assistant Professor in the Department of Social Justice Education at the Ontario Institute for Studies in Education of the University of Toronto. Her main areas of research and teaching are Black radical thinkers and artists, Black Studies in Canada, racialised social relations in Canadian higher education, anti-colonial racial literacy in teacher education, critical ethnography and arts-informed methods of inquiry. She is the author of *Black Racialization and Resistance at an Elite University* (2020: University of Toronto Press).

Alma Maldonado-Maldonado is a researcher at the Educational Research Department, [Departamento de Investigaciones Educativas] of the Center for Advanced Research [Centro de Investigaciones Avanzadas] in Mexico City. Her research focuses on comparative higher education, international organisations, higher education policy and research in Latin America and particularly on Mexico and issues regarding globalisation, mobility and internationalisation of higher education (institutions, faculty and students).

Julie Le Mazier is a post-doctoral researcher in political science at Université Paris 1 Panthéon-Sorbonne, France. In 2015, she defended her political sociology doctoral thesis which dealt with general assemblies in French student mobilisations from 2006 to 2010, and was a contributor to the study of contentious repertoires and democracy in social movements.

Lena Meari is an Assistant Professor of Cultural Anthropology at the Department of Social and Behavioural Sciences and the director of the Institute of Women's Studies at Birzeit University, Palestine. She is a member of Birzeit's administrative board of the union of academics and employees. Her publications include 'Sumud: A Palestinian philosophy of confrontation in colonial prisons', 'Re-signifying "Sexual" Colonial

Power Techniques: The experiences of Palestinian women political prisoners', 'Reconsidering Trauma: Towards a Palestinian community psychology' and the co-edited book *Rethinking Gender in Revolutions and Resistance: Lessons from the Arab World* (2015: Zed Books).

Karlo Mikhail I. Mongaya is an instructor at the Department of Filipino and Philippine Literature, University of the Philippines-Diliman. He is a member of the Congress of Teachers for National Democracy-University of the Philippines (CONTEND-UP) and the International League of People's Struggles (ILPS) Commission 11.

Rhoda Nanre Nafziger is a doctoral candidate at the Pennsylvania State University in the Graduate School of Education pursuing a dual title degree in Education Theory and Policy and Comparative and International Education. Her research focuses on history and cultural education, community participation in public education reform and socio-historical analysis of youth and student movements in education with a geographic focus on Africa. Her other research focuses on Pan-Africanist civic engagement frameworks for Africana youth and the role of racial constructions in education in Black youths' identity development. Nanre is actively involved in social movements and youth engagement, having led a national youth organisation and worked with youth across Nigeria.

Leigh-Ann Naidoo is an educationalist who works at the School of Education at the University of Cape Town, South Africa. She was involved in the #RhodesMustFall and #FeesMustFall struggles at the University of Cape Town and the University of the Witwatersrand.

Dayana Olavarría has an M.Ed in School Counselling, and is currently a Ph.D. student in Education Leadership at the University of Massachusetts, Amherst. Her research topics include teachers' wellbeing, school intervention and the role of the educational psychologist. Dayana has worked as a research assistant in several projects and as consultant for school improvement interventions.

Gülden Özcan is an Assistant Professor in the Department of Sociology at the University of Lethbridge, Canada. She co-edited *A General Police*

System: Political economy and security in the Age of Enlightenment (2009: Red Quill Books) and *Capitalism and Confrontation: Critical readings* (2012: Red Quill Books). She has contributed to *Alternate Routes: A Journal of Critical Social Research, Moment: Journal of Cultural Studies, Kampfplatz* and *The Wiley-Blackwell Encyclopedia of Globalization.* Her commentaries have also appeared in *The Bullet* (Socialist Project, E-Bulletin).

Sarah Raymundo is Assistant Professor and Director at the University of the Philippines-Diliman Center for International Studies. She teaches courses in Global Studies and Social, Political and Economic Theory. Raymundo's research focuses on indigenous knowledge and the revolutionary struggle of Indigenous Peoples in the Philippines. She has published on women and migration, popular culture, semi-colonialism and post-politics. She is an organiser for the International League of People's Struggles Commission 11 (Education Workers Against Neoliberal Attacks on Education) and the current Chair of the Philippine-Venezuela Bolivarian Friendship Association. Her articles on current issues can be read at her Blood Rush column at www.bulatlat. com.

Saliem Shehadeh is a doctoral student in Anthropology and Middle East Studies at the University of California at Los Angeles.

Krystal Strong is an Assistant Professor at the University of Pennsylvania in the Graduate School of Education with affiliations in Anthropology and Africana Studies. Her research and teaching focus on student activism, the cultural and political power of youth and the role of educational spaces as sites of political struggle with a geographic focus on Africa and the African Diaspora. She is currently completing her first book project entitled *Political Training Grounds: Schools and youth power in Nigeria after democracy*, an ethnography of post-military university student politics in southwestern Nigeria. Other research examines the role of educational development in the production of a new leadership class in Africa, and the incidence and causes of contemporary school-based protests in Africa.

Prem Kumar Vijayan teaches in the Department of English at Hindu College, Delhi University. His Ph.D. (from the International Institute of Social Studies, in The Hague, The Netherlands) was on Hindu nationalism and masculinity, and was the basis for a book, titled *Gender and Hindu Nationalism: Understanding masculine hegemony* (2019: Routledge). He has also written and published on a variety of other issues including higher education, state violence, corruption, terrorism, sexuality, etc., in academic and lay journals and books.

Jamie Woodcock is a researcher at the Oxford Internet Institute, University of Oxford. He is the author of *Marx at the Arcade: Consoles, controllers and class struggle* (2019: Haymarket) and *Working the Phones: Control and resistance in call centres* (2016: Pluto), both inspired by workers' inquiry. His research focuses on digital labour, the sociology of work, the gig economy, resistance and videogames. He is on the editorial board of *Notes from Below* and *Historical Materialism*.

Index